THE POEMS OF
CHARLOTTE BRONTË

The Poems of Charlotte Brontë

A NEW ANNOTATED AND ENLARGED EDITION
OF THE SHAKESPEARE HEAD BRONTË

Edited by Tom Winnifrith

PUBLISHED FOR THE SHAKESPEARE HEAD PRESS
BY BASIL BLACKWELL

THIS EDITION © TOM WINNIFRITH
AND THE SHAKESPEARE HEAD PRESS 1984

FIRST PUBLISHED 1984
BASIL BLACKWELL PUBLISHER LTD
108 COWLEY ROAD, OXFORD OX4 1JF, UK

BASIL BLACKWELL INC.
432 PARK AVENUE SOUTH, SUITE 1505,
NEW YORK, NY 10016, USA

British Library Cataloguing in Publication Data

Brontë, Charlotte
   The poems of Charlotte Brontë.
   I. Title   II. Winnifrith, Tom
   821'.8   PR4167.P6
   ISBN 0-631-12563-9

TYPESET BY GLOUCESTER TYPESETTING SERVICES
PRINTED IN GREAT BRITAIN
BY T. J. PRESS LTD, PADSTOW

CONTENTS

ACKNOWLEDGEMENTS

I WOULD like to acknowledge a generous grant from the British Academy and financial help from the University of Warwick which enabled me to examine Brontë manuscripts in America. I am also grateful to the International Baccalaureate, North America. I have to thank the librarians of the Beinecke Library in Yale University, the Berg Collection in the New York Public Library, the British Library, the Brotherton Collection in the University of Leeds, the Henry Huntington Library, the Houghton Library in Harvard University, the Pierpont Morgan Library, New York, the Rare Books Collection in the State University of New York at Buffalo, the Robert Taylor Collection, Princeton, and the Humanities Research Centre in the University of Texas for access to and permission to quote from the manuscripts in their collection. I am also indebted to Mr Roger Barrett, Mr Robert Taylor, and Mr William Self for allowing me to see and copy manuscripts in their private collections. For other kinds of help I am indebted to Dr Christine Alexander, Ms Harriet Barry, Mr Allan Bolton, Mr Edward Chitham, Mrs Val Gladman, Professor and Mrs George Hunter, Mr and Mrs Tony Hutton, Mr David Martin, Dr David Mervin, Professor Victor Neufeldt, Dr Andrew Nicholson, Mr Gil Nicol, and Professor Keith Odom. I would like to dedicate this book to my colleagues at the University of Warwick who in their various ways have kept alive my interest in the Brontës.

GENERAL INTRODUCTION

THE editing of Charlotte's poetry presents a different set of problems from those I outlined in my edition of Branwell's poems (1983). Firstly and most obviously Charlotte published more than Branwell in her lifetime. We can assume, barring printer's errors, that the text of the poems by the three Brontë sisters as printed by Aylott and Jones in 1846, and reprinted by Smith and Elder in 1848, represents the correct and final version that Charlotte would have approved. We hear of the Brontë sisters correcting proofs, and interestingly the four errors mentioned in an errata slip in the Aylott and Jones edition all occur in Charlotte's poems. After her sisters' deaths Charlotte was responsible for the publication of further selections from their poetry, but she did not publish any more of her own, with the exception of one poem in the *Manchester Athenæum*, and we do not have the problem, as we have with Emily, of distinguishing between author and editor. It is true, as I note in the Textual Introduction, that Charlotte's inadequacy in matters of punctuation makes the published version not totally satisfactory as a definitive text. The manuscript of the poems as presented to Aylott and Jones has disappeared, and in some cases we only have early variations of the poems. It is clearly the duty of an editor to print these variations, and this I have done in the notes. Interestingly, there are as a rule not all that many changes between the text printed in 1846 and the original versions, although sometimes we find more than one original version, since Charlotte seems to have revised in the early 1840s what she had written in the 1830s before revising again for publication. There may have been intervening revisions which are missing. Nevertheless the editing of Charlotte's published poems is not a difficult task. Following the editors of the Shakespeare Head edition we have merely copied the Aylott and Jones edition.

There are then a large number of poems which were not published until after Charlotte's death. Many of these poems were published in small private editions sponsored by T. J. Wise, who was also, at any rate in name, partly responsible for the Shakespeare Head edition which collected many previously unpublished poems. Wise is also to blame for scattering so widely so many of Charlotte Brontë's manuscripts, although most of these manuscripts can be found in the Bonnell collections either at Haworth or in the Pierpont Morgan Library in New York. Most of these manuscripts are in minuscule handwriting, and many of them have numerous corrections. They are difficult, but not impossible to read. Wise had them inaccurately copied, and in many cases the Shakespeare Head has followed the inaccurate copy rather than the original manuscript. Where there is more than one version the Shakespeare Head edition has tried, but not very successfully, to record the variant manuscripts. These errors and omissions are important to correct. Many of the manuscripts are unsigned, but the handwriting and subject matter are usually sufficient to make it clear that the poems are by Charlotte. Unsigned manuscripts are usually undated, and dating them tends to be difficult. Unlike Branwell, Charlotte wrote more on loose sheets of paper than in notebooks, and it is less easy than with Branwell to date a poem by reason of its proximity to another poem.

There are also many poems by Charlotte which the editors of the Shakespeare Head did not include in their collected edition of the poetry of Charlotte and Branwell Brontë. Some of these poems were not included because the manuscripts had not been found or because they were illegible or considered too trivial for inclusion. I originally intended to print all known poems, however slight or difficult to read, but I was faced, as the editors of the Shakespeare Head were faced before me, with the very large number of poems which form an integral part of the Angrian prose cycle, and are really better printed as part of Charlotte's prose writings. The same problem arises with Branwell's poetry, but Branwell solved it for us by copying and adapting many of his Angrian poems in his 1837 notebook devoted entirely to poetry. Charlotte too copied poems which had originally been part of a prose narrative, but in nothing like so systematic a fashion. She also wrote a number of poems with an Angrian context, but where the prose narrative has to be taken for granted, and tended to add a poem to the end of a prose narrative, not always making clear whether the poem is part of the narrative or not. We have tried to publish all such poems, leaving to the editor of Charlotte's prose works the large body of poems which form an integral part of the narrative.

Dr Christine Alexander is undertaking the task of editing Charlotte's prose juvenilia, and thus eventually all Charlotte's poetry will be reprinted. For the convenience of readers I list in an appendix those poems which in agreement with Dr Alexander I have left for her edition. Dr Alexander's *Bibliography of the Manuscripts of Charlotte Brontë* (Keighley, 1982) is of course an indispensable guide to the location of Charlotte's manuscripts, and my debt to this volume, as well as my occasional disagreements with it, is clearly visible in the notes. In editing Branwell's poetry I had to locate the scattered manuscripts myself; thanks to Dr Alexander the apparently more difficult task of finding the greater quantity of Charlotte's poems has become much easier.

After setting down the text the editor should comment on it. The interpretation of Charlotte's poetry is not easy. The Angrian context is not always clear, although here again Dr Alexander provides timely help with the recent publication of *The Early Writings of Charlotte Brontë* (Oxford, 1983). Biographical considerations are important in view of the interest in Charlotte's sad life, but it is always dangerous to read poetry as autobiography. It is useful but difficult to trace Charlotte's literary sources, tempting and easy to see traces of her novels in her early poetry; the former is probably the more healthy activity.

Charlotte was probably the worst poet in the family after her father, and we do not make any exaggerated claims for the worth of the poems in this volume. Some of the early poems, not written with publication in mind, have a certain pathos about them, but the published poems cannot stand up to the stark contrast with Emily's, although even these appear to have been weakened in order to conform to popular taste. It is now so rare to find the young interested in poetry that we tend to forget how many young Victorian ladies indulged in writing poems rather like Charlotte's. But Charlotte was not just any Victorian miss; I believe that as the author of two great novels her life and anything she wrote must be of interest, and it is in this belief that I have endeavoured to edit her poetry.

BIOGRAPHICAL NOTE

THE life of Charlotte Brontë has been written many times. Mrs Gaskell's *Life*, composed under the watchful eyes of Charlotte's husband and father, without all the available evidence and with some evidence suppressed, is a remarkable achievement. Subsequent biographers have found themselves unable to get away from Mrs Gaskell in spite of her unreliability about dates, her unwillingness to distinguish hearsay and fact, and her acknowledged and unsuccessful wish to avoid controversy. The discovery of Charlotte's love letters to M. Heger showed that Mrs Gaskell had very understandably not told the whole story, but this encouraged biographers to fill in the gaps in Charlotte's own story by including parts of Charlotte's novels as if they were autobiographical.

Another omission in Mrs Gaskell's account was her handling of the juvenilia. She was aware that they existed, but was not aware of their significance. The juvenile manuscripts were taken with him by Mr Nicholls when he returned to Ireland. He was not totally unappreciative of their significance, because he copied some of them, concentrating especially on Charlotte's poetry. Towards the end of his life he sold them with the help of C. K. Shorter to T. J. Wise, who scattered them widely. Wise and Shorter did print some of the poems and stories, but in limited editions with inaccurate texts. The Shakespeare Head editions of 1934–8 were not much of an improvement. The publication by Fannie E. Ratchford of *The Brontës' Web of Childhood* (New York, 1941) was the first occasion when the juvenilia received proper attention, although Miss Ratchford did not have their whole bulk in front of her, and she exaggerated the merit and the importance of the tales she had seen. Subsequent biographers, charmed by the pathos of the tiny manuscripts and by the fact that they fill in a gap in the Brontë story, have fallen into the same errors. A new life of Charlotte Brontë, based upon a proper study of the juvenile stories and poems, as undertaken by Dr Alexander, is more than overdue. In the absence of such a life I give a brief account of Charlotte's early years, during which she wrote her poetry.

Charlotte was born in 1816 and before she was nine she had lost her mother and two elder sisters. After the disastrous visit to Cowan Bridge, which lasted from 1824 to 1825, she was educated at home until she went to Roe Head in January 1831. Both her father and her aunt left the young Brontës a good deal to their own devices. They appear to have read voraciously. *Blackwood's* and *Fraser's Magazine*, the local newspapers, the books owned by Mr Brontë, the library of the Keighley Mechanics Institute, and the library of the Heatons at Ponden House are all sources for the precocious learning of Charlotte and Branwell Brontë as reflected in their early prose and verse. In 1834 Charlotte recommended a formidable list of poets to her friend Ellen Nussey, including Milton, Shakespeare, Thomson, Goldsmith, Pope, Scott, Byron (with reservations), Campbell, Wordsworth, and Southey.

As well as reading, writing. We can trace the history of the young Brontës' early writing fairly accurately. Branwell records the purchase by his father in Leeds of some toy soldiers on 5 June 1826. Charlotte describes the establishment of 'plays', make-believe worlds in which the young Brontës escaped from reality from 1826 to 1828. The first written records of these plays are found in 1829. Charlotte and Branwell describe the founding in Africa of a new colony by twelve adventurers, based upon the twelve soldiers bought in 1826. Charlotte and Branwell initially collaborated, although there are signs of rivalry between the two. From the beginning the Duke of Wellington, hero of the recent wars against Napoleon and a prominent Tory politician at the time the Brontës were writing, played a major part. From the beginning, too, both Branwell and Charlotte wrote in a mixture of verse and prose, and their early writings, though strongly derivative, are remarkable efforts.

By 1830 the African element dominated the young Brontës' writing. Though they had learnt something of Africa from the travel writings of Mungo Park, their accounts of the setting up of Glass Town, or more grandiosely Verreopolis or Verdopolis, owe nothing to reality, but are rather romantic effusions about aristocratic life, derived largely from imagination but partly based on contemporary accounts of English politics. Gradually Lord Charles Wellesley and the Marquis of Douro, the two sons of the Duke of Wellington, gain prominence at the expense of their father. In 1830 Lord Charles is the narrator of many of Charlotte's poems and tales. Some of these record the love affair between his brother and Marian (Marianne, Marina) Hume, the daughter of his father's physician.

In 1831 Charlotte went to Roe Head, but Branwell continued the saga, in which Charlotte joined during her holidays in June and after she left school in May 1832. In 1831 Branwell had introduced a new hero, Rogue, later Alexander Percy, Viscount Ellrington and the Duke of Northangerland, a rebel against authority. Charlotte was more interested in love than war. Her sisters Anne and Emily would appear at some stage between 1831 and 1834 to have set up their own imaginary world of Gondal, and it may be that it was the influence of her schoolfellows as well as Scott and Byron which drove Charlotte into writing torrid romances centred round the Marquis of Douro. She also takes Branwell's character Rogue and gives him a Byronic past with a variety of wives and mistresses.

In 1834 a new complication appears in the shape of Mary Percy, Rogue's daughter. Marian Hume dies tragically of a broken heart, and Mary becomes Douro's wife. Douro becomes the Duke of Zamorna and Rogue the Earl of Northangerland as a result of a successful defence of the Glass Town Federation's Eastern provinces. It becomes difficult to distinguish the many wives and mistresses of both heroes in the confused and confusing tales of this year, describing the setting up of a new kingdom of Angria with Zamorna as King and Northangerland Prime Minister. A contemporary political crisis in England probably provided the background to the crisis that arose in Angria towards the end of 1834 with King and Prime Minister at loggerheads. But on 29 July 1835 Charlotte went to Roe Head as a teacher.

Charlotte was nineteen when she took this step. Miss Wooler, the Headmistress of Roe Head, seems to have been a kindly if unimaginative woman, whom Charlotte much later invited in lieu of her father to give her away when she married Mr Nicholls. The school appears to have been well run, although the students were hardly intellectual. Nevertheless it is clear that Charlotte was very unhappy in the three years she was at Roe Head. None of the Brontës was happy away from home, nor by temperament suited to the profession of teacher. As well as the normal strains of adolescence Charlotte was troubled by the hold her imagination had over her, and by the way she could escape from the dreary monotony of teaching into the wild world of Angria.

Freed from the influence of Charlotte, Branwell had plunged Angria and Verdopolis into an orgy of war. The battles and politics are extremely complicated, but by July 1836 Zamorna is defeated and exiled, and Northangerland in charge of Verdopolis with Angria virtually crushed. Mary Percy is killed off by Branwell in September 1836, but this event shatters Northangerland, and Zamorna, returning to join the resistance, marches on to Verdopolis to defeat his old rival. Charlotte was not interested in this war, and revived Mary Percy in a story written at the end of 1836.

After 1837 Charlotte seems to have distanced herself from Branwell. His failure in London, probably in 1835, and his inability to get his poems published in *Blackwood's Magazine* cannot have impressed her. It is customary to praise Charlotte's little vignettes of domestic Angrian life in contrast to Branwell's boring accounts of military matters, but neither are very good. Branwell revised his poetry in 1837, and the revised versions in this notebook are better than Charlotte's more sprawling efforts, but Charlotte had less time for composition or revision. She did write one good prose story, *Mina Laury*, dated 17 January 1838, relating the undying love of the lowly Mina for the aristocratic Zamorna, and of the many poems she wrote during this period, untitled and undated, some have a personal note of unhappiness which probably reflects her discontent at Miss Wooler's school. She eventually left the school in a depressed state at the end of May 1838.

Charlotte's remaining Angrian stories show an increasing realism. African aristocratic extravagance gives way to sober Yorkshire realism. Her poetic vein appears temporarily to have dried up; most of her poetic manuscripts dated after 1838 appear to be reworkings of earlier material. She had written and continued to write non-Angrian poetry, but the conventional nature of this poetry, with its stock heroes, forced optimism, and conventional piety renders it inferior to the Angrian. The necessity of earning a living which drove Charlotte to take a post unsuccessfully as governess with the Sedgwicks in 1839 and the Whites in 1840 cannot have helped her poetic inspiration. In March 1839 she had received her first proposal of marriage, an unromantic one from Ellen Nussey's brother, Henry. Branwell cannot be proved disgracefully drunk until 1840, but a hostile portrait of the drunken Henry Hastings in 1839 is a fair indication that Charlotte had become disillusioned with her brother before that date. Branwell continued to write poetry until the end of his life, and some of this was published in local newspapers, but this fact cannot have inspired Charlotte.

Instead she received her inspiration from a different quarter. M. Heger, although imperious like Zamorna, was a very different kind of man, and he inspired Charlotte into creating a less preposterous kind of hero and writing a less purple kind of prose. He is also probably behind some of the poems that she composed during this period, although the dating of most of the poems written in her ordinary hand is uncertain. The years in Brussels, 1842 and 1843, would seem to be the years in which Charlotte revised some of her original poems, many of these being revised again for publication.

The inspiration for publication came from Emily. The story of Charlotte's discovery of Emily's poems in the autumn of 1845, and of Emily's initial reluctance to publish is well known. Charlotte appears to have borne the brunt of corresponding with publishers. The collapse of M. Heger's friendship after Charlotte had written pathetic letters to him, the last of which is dated 18 November 1845, and the disgrace of Branwell in July 1845 had left an unpleasant vacuum in the lives of the three sisters, and the revision of their poems came as something of a godsend. Admittedly the publication by Aylott and Jones in May 1846 led neither to fame nor fortune, although there were a few kind reviews. Charlotte's correspondence reveals that the manuscripts of the poems were dispatched to the publishers on 7 February and proofs began to come in on 11 March 1846. Since the manuscript of *The Professor* is dated 27 June, the Brontës must have been fairly busy during 1846, especially as Charlotte would seem to have started *Jane Eyre* fairly soon after finishing *The Professor*.

With the success of *Jane Eyre*, Charlotte's career as a poet was virtually over. *Jane Eyre* does itself contain two poems, one an interesting adaptation of an earlier poem, and there were two melancholy tributes to her sisters after their deaths. But we are not really concerned with the literary triumphs and personal tragedies which Charlotte suffered in the last seven years of her life. These were the years when she had turned her prosaic poetry into poetic prose; this volume traces earlier stages in this development.

TEXTUAL INTRODUCTION

THE first two sections of this edition are reprinted without change from the Shakespeare Head edition. In editing poems which were published in Charlotte's lifetime Symington and Wise could scarcely go wrong. They did alter for the sake of uniformity Charlotte's slightly eccentric indentation and punctuation which she had adopted in the 1846 Aylott and Jones edition of the poems written by herself and her two sisters, but the alteration is almost always an improvement, and I have not thought it necessary to record every change in the notes. The manuscript of these poems is missing, but there are in several cases manuscripts extant of earlier versions, and these I have recorded in the notes. In the case of poems published in *Jane Eyre*, we have the manuscript and three editions published in Charlotte's lifetime; the fairly small differences between these four versions are described in full in the Clarendon edition of *Jane Eyre* (Oxford, 1969). It is difficult to establish here what the correct reading should be.

In the second section of poems not printed until Charlotte was dead the correct text is taken to be the wording of the latest manuscript. In the case of manuscripts which were, and in almost every case still are, in England, Symington and Wise do not make many errors. Their correction of spelling, punctuation, indentation, and capitalization is usually sensible, and I have followed the same principle as in my edition of Branwell of not worrying unduly about such changes. I have not even recorded whether a manuscript is well punctuated. In almost all of Charlotte's poetic manuscripts, even those written out as fair copies, the punctuation is scanty and irregular, and it hardly seems worth recording this fact. I have also not recorded, as I did in the case of Branwell, whether a manuscript has been corrected or not; in Branwell's case this is useful as an indication of how far a manuscript can be regarded as a fair copy of a final version or a rough draft, but in Charlotte's case we have more copies of individual poems, and there are fewer fair copies. Thus the degree of correction is not usually a guide to which version can be regarded as the final one. Corrections are recorded, where it is possible to read them.

There are a number of poems where it is clear that the editors of the Shakespeare Head did not have access to the original manuscript. Usually this manuscript, if it can be found, is in America. In editing Branwell, and in a chapter on the transmission of Brontë texts in *Brontë Facts and Problems* (London, 1983), I showed the origin of incorrect texts which Symington and Wise copied when a manuscript was not available. They usually copied the earlier printed version of Charlotte's poems, inaccurately entitled *The Complete Poems of Charlotte Brontë*. This edition pays little attention to manuscripts, relying instead on previously printed versions, very often the limited editions printed privately by Wise for his own pecuniary gain. These limited editions have an inaccurate text because Wise did not refer to manuscripts, which he usually had already sold, but to bad copies which he had had made on his acquisition of the manuscripts.

This edition shows just how bad this copying was. Although Charlotte's juvenile handwriting is difficult to read, it sometimes seems impossible to believe that the scribes Wise employed could have been so inefficient. The differences between the printed text of *Found in an Inn belonging to You* and the manuscript led the editors of the Shakespeare Head to suppose there must have been two manuscripts, and in other poems like *Morning* and *Vesper* Dr Alexander has assumed more than one version to account for the discrepancies which seem too great to be explained by faulty transcription. It is possible that Wise, who was a minor versifier as well as a major crook, may have tampered with the text of poems out of a wish to improve them. It is perhaps more probable that he made alterations in the text that he printed in order to increase the value of a manuscript he had retained or was in the process of selling. At all events, if one is interested in the text of Charlotte Brontë's poems as opposed to the iniquities of T. J. Wise, it seems profitable to record in the notes only the manuscript variations without worrying about the printed versions. Dr Alexander has given a full account in her catalogue of the editions where each manuscript is printed.

In the third section I have printed a number of poems which were not published in the Shakespeare Head edition of the poems of Charlotte and Branwell Brontë. Some of these were published in the two-volume *Miscellaneous and Unpublished Writings of Charlotte and Branwell Brontë*, but are more properly considered as poems in their own right. Others have been mistakenly attributed to Emily. Others still have only been published very recently, or not published at all, or have been assumed to be variants of existing poems when, in spite of trivial and superficial resemblances, they are obviously quite different works. Some of these manuscripts are difficult to read and of little literary worth, but at least one poem, 'At first I did attention give', is of great significance to Charlotte's biographers, and perhaps others may be as well.

There are a considerable number of poems written by Charlotte Brontë which I have not published in this edition. I have listed these in an appendix, using Dr Alexander's catalogue as a basis for a list which, thanks to Dr Alexander, is much longer and much more complete than the similar list in the edition of Branwell. These poems will be printed in the forthcoming edition of the juvenilia that Dr Alexander is preparing, and their Angrian context will be clear. Although it is not an Angrian poem, I have also omitted Charlotte's very early translation of Voltaire's *Henriade*.

As explained in the General Introduction, it is difficult to make a hard and fast distinction between poems that are part of the Angrian story and poems which are poems in their own right. A number of poems in this edition refer to Angria, and brief notes have been appended in order to explain them. Other notes have been kept to a minimum, although occasionally it appeared helpful to show possible literary and biographical sources for Charlotte's poetry. Dating Charlotte's poetry is more difficult than Branwell's because Charlotte is less punctilious about giving the date, and because more of her poems are written on loose leaves rather than in notebooks where the date of one poem can suggest the date of another.

There are seven notebooks, six of them in America, where Charlotte has collected more than one poem, but the existence of these notebooks is not much help to dating. The very juvenile *Miscellaneous Poems*, $7\frac{1}{4}'' \times 4\frac{1}{2}''$, contains poems written in 1830, as does the minute *The Violet*, $3\frac{3}{4}'' \times 2\frac{1}{4}''$. *Arthuriana*, $4\frac{1}{2}'' \times 3\frac{3}{4}''$, contains poems and prose written in 1833, and *The Wounded Stag*, $7\frac{1}{4}'' \times 4\frac{1}{2}''$, poems from 1836. Charlotte translated two poems from the French in her French exercise book in 1843. In the same year, she copied some poems into a notebook which I have entitled *Poems*, $9\frac{1}{4}'' \times 7\frac{1}{4}''$, but it is difficult to date all the poems in this notebook with any precision, since there is sometimes confusion between the date of composition and date of transcription. Finally she wrote in 1843 a few poems in a notebook ($7\frac{1}{2}'' \times 5\frac{1}{2}''$), which I have called *German Notebook* as it was originally intended for German exercises.

In some of her other poems Charlotte gives a date, but there are a great many poems where the only guide to dating is subject matter and handwriting. I have distinguished four main types of handwriting by Charlotte Brontë; the copperplate in which she tended to write her fair copies, the normal cursive in which she wrote most of her later poems, the juvenile cursive in which she wrote a few early poems, and the minuscule handwriting in which she wrote the bulk of her juvenile poetry. Sometimes, as in *Poems*, copperplate merges into ordinary cursive, and sometimes in the minuscule poems which are unsigned it is hard to be confident about whether the poems are by Charlotte. In dating most of Charlotte's unsigned minuscule poems to around 1837, and most of her undated cursive poems to around 1843, I am following previous editors, but am uneasily aware that Charlotte's poems after the death of her sisters were written in minuscule.

In both dating and interpretation as well as in textual matters I have erred on the side of caution. Where a word in the manuscript is hard to read I have indicated my doubts by a question mark, and where a correction has made the original version virtually illegible, I have not been unduly active in trying to decipher the original version. Biographical and literary conjecture even from a firmly established text is dangerous, especially when the date of a poem is conjectural, and many versions of the same poem were written at different times. The history of Brontë scholarship is full of horror stories involving hypotheses which become transformed into definite facts. There is probably, however, room for a less cautious and more detailed examination of Charlotte's poetry and the way in which it contributes to an understanding of her life and work. It is to be hoped that in spite of its self-imposed limitations this edition does make some such contribution.

ABBREVIATIONS

A	C. Alexander, *Bibliography of the Manuscripts of Charlotte Brontë* (Keighley, 1982)
AC	C. Alexander, *The Early Writings of Charlotte Brontë* (Oxford, 1983)
BCH	The Bonnell Collection, Haworth
BCL	The Brotherton Collection, Leeds University Library
BCNY	The Berg Collection, New York Public Library
BCPML	The Bonnell Collection, Pierpont Morgan Library, New York
BL	The British Library
BPM	The Brontë Parsonage Museum, Haworth
BST	The *Brontë Society Transactions*
CW	E. Chitham and T. Winnifrith, *Brontë Facts and Problems* (London, 1983)
HLC	The Henry Huntington Library
HLH	The Houghton Library, Harvard University
HRT	The Humanities Research Centre, University of Texas
P	*Poems by Acton Ellis and Currer Bell* (London, 1846)
RB	The Library of Rogert Barrett, Kenilworth, Illinois
RTP	The Robert Taylor Collection, Princeton, New Jersey
SHBB	*The Poems of Branwell Brontë*, edited by T. J. Winnifrith (London, 1983)
SHCBM	*The Miscellaneous and Unpublished Writings of Charlotte Brontë and Patrick Branwell Brontë*, edited by T. J. Wise and J. A. Symington, 2 vols. (Oxford, 1938)
SHCBP	*The Complete Poems of Charlotte Brontë and Patrick Branwell Brontë*, edited by T. J. Wise and J. A. Symington (Oxford, 1934)

SUNY	The Rare Books Collection, The State University of New York at Buffalo
WS	The Library of William Self, Studio City, California
†	indicates a reading that has been crossed out
*	indicates a reading that has been corrected without crossing out
**	indicates the correct or upper reading where there is more than one version
( )	titles in round brackets are those given by the Shakespeare Head editors for which there is no manuscript authority
[ ]	in the notes indicates an incorrect reading in the original Shakespeare Head text
[?]	following a word indicates a doubtful reading
[—]	indicates missing text

Where there is only one manuscript this has been assumed, except on rare occasions, to have the correct reading. Where there is more than one manuscript variant readings are recorded, but the latest version has been assumed to be the correct one. The Shakespeare Head text has been used as a base from which a correct reading may be established; there are occasions when it provides the correct reading, agreeing with the latest manuscript, but earlier manuscript variants are recorded.

CHARLOTTE BRONTË'S POEMS
IN APPROXIMATE
CHRONOLOGICAL ORDER

I

POEMS OF CHARLOTTE BRONTË PUBLISHED IN HER LIFETIME, FROM THE SHAKESPEARE HEAD EDITION

PILATE'S WIFE'S DREAM

I'VE quenched my lamp, I struck it in that start
   Which every limb convulsed, I heard it fall—
The crash blent with my sleep, I saw depart
   Its light, even as I woke, on yonder wall;
5 Over against my bed, there shone a gleam
Strange, faint, and mingling also with my dream.

It sunk, and I am wrapt in utter gloom;
   How far is night advanced, and when will day
Re-tinge the dusk and livid air with bloom,
10   And fill this void with warm, creative ray?
Would I could sleep again till, clear and red,
Morning shall on the mountain-tops be spread!

I'd call my women, but to break their sleep,
   Because my own is broken, were unjust;
15 They've wrought all day, and well-earned slumbers steep
   Their labours in forgetfulness, I trust;
Let me my feverish watch with patience bear,
Thankful that none with me its sufferings share.

Yet Oh! for light! one ray would tranquillize
20   My nerves, my pulses, more than effort can;
I'll draw my curtain and consult the skies:
   These trembling stars at dead of night look wan,
Wild, restless, strange, yet cannot be more drear
Than this my couch, shared by a nameless fear.

25 All black—one great cloud, drawn from east to west,
   Conceals the heavens, but there are lights below;
Torches burn in Jerusalem, and cast
   On yonder stony mount a lurid glow.
I see men stationed there, and gleaming spears;
30 A sound, too, from afar, invades my ears.

Dull, measured strokes of axe and hammer ring
 From street to street, not loud, but through the night
Distinctly heard—and some strange spectral thing
 Is now upreared—and, fixed against the light
35 Of the pale lamps; defined upon that sky,
It stands up like a column, straight and high.

I see it all—I know the dusky sign—
 A cross on Calvary, which Jews uprear
While Romans watch; and when the dawn shall shine
40 Pilate, to judge the victim, will appear,
Pass·sentence—yield Him up to crucify;
And on that cross the spotless Christ must die.

Dreams, then, are true—for thus my vision ran;
 Surely some oracle has been with me,
45 The gods have chosen me to reveal their plan,
 To warn an unjust judge of destiny:
I, slumbering, heard and saw; awake I know,
Christ's coming death, and Pilate's life of woe.

I do not weep for Pilate—who could prove
50 Regret for him whose cold and crushing sway
No prayer can soften, no appeal can move;
 Who tramples hearts as others trample clay,
Yet with a faltering, an uncertain tread,
That might stir up reprisal in the dead.

55 Forced to sit by his side and see his deeds;
 Forced to behold that visage, hour by hour,
In whose gaunt lines the abhorrent gazer reads
 A triple lust of gold, and blood, and power;
A soul whom motives fierce, yet abject, urge—
60 Rome's servile slave, and Judah's tyrant scourge.

How can I love, or mourn, or pity him?
   I, who so long my fettered hands have wrung;
  I, who for grief have wept my eyesight dim;
   Because, while life for me was bright and young,
65 He robbed my youth—he quenched my life's fair ray—
He crushed my mind, and did my freedom slay.

And at this hour—although I be his wife—
  He has no more of tenderness from me
Than any other wretch of guilty life;
70   Less, for I know his household privacy—
I see him as he is—without a screen;
And, by the gods, my soul abhors his mien!

Has he not sought my presence, dyed in blood—
  Innocent, righteous blood, shed shamelessly?
75 And have I not his red salute withstood?
   Ay, when, as èrst, he plunged all Galilee
In dark bereavement—in affliction sore,
Mingling their very offerings with their gore.

Then came he—in his eyes a serpent-smile,
80   Upon his lips some false, endearing word,
And, through the streets of Salem, clanged the while
   His slaughtering, hacking, sacrilegious sword—
And I, to see a man cause men such woe,
Trembled with ire I did not fear to show.

85 And now the envious Jewish priests have brought
   Jesus—whom they in mockery call their king—
To have, by this grim power, their vengeance wrought:
   By this mean reptile, innocence to sting.
Oh! could I but the purposed doom avert,
90 And shield the blameless head from cruel hurt!

Accessible is Pilate's heart to fear,
　　Omens will shake his soul, like autumn leaf;
Could he this night's appalling vision hear,
　　This just man's bonds were loosed, his life were safe,
95　Unless that bitter priesthood should prevail,
And make even terror to their malice quail.

Yet if I tell the dream—but let me pause.
　　What dream? Erewhile the characters were clear,
Graved on my brain—at once some unknown cause
100　Has dimmed and rased the thoughts, which now appear,
Like a vague remnant of some by-past scene;—
Not what will be, but what, long since, has been.

I suffered many things—I heard foretold
　　A dreadful doom for Pilate,—lingering woes,
105　In far barbarian climes, where mountains cold
　　Built up a solitude of trackless snows:
There he and grisly wolves prowled side by side,
There he lived famished—there, methought, he died;

But not of hunger, nor by malady;
110　I saw the snow around him, stained with gore;
I said I had no tears for such as he,
　　And lo! my cheek is wet—mine eyes run o'er.
I weep for mortal suffering, mortal guilt,
I weep the impious deed, the blood self-spilt.

115　More I recall not, yet the vision spread
　　Into a world remote, an age to come—
And still the illumined name of Jesus shed
　　A light, a clearness through the unfolding gloom—
And still I saw that sign which now I see,
120　That cross on yonder brow of Calvary.

What is this Hebrew Christ?—to me unknown
  His lineage—doctrine—mission; yet how clear
Is god-like goodness in his actions shewn,
  How straight and stainless is his life's career!
125 The ray of Deity that rests on him,
In my eyes makes Olympian glory dim.

The world advances; Greek or Roman rite
  Suffices not the inquiring mind to stay;
The searching soul demands a purer light
130   To guide it on its upward, onward way;
Ashamed of sculptured gods, Religion turns
To where the unseen Jehovah's altar burns.

Our faith is rotten, all our rites defiled,
  Our temples sullied, and, methinks, this Man,
135 With His new ordinance, so wise and mild,
  Is come, even as He says, the chaff to fan
And sever from the wheat; but will His faith
Survive the terrors of to-morrow's death?

    .   .   .   .

I feel a firmer trust—a higher hope
140   Rise in my soul—it dawns with dawning day;
Lo! on the Temple's roof—on Moriah's slope
  Appears at length that clear and crimson ray
Which I so wished for when shut in by night;
Oh, opening skies, I hail, I bless your light!

145 Part, clouds and shadows! Glorious Sun, appear!
  Part, mental gloom! Come, insight from on high!
Dusk dawn in heaven still strives with daylight clear,
  The longing soul doth still uncertain sigh.
Oh! to behold the truth—that sun divine,
150 How doth my bosom pant, my spirit pine!

This day, Time travails with a mighty birth;
This day, Truth stoops from heaven and visits earth;
Ere night descends I shall more surely know
What guide to follow, in what path to go;
155 I wait in hope—I wait in solemn fear,
The oracle of God—the sole—true God—to hear.

MEMENTOS

ARRANGING long-locked drawers and shelves
Of cabinets shut up for years,
What a strange task we've set ourselves!
How still the lonely room appears!
5 How strange this mass of ancient treasures,
Mementos of past pains and pleasures;
These volumes, clasped with costly stone,
With print all faded, gilding gone;

These fans of leaves, from Indian trees—
10 These crimson shells, from Indian seas—
These tiny portraits, set in rings—
Once, doubtless, deemed such precious things;
Keepsakes bestowed by Love on Faith,
And worn till the receiver's death,
15 Now stored with cameos, china, shells,
In this old closet's dusty cells.

I scarcely think for ten long years,
A hand has touched these relics old;
And, coating each, slow-formed, appears
20 The growth of green and antique mould.

All in this house is mossing over;
All is unused, and dim, and damp;
Nor light, nor warmth, the rooms discover—
Bereft for years of fire and lamp.

25 The sun, sometimes in summer, enters
     The casements, with reviving ray;
   But the long rains of many winters
     Moulder the very walls away.

   And outside all is ivy, clinging
30   To chimney, lattice, gable grey;
   Scarcely one little red rose springing
     Through the green moss can force its way.

   Unscared, the daw and starling nestle,
     Where the tall turret rises high,
35 And winds alone come near to rustle
     The thick leaves where their cradles lie.

   I sometimes think , when late at even
     I climb the stair reluctantly,
   Some shape that should be well in heaven,
40   Or ill elsewhere, will pass by me.

   I fear to see the very faces,
     Familiar thirty years ago,
   Even in the old accustomed places
     Which look so cold and gloomy now.

45 I've come, to close the window, hither,
     At twilight, when the sun was down,
   And Fear my very soul would wither,
     Lest something should be dimly shown,

   Too much the buried form resembling,
50   Of her who once was mistress here;
   Lest doubtful shade, or moonbeam trembling
     Might take her aspect, once so dear.

   Hers was this chamber; in her time
     It seemed to me a pleasant room,
55 For then no cloud of grief or crime
     Had cursed it with a settled gloom;

I had not seen death's image laid
In shroud and sheet, on yonder bed.
   Before she married, she was blest—
60 Blest in her youth, blest in her worth;
   Her mind was calm, its sunny rest
Shone in her eyes more clear than mirth.

And when attired in rich array,
   Light, lustrous hair about her brow,
65 She yonder sat, a kind of day
   Lit up what seems so gloomy now.
These grim oak walls even then were grim;
   That old carved chair was then antique;
But what around looked dusk and dim
70   Served as a foil to her fresh cheek;
Her neck and arms, of hue so fair,
   Eyes of unclouded, smiling light;
Her soft, and curled, and floating hair,
   Gems and attire, as rainbow bright.

75 Reclined in yonder deep recess,
   Ofttimes she would, at evening, lie
Watching the sun; she seemed to bless
   With happy glance the glorious sky.
She loved such scenes, and as she gazed,
80   Her face evinced her spirit's mood;
Beauty or grandeur ever raised
   In her a deep-felt gratitude.

But of all lovely things, she loved
   A cloudless moon on summer night;
85 Full oft have I impatience proved
   To see how long her still delight
Would find a theme in reverie,
   Out on the lawn, or where the trees
Let in the lustre fitfully,
90 As their boughs parted momently
   To the soft, languid summer breeze.

Alas! that she should e'er have flung
  Those pure though lonely joys away:
Deceived by false and guileful tongue,
95 She gave her hand, then suffered wrong;
Oppressed, ill-used, she faded young,
  And died of grief by slow decay.

Open that casket—look how bright
Those jewels flash upon the sight;
100 The brilliants have not lost a ray
Of lustre since her wedding-day.
But see—upon that pearly chain—
How dim lies Time's discolouring stain!
I've seen that by her daughter worn:
105 For, ere she died, a child was born;
A child that ne'er its mother knew,
That lone, and almost friendless, grew;
For, ever, when its step drew nigh,
Averted was the father's eye;
110 And then a life impure and wild
Made him a stranger to his child:
Absorbed in vice, he little cared
On what she did, or how she fared.

The love withheld she never sought,
115 She grew uncherished—learnt untaught;
To her the inward life of thought
  Full soon was open laid.
I know not if her friendlessness
Did sometimes on her spirit press,
120 But plaint she never made.

The book-shelves were her darling treasure,
She rarely seemed the time to measure
  While she could read alone.
And she too loved the twilight wood,
125 And often, in her mother's mood,
  Away to yonder hill would hie,

Like her, to watch the setting sun,
Or see the stars born, one by one,
   Out of the darkening sky.
130 Nor would she leave that hill till night
Trembled from pole to pole with light;
   Even then, upon her homeward way,
Long—long her wandering steps delayed
To quit the sombre forest shade,
135   Through which her eerie pathway lay.

You ask if she had beauty's grace?
I know not—but a nobler face
   My eyes have seldom seen;
A keen and fine intelligence,
140 And, better still, the truest sense
   Were in her speaking mien.
But bloom or lustre was there none,
Only at moments fitful shone
   An ardour in her eye,
145 That kindled on her cheek a flush,
Warm as a red sky's passing blush
   And quick with energy.

Her speech, too, was not common speech,
No wish to shine, or aim to teach,
150   Was in her words displayed:
She still began with quiet sense,
But oft the force of eloquence
   Came to her lips in aid;
Language and voice unconscious changed,
155 And thoughts, in other words arranged,
   Her fervid soul transfused
Into the hearts of those who heard,
And transient strength and ardour stirred,
   In minds to strength unused.
160 Yet in gay crowd or festal glare,
Grave and retiring was her air;

'Twas seldom, save with me alone,
That fire of feeling freely shone;
She loved not awe's nor wonder's gaze,
165 Nor even exaggerated praise,
Nor even notice, if too keen
The curious gazer searched her mien.
Nature's own green expanse revealed
The world, the pleasures, she could prize;
170 On free hill-side, in sunny field,
In quiet spots by woods concealed,
Grew wild and fresh her chosen joys—
Yet Nature's feelings deeply lay
In that endowed and youthful frame;
175 Shrined in her heart and hid from day,
They burned unseen with silent flame.
In youth's first search for mental light,
She lived but to reflect and learn,
But soon her mind's maturer might
180 For stronger task did pant and yearn;
And stronger task did fate assign,
Task that a giant's strength might strain;
To suffer long and ne'er repine,
Be calm in frenzy, smile at pain.

185 Pale with the secret war of feeling,
Sustained with courage, mute yet high,
The wounds at which she bled revealing
Only by altered cheek and eye;

She bore in silence—but when passion
190 Surged in her soul with ceaseless foam,
The storm at last brought desolation,
And drove her exiled from her home.

And silent still, she straight assembled
The wrecks of strength her soul retained;
195 For though the wasted body trembled,
The unconquered mind, to quail, disdained.

She crossed the sea—now lone she wanders
By Seine's, or Rhine's, or Arno's flow:
Fain would I know if distance renders
200   Relief or comfort to her woe.

Fain would I know if, henceforth, ever,
These eyes shall read in hers again,
That light of love which faded never,
Though dimmed so long with secret pain.

205 She will return, but cold and altered,
Like all whose hopes too soon depart;
Like all on whom have beat, unsheltered,
The bitter blasts that blight the heart.

No more shall I behold her lying
210   Calm on a pillow, smoothed by me;
No more that spirit, worn with sighing,
Will know the rest of infancy.

If still the paths of lore she follow,
'Twill be with tired and goaded will;
215 She'll only toil, the aching hollow,
The joyless blank of life to fill.

And oh! full oft, quite spent and weary,
Her hand will pause, her head decline;
That labour seems so hard and dreary,
220   On which no ray of hope may shine.

Thus the pale blight of time and sorrow
Will shade with grey her soft, dark hair;
Then comes the day that knows no morrow,
And death succeeds to long despair.

225 So speaks experience, sage and hoary;
I see it plainly, know it well,
Like one who, having read a story,
Each incident therein can tell.

Touch not that ring; 'twas his, the sire
230   Of that forsaken child;
And nought his relics can inspire
    Save memories sin-defiled.

I, who sat by his wife's death-bed,
    I, who his daughter loved,
235   Could almost curse the guilty dead,
    For woes the guiltless proved.

And heaven did curse—they found him laid,
    When crime for wrath was ripe[?],
Cold—with the suicidal blade
240   Clutched in his desperate gripe.

'Twas near that long-deserted hut,
    Which in the wood decays,
Death's axe, self-wielded, struck his root,
    And lopped his desperate days.

245   You know the spot, where three black trees,
    Lift up their branches fell,
And moaning, ceaseless as the seas,
Still seem, in every passing breeze,
    The deed of blood to tell.

250   They named him mad, and laid his bones
    Where holier ashes lie;
Yet doubt not that his spirit groans
    In hell's eternity.

But, lo! night, closing o'er the earth,
255   Infects our thoughts with gloom;
Come, let us strive to rally mirth
Where glows a clear and tranquil hearth
    In some more cheerful room.

THE WIFE'S WILL

SIT still—a word—a breath may break
(As light airs stir a sleeping lake)
The glassy calm that soothes my woes—
The sweet, the deep, the full repose.
5   Oh, leave me not! for ever be
Thus, more than life itself to me!

Yes, close beside thee let me kneel—
Give me thy hand, that I may feel
The friend so true—so tried—so dear,
10 My heart's own chosen—indeed is near;
And check me not—this hour divine
Belongs to me—is fully mine.

'Tis thy own hearth thou sitt'st beside,
After long absence, wandering wide;
15 'Tis thy own wife reads in thine eyes
A promise clear of stormless skies;
For faith and true love light the rays
Which shine responsive to her gaze.

Ay,—well that single tear may fall;
20 Ten thousand might mine eyes recall,
Which from their lids ran blinding fast,
In hours of grief, yet scarcely past;
Well may'st thou speak of love to me,
For, oh! most truly—I love thee!

25 Yet smile—for we are happy now.
Whence, then, that sadness on thy brow?
What sayest thou? 'We must once again,
Ere long, be severed by the main!'
I knew not this—I deemed no more
30 Thy step would err from Britain's shore.

'Duty commands!' 'Tis true—'tis just;
Thy slightest word I wholly trust,
Nor by request, nor faintest sigh,
Would I to turn thy purpose try;
35 But, William, hear my solemn vow—
Hear and confirm!—with thee I go.

'Distance and suffering,' didst thou say?
'Danger by night, and toil by day?'
Oh, idle words and vain are these;
40 Hear me! I cross with thee the seas.
Such risk as thou must meet and dare,
I—thy true wife—will duly share.

Passive, at home, I will not pine;
Thy toils, thy perils shall be mine;
45 Grant this—and be hereafter paid
By a warm heart's devoted aid:
'Tis granted—with that yielding kiss,
Entered my soul unmingled bliss.

Thanks, William, thanks! thy love has joy
50 Pure, undefiled with base alloy!
'Tis not a passion, false and blind,
Inspires, enchains, absorbs my mind;
Worthy, I feel, art thou to be
Loved with my perfect energy.

55 This evening now shall sweetly flow,
Lit by our clear fire's happy glow;
And parting's peace-embittering fear
Is warned our hearts to come not near;
For fate admits my soul's decree,
60 In bliss or bale—to go with thee!

THE WOOD

BUT two miles more, and then we rest!
Well, there is still an hour of day,
And long the brightness of the West
    Will light us on our devious way;
5   Sit then, awhile, here in this wood—
So total is the solitude,
    We safely may delay.

These massive roots afford a seat,
    Which seems for weary travellers made.
10 There rest. The air is soft and sweet
    In this sequestered forest glade,
And there are scents of flowers around,
The evening dew draws from the ground;
    How soothingly they spread!

15   Yes; I was tired, but not at heart;
No—that beats full of sweet content,
For now I have my natural part
    Of action with adventure blent;
Cast forth on the wide world with thee,
20 And all my once waste energy
    To weighty purpose bent.

Yet—say'st thou, spies around us roam,
    Our aims are termed conspiracy?
Haply, no more our English home
25   An anchorage for us may be?
That there is risk our mutual blood
May redden in some lonely wood
    The knife of treachery?

Say'st thou, that where we lodge each night,
30   In each lone farm, or lonelier hall
Of Norman Peer—ere morning light
    Suspicion must as duly fall,
As day returns—such vigilance
Presides and watches over France,
35   Such rigour governs all?

I fear not, William; dost thou fear?
    So that the knife does not divide,
It may be ever hovering near:
    I could not tremble at thy side,
40 And strenuous love—like mine for thee—
Is buckler strong 'gainst treachery,
    And turns its stab aside.

I am resolved that thou shalt learn
    To trust my strength as I trust thine;
45 I am resolved our souls shall burn
    With equal, steady, mingling shine;
Part of the field is conquered now,
Our lives in the same channel flow,
    Along the self-same line;

50 And while no groaning storm is heard,
    Thou seem'st content it should be so,
But soon as comes a warning word
    Of danger—straight thine anxious brow
Bends over me a mournful shade,
55 As doubting if my powers are made
    To ford the floods of woe.

Know, then, it is my spirit swells,
    And drinks, with eager joy, the air
Of freedom—where at last it dwells,
60   Chartered, a common task to share
With thee, and then it stirs alert,
And pants to learn what menaced hurt
    Demands for thee its care.

Remember, I have crossed the deep
65   And stood with thee on deck, to gaze
On waves that rose in threatening heap,
    While stagnant lay a heavy haze,
Dimly confusing sea with sky,
And baffling, even, the pilot's eye,
70   Intent to thread the maze—

Of rocks, on Bretagne's dangerous coast,
    And find a way to steer our band
To the one point obscure, which lost,
    Flung us, as victims, on the strand;—
75 All, elsewhere, gleamed the Gallic sword,
And not a wherry could be moored
    Along the guarded land.

I feared not then—I fear not now;
    The interest of each stirring scene
80 Wakes a new sense, a welcome glow,
    In every nerve and bounding vein;
Alike on turbid Channel sea,
Or in still wood of Normandy,
    I feel as born again.

85 The rain descended that wild morn
    When, anchoring in the cove at last,
Our band, all weary and forlorn,
    Ashore, like wave-worn sailors, cast—
Sought for a sheltering roof in vain,
90 And scarce could scanty food obtain
    To break their morning fast.

Thou didst thy crust with me divide,
    Thou didst thy cloak around me fold;
And, sitting silent by thy side,
95   I ate the bread in peace untold:
Given kindly from thy hand, 'twas sweet
As costly fare or princely treat
    On royal plate of gold.

Sharp blew the sleet upon my face,
100   And, rising wild, the gusty wind
Drove on those thundering waves apace,
    Our crew so late had left behind;
But, spite of frozen shower and storm,
So close to thee, my heart beat warm,
105   And tranquil slept my mind.

So now—nor foot-sore, nor oppressed
    With walking all this August day,
I taste a heaven in this brief rest,
    This gipsy-halt beside the way.
110 England's wild flowers are fair to view,
Like balm is England's summer dew,
    Like gold her sunset ray.

But the white violets, growing here,
    Are sweeter than I yet have seen,
115 And ne'er did dew so pure and clear
    Distil on forest mosses green,
As now, called forth by summer heat,
Perfumes our cool and fresh retreat—
    These fragrant limes between.

120 That sunset! Look beneath the boughs,
    Over the copse—beyond the hills;
How soft, yet deep and warm, it glows,
    And heaven with rich suffusion fills;
With hues where still the opal's tint,
125 Its gleam of prisoned fire, is blent,
    Where flame through azure thrills!

Depart we now—for fast will fade
    That solemn splendour of decline,
And deep must be the after-shade,
130   As stars alone to-night will shine;
No moon is destined—pale—to gaze
On such a day's vast phœnix blaze,
    A day in fires decayed!

There—hand-in-hand we tread again
135   The mazes of this varying wood,
And soon, amid a cultured plain,
    Girt in with fertile solitude,
We shall our resting-place descry,
Marked by one roof-tree, towering high
140   Above a farmstead rude.

Refreshed, ere long, with rustic fare,
    We'll seek a couch of dreamless ease;
Courage will guard thy heart from fear,
    And Love give mine divinest peace:
145   To-morrow brings more dangerous toil,
And through its conflict and turmoil
    We'll pass, as God shall please.

The preceding composition refers, doubtless, to the scenes acted in
France during the last year of the Consulate.—C. B.

FRANCES

SHE will not sleep, for fear of dreams,
    But, rising, quits her restless bed,
And walks where some beclouded beams
    Of moonlight through the hall are shed.

5   Obedient to the goad of grief,
    Her steps, now fast, now lingering slow,
In varying motion seek relief
    From the Eumenides of woe.

Wringing her hands, at intervals—
10   But long as mute as phantom dim—
She glides along the dusky walls,
    Under the black oak rafters grim.

The close air of the grated tower
    Stifles a heart that scarce can beat,
15 And, though so late and lone the hour,
    Forth pass her wandering, faltering feet;

And on the pavement spread before
    The long front of the mansion grey,
Her steps imprint the night-frost hoar,
20   Which pale on grass and granite lay.

Not long she stayed where misty moon
    And shimmering stars could on her look,
But through the garden archway soon
    Her strange and gloomy path she took.

25 Some firs, coëval with the tower,
    Their straight black boughs stretched o'er her head;
Unseen, beneath this sable bower,
    Rustled her dress and rapid tread.

There was an alcove in that shade,
30   Screening a rustic seat and stand;
Weary, she sat her down, and laid
    Her hot brow on her burning hand.

To solitude and to the night
    Some words she now, in murmurs, said;
35 And trickling through her fingers white,
    Some tears of misery she shed.

'God help me in my grievous need,
    God help me in my inward pain;
Which cannot ask for pity's meed,
40   Which has no licence to complain;

'Which must be borne; yet who can bear,
    Hours long, days long, a constant weight—
The yoke of absolute despair,
    A suffering wholly desolate?

45 'Who can for ever crush the heart,
    Restrain its throbbing, curb its life?
Dissemble truth with ceaseless art,
    With outward calm mask inward strife?'

She waited—as for some reply;
50   The still and cloudy night gave none;
Ere long, with deep-drawn, trembling sigh,
    Her heavy plaint again begun.

'Unloved—I love; unwept—I weep;
    Grief I restrain—hope I repress:
55 Vain is this anguish—fixed and deep;
    Vainer, desires and dreams of bliss:[1]

'My love awakes no love again,
    My tears collect, and fall unfelt;
My sorrow touches none with pain,
60   My humble hopes to nothing melt.

'For me the universe is dumb,
    Stone-deaf, and blank, and wholly blind;
Life I must bound, existence sum
    In the strait limits of one mind;

65 'That mind my own. Oh! narrow cell;
    Dark—imageless—a living tomb!
There must I sleep, there wake and dwell
    Content,—with palsy, pain, and gloom.'

[1]Compare with the first verse of the poem 'Reason.'

Again she paused; a moan of pain,
70   A stifled sob, alone was heard;
Long silence followed—then again
    Her voice the stagnant midnight stirred:

'Must it be so? Is this my fate?
    Can I nor struggle, nor contend?
75 And am I doomed for years to wait,
    Watching death's lingering axe descend?

'And when it falls, and when I die,
    What follows? Vacant nothingness?
The blank of lost identity?
80   Erasure both of pain and bliss?

'I've heard of Heaven—I would believe;
    For if this earth indeed be all,
Who longest lives may deepest grieve;
    Most blest, whom sorrows soonest call.

85 'Oh! leaving disappointment here,
    Will man find hope on yonder coast?
Hope, which, on earth, shines never clear,
    And oft in clouds is wholly lost.

'Will he hope's source of light behold,
90   Fruition's spring, where doubts expire,
And drink, in waves of living gold,
    Contentment, full, for long desire?

'Will he find bliss, which here he dreamed?
    Rest, which was weariness on earth?
95 Knowledge, which, if o'er life it beamed,
    Served but to prove it void of worth?

'Will he find love without lust's leaven,
  Love fearless, tearless, perfect, pure,
To all with equal bounty given;
100 In all, unfeigned, unfailing, sure?

'Will he, from penal sufferings free,
  Released from shroud and wormy clod,
All calm and glorious, rise and see
  Creation's Sire—Existence' God?

105 'Then, glancing back on Time's brief woes,
  Will he behold them, fading, fly;
Swept from Eternity's repose,
  Like sullying cloud from pure blue sky?

'If so, endure, my weary frame;
110 And when thy anguish strikes too deep,
And when all troubled burns life's flame,
  Think of the quiet, final sleep;

'Think of the glorious waking-hour,
  Which will not dawn on grief and tears,
115 But on a ransomed spirit's power,
  Certain and free from mortal fears.

'Seek now thy couch, and lie till morn,
  Then from thy chamber, calm, descend,
With mind nor tossed, nor anguish-torn,
120 But tranquil, fixed, to wait the end.

'And when thy opening eyes shall see
  Mementos on the chamber wall,
Of one who has forgotten thee,
  Shed not the tear of acrid gall.

125 'The tear which, welling from the heart,
  Burns where its drop corrosive falls,
And makes each nerve in torture start,
  At feelings it too well recalls:

'When the sweet hope of being loved
130   Threw Eden-sunshine on Life's way;
When every sense and feeling proved
  Expectancy of brightest day:

'When the hand trembled to receive
  A thrilling clasp, which seemed so near,
135 And the heart ventured to believe
  Another heart esteemed it dear:

'When words, half love, all tenderness,
  Were hourly heard, as hourly spoken,
When the long sunny days of bliss
140   Only by moonlight nights were broken:

'Till, drop by drop, the cup of joy,
  Filled full, with purple light was glowing,
And Faith, which watched it sparkling high,
  Still never dreamt the overflowing.

145 'It fell not with a sudden crashing,
  It poured not out like open sluice;
No, sparkling still, and redly flashing,
  Drained, drop by drop, the generous juice.

'I saw it sink, and strove to taste it—
150   My eager lips approached the brim;
The movement only seemed to waste it—
  It sank to dregs, all harsh and dim.

'These I have drunk, and they for ever
 Have poisoned life and love for me;
155 A draught from Sodom's lake could never
  More fiery, salt, and bitter be.

'Oh! Love was all a thin illusion;
 Joy but the desert's flying stream;
And glancing back on long delusion
160 My memory grasps a hollow dream.

'Yet whence that wondrous change of feeling,
 I never knew, and cannot learn;
Nor why my lover's eye, congealing,
 Grew cold and clouded, proud and stern.

165 'Nor wherefore, friendship's forms forgetting,
 He careless left and cool withdrew,
Nor spoke of grief nor fond regretting,
 Nor even one glance of comfort threw.

'And neither word nor token sending,
170 Of kindness, since the parting day,
His course, for distant regions bending,
 Went, self-contained and calm, away.

'O bitter, blighting, keen sensation,
 Which will not weaken, cannot die,
175 Hasten thy work of desolation,
 And let my tortured spirit fly!

'Vain as the passing gale, my crying;
 Though lightning-struck, I must live on;
I know at heart there is no dying
180 Of love, and ruined hope, alone.

'Still strong and young, and warm with vigour,
   Though scathed, I long shall greenly grow;
And many a storm of wildest rigour
   Shall yet break o'er my shivered bough.

185 'Rebellious now to blank inertion,
   My unused strength demands a task;
Travel, and toil, and full exertion
   Are the last, only boon I ask.

'Whence, then, this vain and barren dreaming
190   Of death, and dubious life to come?
I see a nearer beacon gleaming
   Over dejection's sea of gloom.

'The very wildness of my sorrow
   Tells me I yet have innate force;
195 My track of life has been too narrow,
   Effort shall trace a broader course.

'The world is not in yonder tower,
   Earth is not prisoned in that room,
'Mid whose dark panels, hour by hour,
200   I've sat, the slave and prey of gloom.

'One feeling— turned to utter anguish,
   Is not my being's only aim;
When, lorn and loveless, life will languish,
   But courage can revive the flame.

205 'He, when he left me, went a-roving
   To sunny climes beyond the sea;
And I, the weight of woe removing,
   Am free and fetterless as he.

'New scenes, new language, skies less clouded,
210   May once more wake the wish to live;
Strange foreign towns, astir and crowded,
    New pictures to the mind may give.

'New forms and faces, passing ever,
    May hide the one I still retain,
215 Defined and fixed, and fading never,
    Stamped deep on vision, heart, and brain.

'And we might meet—time may have changed him;
    Chance may reveal the mystery,
The secret influence which estranged him;
220   Love may restore him yet to me.

'False thought—false hope—in scorn be banished!
    I am not loved—nor loved have been!
Recall not, then, the dreams scarce vanished;
    Traitors! mislead me not again!

225 'To words like yours I bid defiance,
    'Tis such my mental wreck have made;
Of God alone, and self-reliance,
    I ask for solace—hope for aid.

'Morn comes—and ere meridian glory
230   O'er these, my natal woods, shall smile,
Both lonely wood and mansion hoary
    I'll leave behind, full many a mile.'

GILBERT

I. THE GARDEN

ABOVE the city hung the moon,
 Right o'er a plot of ground
Where flowers and orchard-trees were fenced
 With lofty walls around:
5 'Twas Gilbert's garden—there to-night
 Awhile he walked alone;
And, tired with sedentary toil,
 Mused where the moonlight shone.

This garden, in a city heart,
10 Lay still as houseless wild,
Though many-windowed mansion fronts
 Were round it closely piled;
But thick their walls, and those within
 Lived lives by noise unstirred;
15 Like wafting of an angel's wing,
 Time's flight by them was heard.

Some soft piano-notes alone
 Were sweet as faintly given,
Where ladies, doubtless, cheered the hearth
20 With song that winter-even.
The city's many-mingled sounds
 Rose like the hum of ocean;
They rather lulled the heart than roused
 Its pulse to faster motion.

25 Gilbert has paced the single walk
 An hour, yet is not weary;
And, though it be a winter night,
 He feels nor cold nor dreary.

The prime of life is in his veins,
    And sends his blood fast flowing,
And Fancy's fervour warms the thoughts
    Now in his bosom glowing.

Those thoughts recur to early love,
    Or what he love would name,
Though haply Gilbert's secret deeds
    Might other title claim.
Such theme not oft his mind absorbs,
    He to the world clings fast,
And too much for the present lives,
    To linger o'er the past.

But now the evening's deep repose
    Has glided to his soul;
That moonlight falls on Memory,
    And shows her fading scroll.
One name appears in every line
    The gentle rays shine o'er,
And still he smiles and still repeats
    That one name—Elinor.

There is no sorrow in his smile,
    No kindness in his tone;
The triumph of a selfish heart
    Speaks coldly there alone.
He says: 'She loved me more than life;
    And truly it was sweet
To see so fair a woman kneel
    In bondage at my feet.

'There was a sort of quiet bliss
    To be so deeply loved,
To gaze on trembling eagerness
    And sit myself unmoved;
And when it pleased my pride to grant
    At last some rare caress,
To feel the fever of that hand
    My fingers deigned to press.

65 ' 'Twas sweet to see her strive to hide
    What every glance revealed;
Endowed, the while, with despot-might
    Her destiny to wield.
I knew myself no perfect man,
70   Nor, as she deemed, divine;
I knew that I was glorious—but
    By her reflected shine;

'Her youth, her native energy,
    Her powers new-born and fresh—
75 'Twas these with Godhead sanctified
    My sensual frame of flesh.
Yet, like a god did I descend
    At last to meet her love;
And, like a god, I then withdrew
80   To my own heaven above.

'And never more could she invoke
    My presence to her sphere;
No prayer, no plaint, no cry of hers
    Could win my awful ear.
85 I knew her blinded constancy
    Would ne'er my deeds betray,
And, calm in conscience, whole in heart,
    I went my tranquil way.

'Yet, sometimes, I still feel a wish,
90   The fond and flattering pain
Of passion's anguish to create
    In her young breast again.
Bright was the lustre of her eyes
    When they caught fire from mine;
95 If I had power—this very hour,
    Again I'd light their shine.

'But where she is, or how she lives,
    I have no clue to know;
I've heard she long my absence pined,
100   And left her home in woe.

But busied, then, in gathering gold,
    As I am busied now,
I could not turn from such pursuit,
    To keep[?] a broken vow.

105 'Nor could I give to fatal risk
    The fame I ever prized;
Even now, I fear, that precious fame
    Is too much compromised.'
An inward trouble dims his eye,
110   Some riddle he would solve;
Some method to unloose a knot,
    His anxious thoughts revolve.

He, pensive, leans against a tree,
    A leafy evergreen—
115 The boughs the moonlight intercept,
    And hide him like a screen;
He starts—the tree shakes with his tremor,
    Yet nothing near him passed;
He hurries up the garden alley
120   In strangely sudden haste.

With shaking hand he lifts the latchet,
    Steps o'er the threshold stone;
The heavy door slips from his fingers—
    It shuts, and he is gone.
125 What touched, transfixed, appalled his soul?—
    A nervous thought, no more;
'Twill sink like stone in placid pool,
    And calm close smoothly o'er.

2. THE PARLOUR

Warm is the parlour atmosphere,
130   Serene the lamp's soft light;
The vivid embers, red and clear,
    Proclaim a frosty night.
Books, varied, on the table lie,
    Three children o'er them bend,
135 And all, with curious, eager eye,
    The turning leaf attend.

Picture and tale alternately
    Their simple hearts delight,
And interest deep, and tempered glee,
140   Illume their aspects bright.
The parents, from their fireside place,
    Behold that pleasant scene,
And joy is on the mother's face,
    Pride in the father's mien.

145 As Gilbert sees his blooming wife,
    Beholds his children fair,
No thought has he of transient strife,
    Or past though piercing fear.
The voice of happy infancy
150   Lisps sweetly in his ear,
His wife, with pleased and peaceful eye,
    Sits, kindly smiling, near.

The fire glows on her silken dress,
    And shows its ample grace,
155 And warmly tints each hazel tress,
    Curled soft around her face.
The beauty that in youth he wooed
    Is beauty still, unfaded;
The brow of ever placid mood
160   No churlish grief has shaded.

Prosperity, in Gilbert's home,
   Abides, the guest of years;
There Want or Discord never come,
   And seldom Toil or Tears.
165 The carpets bear the peaceful print
   Of Comfort's velvet tread,
And golden gleams, from plenty sent,
   In every nook are shed.

The very silken spaniel seems
170   Of quiet ease to tell,
As near its mistress' feet it dreams,
   Sunk in a cushion's swell;
And smiles seem native to the eyes
   Of those sweet children three;
175 They have but looked on tranquil skies,
   And know not Misery.

Alas! that Misery should come
   In such an hour as this;
Why could she not so calm a home
180   A little longer miss?
But she is now within the door,
   Her steps advancing glide;
Her sullen shade has crossed the floor,
   She stands at Gilbert's side.

185 She lays her hand upon his heart,
   It bounds with agony;
His fireside chair shakes with the start
   That shook the garden tree.
His wife towards the children looks,
190   She does not mark his mien;
The children, bending o'er their books,
   His terror have not seen.

In his own home, by his own hearth,
    He sits in solitude,
195 And circled round with light and mirth,
    Cold horror chills his blood.
His mind would hold with desperate clutch
    The scene that round him lies;
No—changed, as by some wizard's touch,
200   The present prospect flies.

A tumult vague—a viewless strife
    His futile struggles crush;
'Twixt him and his, an unknown life
    And unknown feelings rush.
205 He sees—but scarce can language paint
    The tissue Fancy weaves;
For words oft give but echo faint
    Of thoughts the mind conceives.

Noise, tumult strange, and darkness dim
210   Efface both light and quiet;
No shape is in those shadows grim,
    No voice in that wild riot.
Sustained and strong, a wondrous blast
    Above and round him blows;
215 A greenish gloom, dense overcast,
    Each moment denser grows.

He nothing knows—nor clearly sees,
    Resistance checks his breath,
The high, impetuous, ceaseless breeze
220   Blows on him, cold as death.
And still the undulating gloom
    Mocks sight with formless motion:
Was such sensation Jonah's doom,
    'Gulfed in the depths of ocean?

225 Streaking the air, the nameless vision,
　　　Fast-driven, deep-sounding, flows;
　　Oh! whence its source, and what its mission?
　　　How will its terrors close?
　　Long-sweeping, rushing, vast and void,
230　　The Universe it swallows;
　　And still the dark, devouring tide
　　　A Typhoon tempest follows.

　　More slow it rolls; its furious race
　　　Sinks to a solemn gliding;
235　The stunning roar, the wind's wild chase,
　　　To stillness are subsiding;
　　And, slowly borne along, a form
　　　The shapeless chaos varies;
　　Poised in the eddy of the storm,
240　　Before the eye it tarries:

　　A woman drowned—sunk in the deep,
　　　On a long wave reclining;
　　The circling waters' crystal sweep,
　　　Like glass, her shape enshrining.
245　Her pale dead face, to Gilbert turned,
　　　Seems as in sleep reposing;
　　A feeble light, now first discerned,
　　　The features well disclosing.

　　No effort from the haunted air
250　　The ghastly scene could banish;
　　That hovering wave, arrested there,
　　　Rolled—throbbed—but did not vanish.
　　If Gilbert upward turned his gaze,
　　　He saw the ocean-shadow;
255　If he looked down, the endless seas
　　　Lay green as summer meadow.

And straight before, the pale corpse lay,
   Upborne by air or billow,
So near, he could have touched the spray
260   That churned around its pillow.
The hollow anguish of the face
   Had moved a fiend to sorrow;
Not death's fixed calm could rase the trace
   Of suffering's deep-worn furrow.

265 All moved; a strong returning blast,
   The mass of waters raising,
Bore wave and passive carcase past,
   While Gilbert yet was gazing.
Deep in her isle-conceiving womb,
270   It seemed the ocean thundered,
And soon, by realms of rushing gloom,
   Were seer and phantom sundered.

Then swept some timbers from a wreck,
   On following surges riding;
275 Then seaweed, in the turbid rack
   Uptorn, went slowly gliding.
The horrid shade, by slow degrees,
   A beam of light defeated,
And then the roar of raving seas,
280   Fast, far, and faint, retreated.

And all was gone—gone like a mist,
   Corse, billows, tempest, wreck;
Three children close to Gilbert pressed,
   And clung around his neck.
285 'Good-night! good-night!' the prattlers said,
   And kissed their father's cheek;
'Twas now the hour their quiet bed
   And placid rest to seek.

The mother with her offspring goes
290 To hear their evening prayer;
She nought of Gilbert's vision knows,
And nought of his despair.
Yet, pitying God, abridge the time
Of anguish, now his fate!
295 Though, haply, great has been his crime,
Thy mercy, too, is great.

Gilbert, at length, uplifts his head,
Bent for some moments low,
And there is neither grief nor dread
300 Upon his subtle brow.
For well can he his feelings task,
And well his looks command;
His features well his heart can mask,
With smiles and smoothness bland.

305 Gilbert has reasoned with his mind—
He says 'twas all a dream;
He strives his inward sight to blind
Against truth's inward beam.
He pitied not that shadowy thing,
310 When it was flesh and blood;
Nor now can pity's balmy spring
Refresh his arid mood.

'And if that dream has spoken truth,'
Thus musingly he says;
315 'If Elinor be dead, in sooth,
Such chance the shock repays:
A net was woven round my feet,
I scarce could further go,
Ere shame had forced a fast retreat,
320 Dishonour brought me low.

'Conceal her then, deep, silent Sea,
   Give her a secret grave!
She sleeps in peace, and I am free,
   No longer Terror's slave:
325 And homage still, from all the world,
   Shall greet my spotless name,
Since surges break and waves are curled
   Above its threatened shame.'

3. THE WELCOME HOME

Above the city hangs the moon,
330   Some clouds are boding rain;
Gilbert, erewhile on journey gone,
   To-night comes home again.
Ten years have passed above his head,
   Each year has brought him gain;
335 His prosperous life has smoothly sped,
   Without or tear or stain.

'Tis somewhat late—the city clocks
   Twelve deep vibrations toll,
As Gilbert at the portal knocks,
340   Which is his journey's goal.
The street is still and desolate,
   The moon hid by a cloud;
Gilbert, impatient, will not wait,—
   His second knock peals loud.

345 The clocks are hushed; there's not a light
   In any window nigh,
And not a single planet bright
   Looks from the clouded sky;
The air is raw, the rain descends,
350   A bitter north-wind blows;
His cloak the traveller scarce defends—
   Will not the door unclose?

He knocks the third time, and the last;
   His summons now they hear:
355 Within, a footstep, hurrying fast,
   Is heard approaching near.
The bolt is drawn, the clanking chain
   Falls to the floor of stone;
And Gilbert to his heart will strain
360   His wife and children soon.

The hand that lifts the latchet, holds
   A candle to his sight,
And Gilbert, on the step, beholds
   A woman clad in white.
365 Lo! water from her dripping dress
   Runs on the streaming floor;
From every dark and clinging tress
   The drops incessant pour.

There's none but her to welcome him;
370   She holds the candle high,
And, motionless in form and limb,
   Stands cold and silent nigh;
There's sand and seaweed on her robe,
   Her hollow eyes are blind;
375 No pulse in such a frame can throb,
   No life is there defined.

Gilbert turned ashy-white, but still
   His lips vouchsafed no cry;
He spurred his strength and master-will
380   To pass the figure by,—
But, moving slow, it faced him straight,
   It would not flinch nor quail:
Then first did Gilbert's strength abate,
   His stony firmness fail.

385 He sank upon his knees and prayed;
    The shape stood rigid there;
He called aloud for human aid,
    No human aid was near.
An accent strange did thus repeat
390   Heaven's stern but just decree:
'The measure thou to her didst mete,
    To thee shall measured be!'

Gilbert sprang from his bended knees,
    By the pale spectre pushed,
395 And, wild as one whom demons seize,
    Up the hall-staircase rushed;
Entered his chamber—near the bed
    Sheathed steel and firearms hung—
Impelled by maniac purpose dread
400   He chose those stores among.

Across his throat a keen-edged knife
    With vigorous hand he drew;
The wound was wide—his outraged life
    Rushed rash and redly through.
405 And thus died, by a shameful death,
    A wise and worldly man,
Who never drew but selfish breath
    Since first his life began.

LIFE

LIFE, believe, is not a dream
  So dark as sages say;
Oft a little morning rain
  Foretells a pleasant day.
5 Sometimes there are clouds of gloom,
    But these are transient all;
  If the shower will make the roses bloom,
    Oh, why lament its fall?
      Rapidly, merrily,
10   Life's sunny hours flit by,
      Gratefully, cheerily,
    Enjoy them as they fly!

  What though Death at times steps in,
    And calls our Best away?
15 What though Sorrow seems to win,
    O'er Hope, a heavy sway?
  Yet Hope again elastic springs,
    Unconquered, though she fell;
  Still buoyant are her golden wings,
20   Still strong to bear us well.
      Manfully, fearlessly,
    The day of trial bear,
      For gloriously, victoriously,
    Can courage quell despair!

This poem appears on the last page of the MS. of an unpublished story by Charlotte Brontë, entitled 'Caroline Vernon,' dated March 26, 1839. On another MS. copy of the poem Charlotte Brontë has written, 'Copied at Bruxelles, 1843.'

THE LETTER

WHAT is she writing? Watch her now,
 How fast her fingers move!
How eagerly her youthful brow
 Is bent in thought above!
5 Her long curls, drooping, shade the light,
 She puts them quick aside,
Nor knows that band of crystals bright
 Her hasty touch untied.
It slips adown her silken dress,
10 Falls glittering at her feet;
Unmarked it falls, for she no less
 Pursues her labour sweet.

The very loveliest hour that shines
 Is in that deep blue sky;
15 The golden sun of June declines,
 It has not caught her eye.
The cheerful lawn, and unclosed gate,
 The white road, far away,
In vain for her light footsteps wait,
20 She comes not forth to-day.
There is an open door of glass
 Close by that lady's chair,
From thence, to slopes of mossy grass,
 Descends a marble stair.

25 Tall plants of bright and spicy bloom
 Around the threshold grow;
Their leaves and blossoms shade the room
 From that sun's deepening glow.
Why does she not a moment glance
30 Between the clustering flowers,

And mark in heaven the radiant dance
   Of evening's rosy hours?
Oh, look again! Still fixed her eye,
   Unsmiling, earnest, still,
35 And fast her pen and fingers fly,
   Urged by her eager will.

Her soul is in the absorbing task;
   To whom, then, doth she write?
Nay, watch her still more closely, ask
40   Her own eyes' serious light;
Where do they turn, as now her pen
   Hangs o'er the unfinished line?
Whence fell the tearful gleam that then
   Did in their dark spheres shine?
45 The summer-parlour looks so dark,
   When from that sky you turn,
And from the expanse of that green park
   You scarce may aught discern.

Yet o'er the piles of porcelain rare,
50   O'er flower-stand, couch, and vase,
Sloped, as if leaning on the air,
   One picture meets the gaze.
'Tis there she turns; you may not see,
   Distinct, what form defines
55 The clouded mass of mystery
   Yon broad gold frame confines.
But look again; inured to shade
   Your eyes now faintly trace
A stalwart form, a massive head,
60   A firm, determined face.

Black Spanish locks, a sunburnt cheek,
   A brow high, broad, and white,
Where every furrow seems to speak
   Of mind and moral might.

65 Is that her god? I cannot tell;
        Her eye a moment met
    The impending picture, then it fell
        Darkened and dimmed and wet.
    A moment more, her task is done,
70   And sealed the letter lies;
    And now, towards the setting sun
        She turns her tearful eyes.

    Those tears flow over, wonder not,
        For by the inscription see
75 In what a strange and distant spot
        Her heart of hearts must be!
    Three seas and many a league of land
        That letter must pass o'er,
    Ere read by him to whose loved hand
80   'Tis sent from England's shore.
    Remote colonial wilds detain
        Her husband, loved though stern;
    She, 'mid that smiling English scene,
        Weeps for his wished return.

An early draft of this poem is dated June, 1837.

REGRET

L ONG ago I wished to leave
        'The house where I was born';
    Long ago I used to grieve,
        My home seemed so forlorn.
5   In other years, its silent rooms
        Were filled with haunting fears;
    Now, their very memory comes
        O'ercharged with tender tears.

Life and marriage I have known,
10   Things once deemed so bright;
Now, how utterly is flown
     Every ray of light!
'Mid the unknown sea of life
     I no blest isle have found;
15 At last, through all its wild waves' strife,
     My bark is homeward bound.

Farewell, dark and rolling deep!
     Farewell, foreign shore!
Open, in unclouded sweep,
20   Thou glorious realm before!
Yet, though I had safely passed
     That weary, vexèd main,
One loved voice, through surge and blast,
     Could call me back again.

25 Though the soul's bright morning rose
     O'er Paradise for me,
William! even from Heaven's repose
     I'd turn, invoked by thee!
Storm nor surge should e'er arrest
30   My soul, exulting then:
All my Heaven was once thy breast,
     Would it were mine again!

An early draft of the above poem is contained in a MS. of a story without a title, dated July 21, 1837. Another MS. of the poem is entitled 'Lament,' and dated July 1837. There is also a draft of the poem, in the author's autograph, which has no title, and is dated May 30, 1837.

PRESENTIMENT

'SISTER, you've sat there all the day,
  Come to the hearth awhile;
The wind so wildly sweeps away,
  The clouds so darkly pile.
5 That open book has lain, unread,
  For hours upon your knee;
You've never smiled nor turned your head;
  What can you, sister, see?'

'Come hither, Jane, look down the field;
10   How dense a mist creeps on!
The path, the hedge, are both concealed,
  Even the white gate is gone;
No landscape through the fog I trace,
  No hill with pastures green;
15 All featureless is Nature's face,
  All masked in clouds her mien.

'Scarce is the rustle of a leaf
  Heard in our garden now;
The year grows old, its days wax brief,
20   The tresses leave its brow.
The rain drives fast before the wind,
  The sky is blank and grey;
O Jane, what sadness fills the mind
  On such a dreary day!'

25 'You think too much, my sister dear;
  You sit too long alone;
What though November days be drear?
  Full soon will they be gone.

I've swept the hearth, and placed your chair,
30   Come, Emma, sit by me;
Our own fireside is never drear,
Though late and wintry wane the year,
     Though rough the night may be.'

'The peaceful glow of our fireside
35   Imparts no peace to me:
My thoughts would rather wander wide
     Than rest, dear Jane, with thee.
I'm on a distant journey bound,
     And if, about my heart,
40 Too closely kindred ties were bound,
     'Twould break when forced to part.

' "Soon will November days be o'er"—
     Well have you spoken, Jane:
My own forebodings tell me more—
45 For me, I know by presage sure,
     They'll ne'er return again.
Ere long, nor sun nor storm to me
     Will bring or joy or gloom;
They reach not that Eternity
50   Which soon will be my home.'

      .   .   .   .   .

Eight months are gone, the summer sun
     Sets in a glorious sky;
A quiet field, all green and lone,
     Receives its rosy dye.
55 Jane sits upon a shaded stile,
     Alone she sits there now;
Her head rests on her hand the while
     And thought o'ercasts her brow.

She's thinking of one winter's day,
60   A few short months ago,
When Emma's bier was borne away
O'er wastes of frozen snow.
She's thinking how that drifted snow
Dissolved in spring's first gleam,
65   And how her sister's memory now
Fades, even as fades a dream.

The snow will whiten earth again,
But Emma comes no more;
She left, 'mid winter's sleet and rain,
70   This world for Heaven's far shore.
On Beulah's hills she wanders now,
On Eden's tranquil plain;
To her shall Jane hereafter go,
She ne'er shall come to Jane!

The original draft of this poem is dated May 1837. Another MS.
copy is dated July 11, 1837.

THE TEACHER'S MONOLOGUE

THE room is quiet, thoughts alone
People its mute tranquillity;
The yoke put off, the long task done,—
I am, as it is bliss to be,
5   Still and untroubled. Now, I see,
For the first time, how soft the day
O'er waveless water, stirless tree,
Silent and sunny, wings its way.
Now, as I watch that distant hill,
10   So faint, so blue, so far removed,
Sweet dreams of home my heart may fill,
That home where I am known and loved:

It lies beyond; yon azure brow
 Parts me from all Earth holds for me;
15 And, morn and eve, my yearnings flow
 Thitherward tending, changelessly.
My happiest hours, ay! all the time,
 I love to keep in memory,
Lapsed among moors, ere life's first prime
20 Decayed to dark anxiety.

Sometimes, I think a narrow heart
 Makes me thus mourn those far away,
And keeps my love so far apart
 From friends and friendships of to-day;
25 Sometimes, I think 'tis but a dream
 I treasure up so jealously,
All the sweet thoughts I live on seem
 To vanish into vacancy:
And then, this strange, coarse world around
30 Seems all that's palpable and true;
And every sight and every sound
 Combines my spirit to subdue
To aching grief; so void and lone
 Is Life and Earth—so worse than vain,
35 The hopes that, in my own heart sown,
 And cherished by such sun and rain
As Joy and transient Sorrow shed,
 Have ripened to a harvest there:
Alas! methinks I hear it said,
40 'Thy golden sheaves are empty air.'
All fades away; my very home
 I think will soon be desolate;
I hear, at times, a warning come
 Of bitter partings at its gate;
45 And, if I should return and see
 The hearth-fire quenched, the vacant chair;

And hear it whispered mournfully,
    That farewells have been spoken there,
What shall I do, and whither turn?
50 Where look for peace? When cease to mourn?

The original MS. of the first part of 'The Teacher's Monologue' is
dated May 15, 1837.

·   ·   ·   ·   ·

    'Tis not the air I wished to play,
        The strain I wished to sing;
    My wilful spirit slipped away
        And struck another string.
55 I neither wanted smile nor tear,
        Bright joy nor bitter woe,
    But just a song that sweet and clear,
        Though haply sad, might flow.

    A quiet song, to solace me
60   When sleep refused to come;
    A strain to chase despondency
        When sorrowful for home.
    In vain I try; I cannot sing;
        All feels so cold and dead;
65 No wild distress, no gushing spring
        Of tears in anguish shed;

    But all the impatient gloom of one
        Who waits a distant day,
    When, some great task of suffering done,
70   Repose shall toil repay.
    For youth departs, and pleasure flies,
        And life consumes away,
    And youth's rejoicing ardour dies
        Beneath this drear delay;

75 And Patience, weary with her yoke,
       Is yielding to despair,
   And Health's elastic spring is broke
       Beneath the strain of care.
   Life will be gone ere I have lived;
80   Where now is Life's first prime?
   I've worked and studied, longed and grieved,
       Through all that rosy time.

   To toil, to think, to long, to grieve,—
       Is such my future fate?
85 The morn was dreary, must the eve
       Be also desolate?
   Well, such a life at least makes Death
       A welcome, wished-for friend;
   Then, aid me, Reason, Patience, Faith,
90   To suffer to the end!

The original MS. of the second part of 'The Teacher's Monologue'
is dated May 12, 1837.

PASSION

SOME have won a wild delight,
    By daring wilder sorrow;
Could I gain thy love to-night,
    I'd hazard death to-morrow.

5 Could the battle-struggle earn
       One kind glance from thine eye,
   How this withering heart would burn,
       The heady fight to try!

   Welcome nights of broken sleep,
10   And days of carnage cold,
   Could I deem that thou wouldst weep
       To hear my perils told.

Tell me, if with wandering bands
 I roam full far away,
15 Wilt thou to those distant lands
 In spirit ever stray!

Wild, long, a trumpet sounds afar;
 Bid me—bid me go
Where Seik and Briton meet in war,
20 On Indian Sutlej's flow.

Blood has dyed the Sutlej's waves
 With scarlet stain, I know;
Indus' borders yawn with graves,
 Yet, command me go!

25 Though rank and high the holocaust
 Of nations steams to heaven,
Glad I'd join the death-doomed host,
 Were but the mandate given.

Passion's strength should nerve my arm,
30 Its ardour stir my life,
Till human force to that dread charm
Should yield and sink in wild alarm,
 Like trees to tempest-strife.

If, hot from war, I seek thy love,
35 Darest thou turn aside?
Darest thou then my fire reprove,
 By scorn, and maddening pride?

No—my will shall yet control
 Thy will, so high and free,
40 And love shall tame that haughty soul—
 Yes—tenderest love for me.

I'll read my triumph in thine eyes,
  Behold, and prove the change;
Then leave, perchance, my noble prize,
45   Once more in arms to range.

I'd die when all the foam is up,
  The bright wine sparkling high;
Nor wait till in the exhausted cup
  Life's dull dregs only lie.

50 Then Love thus crowned with sweet reward,
  Hope blessed with fulness large,
I'd mount the saddle, draw the sword,
  And perish in the charge!

The MS. of this poem is dated December 12, 1841, and is marked 'Finished at Upperwood.' Charlotte Brontë was a governess at Upperwood House, Rawdon, Yorkshire, from March 2 until December 24, 1841.

PREFERENCE

NOT in scorn do I reprove thee,
  Not in pride thy vows I waive,
But, believe, I could not love thee,
  Wert thou prince and I a slave.
5 These, then, are thine oaths of passion?
  This, thy tenderness for me?
Judged, even, by thine own confession,
  Thou art steeped in perfidy.
Having vanquished, thou wouldst leave me!
10   Thus I read thee long ago;
Therefore, dared I not deceive thee,
  Even with friendship's gentle show.
Therefore, with impassive coldness
  Have I ever met thy gaze;
15 Though, full oft, with daring boldness,
  Thou thine eyes to mine didst raise.

Why that smile? Thou now art deeming
 This my coldness all untrue,—
But a mask of frozen seeming,
20 Hiding secret fires from view.
Touch my hand, thou self-deceiver;
 Nay—be calm, for I am so:
Does it burn? Does my lip quiver?
 Has mine eye a troubled glow?
25 Canst thou call a moment's colour
 To my forehead—to my cheek?
Canst thou tinge their tranquil pallor
 With one flattering, feverish streak?
Am I marble? What! no woman
30 Could so calm before thee stand?
Nothing living, sentient, human,
 Could so coldly take thy hand?
Yes—a sister might, a mother:
 My good-will is sisterly:
35 Dream not, then, I strive to smother
 Fires that inly burn for thee.
Rave not, rage not, wrath is fruitless,
 Fury cannot change my mind;
I but deem the feeling rootless
40 Which so whirls in passion's wind.
Can I love? Oh, deeply—truly—
 Warmly—fondly—but not thee;
And my love is answered duly,
 With an equal energy.
45 Wouldst thou see thy rival? Hasten,
 Draw that curtain soft aside,
Look where yon thick branches chasten
 Noon, with shades of eventide.
In that glade, where foliage blending
50 Forms a green arch overhead,
Sits thy rival, thoughtful bending
 O'er a stand with papers spread—

Motionless, his fingers plying
That untired, unresting pen;
55   Time and tide unnoticed flying,
There he sits—the first of men!
Man of conscience—man of reason;
Stern, perchance, but ever just;
Foe to falsehood, wrong, and treason,
60   Honour's shield, and virtue's trust!
Worker, thinker, firm defender
Of Heaven's truth—man's liberty;
Soul of iron—proof to slander,
Rock where founders tyranny.
65   Fame he seeks not—but full surely
She will seek him, in his home;
This I know, and wait securely
For the atoning hour to come.
To that man my faith is given,
70   Therefore, soldier, cease to sue;
While God reigns in earth and Heaven,
I to him will still be true!

EVENING SOLACE

THE human heart has hidden treasures,
In secret kept, in silence sealed; —
The thoughts, the hopes, the dreams, the pleasures,
Whose charms were broken if revealed.
5   And days may pass in gay confusion,
And nights in rosy riot fly,
While, lost in Fame's or Wealth's illusion,
The memory of the Past may die.

But there are hours of lonely musing,
10   Such as in evening silence come,
When, soft as birds their pinions closing,
The heart's best feelings gather home.

Then in our souls there seems to languish
   A tender grief that is not woe;
15 And thoughts that once wrung groans of anguish,
   Now cause but some mild tears to flow.

And feelings, once as strong as passions,
   Float softly back—a faded dream;
Our own sharp griefs and wild sensations,
20   The tale of others' sufferings seem.
Oh! when the heart is freshly bleeding,
   How longs it for that time to be,
When, through the mist of years receding,
   Its woes but live in reverie!

25 And it can dwell on moonlight glimmer,
      On evening shade and loneliness;
And, while the sky grows dim and dimmer,
      Feel no untold and strange distress—
Only a deeper impulse given
30   By lonely hour and darkened room,
To solemn thoughts that soar to heaven,
   Seeking a life and world to come.

The original draft of this poem is entitled 'Remembrance,' and is
marked 'Haworth.'

STANZAS

IF thou be in a lonely place,
   If one hour's calm be thine,
As Evening bends her placid face
   O'er this sweet day's decline;
5 If all the earth and all the heaven
   Now look serene to thee,
As o'er them shuts the summer even,
   One moment—think of me!

Pause, in the lane, returning home;
10   'Tis dusk, it will be still:
Pause near the elm, a sacred gloom
     Its breezeless boughs will fill.
Look at that soft and golden light,
     High in the unclouded sky;
15 Watch the last bird's belated flight,
     As it flits silent by.

Hark! for a sound upon the wind,
     A step, a voice, a sigh;
If all be still, then yield thy mind,
20   Unchecked, to memory.
If thy love were like mine, how blest
That twilight hour would seem,
When, back from the regretted Past,
     Returned our early dream!

25 If thy love were like mine, how wild
     Thy longings, even to pain,
For sunset soft, and moonlight mild,
     To bring that hour again!
But oft, when in thine arms I lay,
30   I've seen thy dark eyes shine,
And deeply felt their changeful ray
     Spoke other love than mine.

My love is almost anguish now,
     It beats so strong and true;
35 'Twere rapture, could I deem that thou
     Such anguish ever knew.
I have been but thy transient flower,
     Thou wert my god divine;
Till, checked by death's congealing power,
40   This heart must throb for thine.

And well my dying hour were blest,
   If life's expiring breath
Should pass, as thy lips gently prest
   My forehead cold in death;
45 And sound my sleep would be, and sweet,
   Beneath the churchyard tree,
If sometimes in thy heart should beat
   One pulse, still true to me.

The MS. of this poem is dated May 14, 1837, and is marked 'Written at Roe Head; copied at Haworth, Aug. 30th, 1845.'

PARTING

THERE'S no use in weeping,
   Though we are condemned to part;
There's such a thing as keeping
   A remembrance in one's heart:

5 There's such a thing as dwelling
   On the thought ourselves have nursed,
And with scorn and courage telling
   The world to do its worst.

We'll not let its follies grieve us,
10   We'll just take them as they come;
And then every day will leave us
   A merry laugh for home.

When we've left each friend and brother,
   When we're parted, wide and far,
15 We will think of one another,
   As even better than we are.

Every glorious sight above us,
   Every pleasant sight beneath,
We'll connect with those that love us,
20   Whom we truly love till death!

In the evening, when we're sitting
  By the fire, perchance alone,
Then shall heart with warm heart meeting,
  Give responsive tone for tone.

25 We can burst the bonds which chain us,
  Which cold human hands have wrought,
And where none shall dare restrain us
  We can meet again, in thought.

So there's no use in weeping,
30   Bear a cheerful spirit still:
Never doubt that Fate is keeping
  Future good for present ill!

One MS. of the above poem is dated January 29, 1838 (the last day of the Christmas holidays, which Charlotte Brontë spent at home, before returning to her situation as governess in Miss Wooler's school at Heald's House, Dewsbury Moor, Yorkshire). Another MS. copy of the poem is marked 'Written at Haworth, 1838; copied at Bruxelles, 1843.' The poem was set to music by J. E. Field, London, and published in the year 1853.

APOSTASY

THIS last denial of my faith,
  Thou, solemn Priest, hast heard;
And, though upon my bed of death,
  I call not back a word.
5 Point not to thy Madonna, Priest,—
  Thy sightless saint of stone:
She cannot, from this burning breast,
  Wring one repentant moan.

Thou say'st that, when a sinless child,
10   I duly bent the knee,
And prayed to what in marble smiled
  Cold, lifeless, mute on me.

I did. But listen! Children spring
    Full soon to riper youth;
15 And, for Love's vow and Wedlock's ring,
    I sold my early truth.

'Twas not a grey, bare head, like thine,
    Bent o'er me, when I said,
'That land and God and Faith are mine,
20   For which thy fathers bled.'
I see thee not: my eyes are dim;
    But well I hear thee say,
'O daughter, cease to think of him
    Who led thy soul astray.

25 'Between you lies both space and time;
    Let leagues and years prevail
To turn thee from the path of crime,
    Back to the Church's pale.'
And did I need that thou shouldst tell
30   What mighty barriers rise
To part me from that dungeon-cell,
    Where my loved Walter lies?

And did I need that thou shouldst taunt
    My dying hour at last,
35 By bidding this worn spirit pant
    No more for what is past?
Priest—*must* I cease to think of him?
    How hollow rings that word!
Can time, can tears, can distance dim
40   The memory of my lord?

I said before, I saw not thee,
    Because, an hour agone,
Over my eyeballs, heavily,
    The lids fell down like stone.

45 But still my spirit's inward sight
   Beholds his image beam
As fixed, as clear, as burning bright,
   As some red planet's gleam.

Talk not of thy Last Sacrament,
50   Tell not thy beads for me;
Both rite and prayer are vainly spent,
   As dews upon the sea.
Speak not one word of Heaven above,
   Rave not of Hell's alarms;
55 Give me but back my Walter's love,
   Restore me to his arms!

Then will the bliss of Heaven be won;
   Then will Hell shrink away,
As I have seen night's terrors shun
60   The conquering steps of day.
'Tis my religion thus to love,
   My creed thus fixed to be;
Not death shall shake, nor Priestcraft break
   My rock-like constancy!

65 Now go; for at the door there waits
   Another stranger guest;
He calls—I come—my pulse scarce beats,
   My heart fails in my breast.
Again that voice—how far away,
70   How dreary sounds that tone!
And I, methinks, am gone astray,
   In trackless wastes and lone.

I fain would rest a little while:
   Where can I find a stay,
75 Till dawn upon the hills shall smile,
   And show some trodden way?

'I come! I come!' in haste she said,
  "'Twas Walter's voice I heard!'
Then up she sprang—but fell back dead,
80   His name her latest word.

A draft of part of the above poem (60 lines) is dated May 29, 1837, and is marked 'Roe Head.'

WINTER STORES

WE take from life one little share,
  And say that this shall be
A space, redeemed from toil and care,
  From tears and sadness free.

5 And, haply, Death unstrings his bow,
  And Sorrow stands apart,
And, for a little while, we know
  The sunshine of the heart.

Existence seems a summer eve,
10   Warm, soft, and full of peace;
Our free, unfettered feelings give
  The soul its full release.

A moment, then, it takes the power
  To call up thoughts that throw,
15 Around that charmed and hallowed hour,
  This life's divinest glow.

But Time, though viewlessly it flies,
  And slowly, will not stay;
Alike, through clear and clouded skies,
20   It cleaves its silent way.

Alike the bitter cup of grief,
  Alike the draught of bliss,
Its progress leaves but moment brief
  For baffled lips to kiss.

25 The sparkling draught is dried away,
   The hour of rest is gone,
And urgent voices, round us, say,
   'Ho, lingerer, hasten on!'

And has the soul, then, only gained,
30   From this brief time of ease,
A moment's rest, when overstrained,
   One hurried glimpse of peace?

No; while the sun shone kindly o'er us,
   And flowers bloomed round our feet,—
35 While many a bud of joy before us
   Unclosed its petals sweet,—

An unseen work within was plying;
   Like honey-seeking bee,
From flower to flower, unwearied, flying,
40   Laboured one faculty,—

Thoughtful for Winter's future sorrow,
   Its gloom and scarcity;
Prescient to-day of want to-morrow,
   Toiled quiet Memory.

45 'Tis she that from each transient pleasure
   Extracts a lasting good;
'Tis she that finds, in summer, treasure
   To serve for winter's food.

And when Youth's summer day is vanished,
50   And Age brings Winter's stress,
Her stores, with hoarded sweets replenished,
   Life's evening hours will bless.

THE MISSIONARY

PLOUGH, vessel, plough the British main,
  Seek the free ocean's wider plain;
Leave English scenes and English skies,
Unbind, dissever English ties;
5 Bear me to climes remote and strange,
Where altered life, fast-following change,
Hot action, never-ceasing toil,
Shall stir, turn, dig, the spirit's soil;
Fresh roots shall plant, fresh seed shall sow,
10 Till a new garden there shall grow,
Cleared of the weeds that fill it now,—
Mere human love, mere selfish yearning,
Which, cherished, would arrest me yet.
I grasp the plough, there's no returning,
15 Let me, then, struggle to forget.

But England's shores are yet in view,
And England's skies of tender blue
Are arched above her guardian sea.
I cannot yet Remembrance flee;
20 I must again, then, firmly face
That task of anguish, to retrace.
Wedded to home—I home forsake;
Fearful of change—I changes make;
Too fond of ease—I plunge in toil;
25 Lover of calm—I seek turmoil:
Nature and hostile Destiny
Stir in my heart a conflict wild;
And long and fierce the war will be
Ere duty both has reconciled.

30 What other tie yet holds me fast
To the divorced, abandoned past?
Smouldering, on my heart's altar lies
The fire of some great sacrifice,

Not yet half quenched. The sacred steel
35 But lately struck my carnal will,
My life-long hope, first joy and last,
What I loved well, and clung to fast;
What I wished wildly to retain,
What I renounced with soul-felt pain;
40 What—when I saw it, axe-struck, perish—
Left me no joy on earth to cherish;
A man bereft—yet sternly now
I do confirm that Jephtha vow:
Shall I retract, or fear, or flee?
45 Did Christ, when rose the fatal tree
Before Him, on Mount Calvary?
'Twas a long fight, hard fought, but won,
And what I did was justly done.

Yet, Helen! from thy love I turned,
50 When my heart most for thy heart burned;
I dared thy tears, I dared thy scorn—
Easier the death-pang had been borne.
Helen, thou might'st not go with me,
I could not—dared not stay for thee!
55 I heard afar, in bonds complain
The savage from beyond the main;
And that wild sound rose o'er the cry
Wrung out by passion's agony;
And even when, with the bitterest tear
60 I ever shed, mine eyes were dim,
Still, with the spirit's vision clear,
I saw Hell's empire, vast and grim,
Spread on each Indian river's shore,
Each realm of Asia covering o'er.
65 There the weak, trampled by the strong,
Live but to suffer—hopeless die;
There pagan-priests, whose creed is Wrong,
Extortion, Lust, and Cruelty,

Crush our lost race—and brimming fill
70 The bitter cup of human ill;
And I—who have the healing creed,
The faith benign of Mary's Son,
Shall I behold my brother's need,
And selfishly to aid him shun?
75 I—who upon my mother's knees,
In childhood, read Christ's written word,
Received His legacy of peace,
His holy rule of action heard;
I—in whose heart the sacred sense
80 Of Jesus' love was early felt;
Of His pure, full benevolence,
His pitying tenderness for guilt;
His shepherd-care for wandering sheep,
For all weak, sorrowing, trembling things,
85 His mercy vast, His passion deep
Of anguish for man's sufferings;
I—schooled from childhood in such lore—
Dared I draw back or hesitate,
When called to heal the sickness sore
90 Of those far off and desolate?
Dark, in the realm and shades of Death,
Nations, and tribes, and empires lie,
But even to them the light of Faith
Is breaking on their sombre sky:
95 And be it mine to bid them raise
Their drooped heads to the kindling scene,
And know and hail the sunrise blaze
Which heralds Christ the Nazarene.
I know how Hell the veil will spread
100 Over their brows and filmy eyes,
And earthward crush the lifted head
That would look up and seek the skies;
I know what war the fiend will wage
Against that soldier of the Cross,

105 Who comes to dare his demon—rage,
　　And work his kingdom shame and loss.
　　Yes, hard and terrible the toil
　　Of him who steps on foreign soil,
　　Resolved to plant the gospel vine,
110 Where tyrants rule and slaves repine;
　　Eager to lift Religion's light
　　Where thickest shades of mental night
　　Screen the false god and fiendish rite;
　　Reckless that missionary blood,
115 Shed in wild wilderness and wood,
　　Has left, upon the unblest air,
　　The man's deep moan—the martyr's prayer.
　　I know my lot—I only ask
　　Power to fulfil the glorious task;
120 Willing the spirit, may the flesh
　　Strength for the day receive afresh.
　　May burning sun or deadly wind
　　Prevail not o'er an earnest mind;
　　May torments strange or direst death
125 Nor trample truth, nor baffle faith.
　　Though such blood-drops should fall from me
　　As fell in old Gethsemane,
　　Welcome the anguish, so it gave
　　More strength to work—more skill to save.
130 And, oh! if brief must be my time,
　　If hostile hand or fatal clime
　　Cut short my course—still o'er my grave,
　　Lord, may Thy harvest whitening wave.
　　So I the culture may begin,
135 Let others thrust the sickle in;
　　If but the seed will faster grow,
　　May my blood water what I sow!
　　What! have I ever trembling stood,
　　And feared to give to God that blood?
140 What! has the coward love of life
　　Made me shrink from the righteous strife?

Have human passions, human fears
Severed me from those Pioneers
Whose task is to march first, and trace
145 Paths for the progress of our race?
It has been so; but grant me, Lord,
Now to stand steadfast by Thy word!
Protected by salvation's helm,
Shielded by faith, with truth begirt,
150 To smile when trials seek to whelm
And stand 'mid testing fires unhurt
Hurling Hell's strongest bulwarks down,
Even when the last pang thrills my breast,
When Death bestows the Martyr's crown,
155 And calls me into Jesus' rest.
Then for my ultimate reward—
Then for the world-rejoicing word—
The voice from Father—Spirit—Son:
'Servant of God, well hast thou done!'

Poems from 'Jane Eyre'

1. THE ORPHAN CHILD

MY feet they are sore, and my limbs they are weary;
Long is the way, and the mountains are wild;
Soon will the twilight close moonless and dreary
Over the path of the poor orphan child.

5 Why did they send me so far and so lonely,
Up where the moors spread and grey rocks are piled?
Men are hard-hearted, and kind angels only
Watch o'er the steps of a poor orphan child.

Yet distant and soft the night-breeze is blowing,
10 Clouds there are none, and clear stars beam mild;
God, in His mercy, protection is showing,
Comfort and hope to the poor orphan child.

Even should I fall o'er the broken bridge passing,
  Or stray in the marshes, by false lights beguiled,
15 Still will my Father, with promise and blessing,
  Take to His bosom the poor orphan child.

There is a thought that for strength should avail me,
  Though both of shelter and kindred despoiled:
Heaven is a home, and a rest will not fail me;
20   God is a friend to the poor orphan child.

2. ROCHESTER'S SONG TO JANE EYRE

THE truest love that ever heart
  Felt at its kindled core
Did through each vein, in quickened start,
  The tide of being pour.

5   Her coming was my hope each day,
    Her parting was my pain;
  The chance that did her steps delay,
    Was ice in every vein.

I dreamed it would be nameless bliss,
10   As I loved, loved to be;
  And to this object did I press
    As blind as eagerly.

But wide as pathless was the space
  That lay, our lives, between,
15 And dangerous as the foamy race
  Of ocean-surges green.

And haunted as a robber-path
  Through wilderness or wood;
For Might and Right, and Woe and Wrath,
20   Between our spirits stood.

I dangers dared; I hindrance scorned;
   I omens did defy:
Whatever menaced, harassed, warned,
   I passed impetuous by.

25 On sped my rainbow, fast as light;
   I flew as in a dream;
For glorious rose upon my sight
   That child of Shower and Gleam.

Still bright on clouds of suffering dim
30   Shines that soft, solemn joy;
Nor care I now, how dense and grim
   Disasters gather nigh:

I care not in this moment sweet,
   Though all I have rushed o'er
35 Should come on pinion, strong and fleet,
   Proclaiming vengeance sore:

Though haughty Hate should strike me down,
   Right, bar approach to me,
And grinding Might, with furious frown,
40   Swear endless enmity.

My love has placed her little hand
   With noble faith in mine,
And vowed that wedlock's sacred band
   Our natures shall entwine.

45 My love has sworn, with sealing kiss,
   With me to live—to die;
I have at last my nameless bliss:
   As I love—loved am I!

THE ORPHANS

Translated from the French of Louis Belmontet.

'TWAS New Year's night; the joyous throng
　　Of guests from banquet rose,
And lightly took their homeward path
　　Across the drifted snows.
5　That night, e'en to the peasants' shed,
　Some little gleam of gladness spread.

That night, beside a chapel door,
　　Two lonely children stood;
In timid tone, with utterance faint,
10　　They asked a little food:
　Careless, the laughing guests passed by,
　Too gay to mark the Orphans' cry.

A lamp that lit the sacred shrine
　　The children's pale cheeks shewed;
15　The elder stretched his trembling hand
　　For what was not bestowed;
　The younger sang a plaintive strain,
　Oft dropped, then feebly raised again:—

'Two friendless, helpless children, we,
20　　Our mother's death we weep;
　Together, in one narrow grave,
　　She and our father sleep!
　We too of cold and want must die,
　If none will help or hear our cry!'

25　This voice was lost; the winter-wind
　　Bore off its tones subdued,
　And soon the merry feasters gone,
　　Left all in solitude;
　And none had looked towards the church,
30　Or marked the Orphans in its porch.

Then turned they to the chapel door;
   Their mother oft had said
That God will shield the friendless poor,
   When other aid is fled.
35 They knocked—an echo mocked the ear;
They waited—Death alone drew near!

Time speeds; the lamp shines feebly still,
   The chimes of midnight sound;
Heard now from far, a chariot's wheels
40   Ring o'er the frozen ground.
Rise, Orphans! Call! No!—hushed their cry.
Unchecked, the chariot thunders by.

A Priest his matins came to say,
   When dawn first lit the skies;
45 He found them on the threshold laid;
   He called—they would not rise!
The icy steps of stone, their bed,
The white snow for their covering spread.

Clasped closely in each other's arms
50   As if for warmth, they lay;
But perished is the fire of Life,
   And stilled the pulses' play;
Mute, motionless, and ashen pale,
They slept, no more to wake or wail!

55 The elder pressed the younger's lips,
   As if to check a prayer;
As if to say, ''Tis vain to ask!
   Compassion dwells not here!'
And half he screened his brother's form,
60 To hide him from the frozen storm.

Lulled thus in everlasting sleep,
  The Orphan Babes are laid;
Now those their piteous fate may weep
  Who would not give them aid:
65 Crowds thronged the church by morning light,
  But none came near, that winter-night!

The original MS. of the above translation is dated February 1843. It was printed in *The Manchester Athenæum Album*, 1850, with the exception of the first stanza, which is as follows:

The summer days are passed away,
  The fields are frozen o'er;
Now, reft of hope and far from aid,
  Woe to the houseless poor:
By cold hearts spurned, how hard their fate
To die unpitied, desolate!

2

POEMS OF CHARLOTTE BRONTË PUBLISHED AFTER HER DEATH, FROM THE SHAKESPEARE HEAD EDITION

FOUND IN
AN INN BELONGING TO E.

THOU art a sweet and lovely flower
  Planted in a fairy's bower,
Cherished by a bright sunbeam,
Watered by a silver stream;

5 Thou art a palm tree green and fair
    Rising from the desert plain;
Thou art a ray of silver light
    Streaming o'er the stormy main,

When the mighty billows mix
10   With the over-hanging cloud,
When the vivid lightings flash
    And the thunder roars aloud;

Then, when some pale star sends out
    Through the night a pearly ray,
15 The weary seaman's fainting heart
    Hails the herald of the day

When the radiant sun shall rise,
    Fling its beams upon the foam,
Bidding with its colours bright
20   Welcome to the mariner's home;

Then the rocking ship shall rest
    On the ocean's glassy calm,
Its flag shall flutter on the gale
Whose breath is sweet and soothing
      balm,

25   Blowing from Britannia's shores
      O'er her roses red and white,
  Over Scotia's thistle wild,
      Over Erin's emerald bright;

  While the music of the harp
30   And the echo of the song
  Borne upon the passing wind
      Float in solemn strains along.

U. T.

September 28, 1829.

An earlier draft of these lines is dated September 18, 1829. Many other similar poems are to be found among the very early MSS. of Charlotte and Branwell Brontë. Most of them appear in the First Series of the *Young Men's Magazine*, where many of the verses are signed with the initials 'U.T.' (Us Two), or 'W.T.' (We Two), indicating that they are the joint production of the two young authors. See the volumes of *Miscellaneous and Unpublished Works* in this edition.

LINES ADDRESSED TO 'THE TOWER OF ALL NATIONS'[1]

OH, thou great, thou mighty tower!
    Rising up so solemnly
O'er all this splendid, glorious city:
    This city of the sea;

5   Thou seem'st, as silently I gaze,
    Like a pillar of the sky:
  So lofty is thy structure grey;
    So massive, and so high!

  The dome of Heaven is o'er thee hung
10   With its maze of silver stars;
  The earth is round about thee spread
    With its eternal bars.

[1]The wonderful Tower of All Nations is frequently mentioned by Charlotte and Branwell Brontë in their early Angrian Stories.

And such a charming doggerel
  As this was never wrote,
15 Not even by the mighty
  And high Sir Walter Scott!

U. T. *October* 7, 1829.

SUNSET

BENEATH a shady tree I sat
  Through which, with wondrous lustre, gleamed
The rays of the departing sun
  Which, in its golden glory, beamed

5 Among the shady verdant boughs,
  Tinging with crimson light
The beauteous emerald foliage
  Now like a ruby bright.

All still and peaceful was the scene,
10 And silence reigned around,
Save the music of a murmuring stream
  Which, with its gentle sound,

Filled the shady valley where I sat
  With a low melodious tone,
15 In concert with the nightingale,
  And zephyr's gentle moan.

At length the robe of twilight spread
  O'er all the darkening earth,
And still and peaceful were the sounds
20 Of sorrow and of mirth;

And silently the little stars
  Looked from the azure sky,
While Orion's golden belt
  Shone gloriously on high.

C. B. *October* 8, 1829.

SUNRISE

BEHOLD that silvery streak of light
　　Circling the heavens gray,
Encroaching on the reign of night
　　And heralding the day.

5　Now of a richer, deeper tint
　　　The sunny glory grows.
Until a stream of heavenly light
　　　Along the horizon flows.

Rising it melts into the pale
10　　　Soft azure of the sky:
How beautiful, how glowing bright,
　　　Is its ethereal dye!

Hung in the sapphire arch of heaven,
　　　Above this golden light,
15　The silver crescent of the moon
　　　Seems to the wondering sight

A world in which fair spirits dwell,
　　　So pure and fair it beams,
So gentle is the pearly light
20　　　That softly from it streams.

But rises now the glorious sun
　　　Casting the clouds aside,
And in his burning chariot forth
　　　Triumphantly doth ride;

25　And at his blazing presence bright
　　　All nature doth rejoice:
Earth, sky, and sea join in his praise
　　　With one united voice.

Sweetly the little birds do sing,
30   Warbling their notes in air,
While flowerets in their tiny cups
Bright gem-like dewdrops bear.

CHARLOTTE BRONTË.

October 9, 1829.

A facsimile of the original manuscript of the two poems 'Sunset'
and 'Sunrise' is given as a frontispiece in a small volume entitled
Poems by Charlotte, Emily, and Anne Brontë, which was issued for
private circulation only, in an edition limited to one hundred and ten
copies, by Dodd, Mead and Company, New York, in the year 1902.
The MS. contains several pen and ink sketches by Charlotte Brontë,
including portraits of herself, and 'Young Soult,' i.e. her brother,
Patrick Branwell Brontë.

THE CHURCHYARD

'TWAS one fair evening,—when the closing day
Shines lustrous in Apollo's parting beam,
Who, as he sinks within his azure palace
And draws the splendid curtains ruby-red
5   Of his sublime pavilion, casts a glance
O'er this round globe terrestrial, then bids
A bright farewell, and drops the veil which hides
His glories in its cloud-like crimson folds,—
'Twas in that hour I entered the high gates
10   Of consecrated ground. There stood a Church
Whose grey and ruined form seemed to have felt
The storms and blasts of centuries. It was
Enrobed with ivy, and its pillared portals,
All wreathed with green young tendrils, seemed in their
15   Massive grandeur to have been formed in ages
When the British chivalry rode forth with might
To meet the Saracen, and free the land,—

The sacred land of Palestine—from their
Unhallowed presence. Through the dark yew-trees,
20 Gloomy cypresses and high black firs
Which grew around, a soft and faint light stole,
Investing with a holy solemness
The ancient building, and illumining
The tombs and grave-mounds where the still dead slept,
25 Among those monuments there stood a figure
Clothed in deep mourning, from whose dark eye beamed
The sad and wild light of insanity;
And as she stood she poured a thrilling strain
Which echoed 'mid the Churchyard, from whose walls
30 A soft response came forth as thus she sang;—

I know my sister, thou art gone;—
For the mild peaceful light
Which ever in thy fair eye shone
Has vanished from my sight;

35 And when black midnight cast her pall
O'er the reposing earth,
I heard a faint voice on thee call,
And bid thy soul come forth.

I saw thee in a sombre shroud
40 Within the chamber lie,
And when with grief my heart was bowed
A whisper from on high,

Has told me that thou dwell'st among
Bright bands of Seraphim
45 Who with a sweet eternal song
The triune Godhead hymn.

One night when silence reigned around
I heard sweet music rise,
Whose harp-like and harmonious sound
50 Came from the star-hung skies;

And when had died each soft sweet tone,
  The spirit passed away,
And left me a sad mourner here
  On this dark earth to stay.

55 Then ceased the requiem, and the figure moved
With slow and noiseless step from the dark grove
Amid grey mantled twilight's deepening gloom,
Now hovering over all the silent earth.

CHARLOTTE BRONTË. *Dec.* 24, 1829.

There is another manuscript of the poem entitled *The Churchyard*
from which the following four stanzas were printed in *Brontë Poems,*
1915, p. 3; also in *Complete Poems,* p. 76:

.   .   .   .

ONE night, when silence reigned around,
  I heard sweet music rise,
Whose harp-like and harmonious sound
  Came from the star-decked skies.

5 And when had died each silver tone,
  Thy spirit passed away,
And left me a sad mourner lone,
  On this dark earth to stay.

My sister, may it ever be
10   That from thy home on high
A hymn of peace may check in me
  Each dark rebellious sigh.

Then, sister, shall I truly know
  That mansions of the blest
15 Wait, till from weariness below
  My spirit enters rest!

.   .   .   .

December 24, 1829.

WRITTEN UPON THE OCCASION OF THE DIN-
NER GIVEN TO THE LITERATI OF THE GLASS-
TOWN, which was attended by all the Great Men of the
present time: Soldier, Sailor, Poet and Painter, Archi-
tect, Politician, Novelist, and Romancer.

THE splendid Hall is blazing with many a glowing light,
   And a spirit-like effulgence mild, a flood of glory bright,
Flows round the stately pillars, nor dimly dies away
In the arched roof of solid stone, but there each golden ray
5   Shines with a brightened splendour, a radiance rich and fair,
And then falls amid the palace vast, and lightens up the air,
Till the atmosphere around is one continuous flow
Of streaming lustre, brilliant light, and liquid topaz glow.
All beneath this gorgeousness there sits a chosen band
10   Of genius high and courage bold: the noblest of the land.
The feast is spread, and brightly the purple juice doth shine
In the yellow gold magnificent: the sparkling generous wine!
And all between the thunders of patriotic cheers
Is heard the sounding orchestra, while the inspiring tears
15   Of a rich southern vineyard are quaffed to wish the health
Of some most noble warrior fierce, a nation's power and
    wealth.
And then arises slowly an orator of might
And pours a flood of eloquence upon this festal night.
The gentle stream flows dimpling 'mong rhetoric's bright
    flowers,
20   Poises in wild sublimity on eagle's wing-high towers;
And lost amid the cloudy curtains of his might,
Far beyond the common ken his spirit has taken flight.
For awhile he dwells in glory within the solemn veil,
Then returns upon the smoother seas of beauty fair to sail.
25   The scene this night is joyous within these palace walls,
But ere ten passing centuries are gone these lofty halls

May stand in darksome ruin: these stately pillars high
May echo back far other sounds than those which sweetly fly
Among their light bold arches, and mingling softly rise
30 In a wild enchanting melody, which tremulously dies;
The yell of the hyena, the bloody-tiger's howl,
May be heard in this magnificence, mixed with the lion's
    growl;
While in the cold pale moonlight may stand the ruins grey,
These marble columns mouldering, and gladness fled away!

C. Brontë. *January* 9, 1830.

WRITTEN ON THE SUMMIT OF A HIGH MOUNTAIN IN THE NORTH OF ENGLAND

HOW lonely is this spot! Deep silence reigns;
    For ceased has every human stir and sound;
But Nature's voice is heard in gentle strains
    Which with a stilly noise float softly round.

5 Each leaf which quivers in those giant elms
    Falls audibly upon the listening ear
As if it came from distant spirit realms,
    A warning of some death or danger near.

And now strange thoughts and mournful slowly rise
10   Each after other in a gloomy train;
Each quickly born, and each as quickly dies,
    Drunk by the whirlpool of oblivion's main.

But sudden, bursting from a thick, dark cloud,
    Lo! the bright sun illumines all the earth,
15 Tinting with amber light that watery shroud,
    Radiant with beauty as he now walks forth.

Behold, the valley glows with life and light:
    Each rain-drop bears a glory in its cell
Of sapphire, ruby, or fair emerald bright,
20   Rejoicing in its palace clear to dwell.

A wilderness of sweets yon wood appears;
    Before, a forest full of darksome gloom;
But now a smiling face of joy it wears:
    Not such as would befit the churchyard's tomb.

25 But, all unseemly 'mid the gladness, stands
    That ancient castle, mossed and grey with age;
Once the resort of war-like, feudal bands,
    Where oft was heard the battle's bloody rage.

Now an unbroken stillness reigns around:
30   No warrior's step rings through the archèd halls;
No hunting horn's sweet, thrilling, mellow sound,
    Or blood-hounds' yell, reverberates 'mid those walls.

The gladsome sunshine suits not with this place:
    The golden light seems but to mock the grey
35 And sorrowing aspect of its furrowed face,
    Too time-worn to be joyous with the day.

But when black night o'ershadows with her wing
    The prospect, and the solemn nightingale
Sings, while the moon her silver light doth fling
40   In tremulous lustre o'er the sleeping vale,

Then awfully that ancient castle towers
    From out its grave of venerable trees,
Amid whose scathed and withered, leafless bowers
    Howls mournfully the piercing winter breeze;

45 Or on some day when dark and sombre clouds
    Veil dismally the blue ethereal sky,
When the deep grandeur of their blackness shrouds
    The sun with all its majesty on high;

When fitful shadows hurry o'er the plain
50   And curtain round this mountain's hoary brow,
Rolling voluminous, a misty train,
      Or curled in floating vapours, e'en as now,
Those light soft clouds piled in the ambient air,
      Of gentle lustre and of pearly hue,
55 Calm in the summer twilight, mild and fair,
      Distilling from their pureness crystal dew.

                    CHARLOTTE BRONTË. *January* 14, 1830.

A WRETCH IN PRISON

By MURRY

OH, for the song of the gladsome lark,
      For the morning sun's fair beam,
Instead of this dungeon, deeply dark,
      Where ne'er its light doth gleam!

5   Oh, for the breath of the fragrant vale,
      For the woodland's bracing breeze,
Blowing like Araby's spicy gale
      Amid the forest trees!

Oh, for the light, elastic spring,
10   For the swift, unwearied step,
When the sound of the horn makes the high hills ring
      And the bounding hunter leap!

Oh, for the noise of Freedom's voice
      Heard in the hunter's cry,
15   When the deer has fled like an arrow sped,
      Or a lightning flash on high!

Oh, for the rush, for the bold free rush
      Of the mighty mountain breeze
Down the rocks away to the dashing spray
20   Of the roaring, rolling seas!

Oh, for the light most fierce and bright
Of the heavens' cloudy gloom!
Oh, for the sound like an earthquake bound
Of the thunder's hollow boom!

25 Oh, that the glad stars through my dungeon-bars
Would shed their lustre clear;
That the solemn moon would lighten the gloom
Which reigns in silence here!

Oh, for some fair light to illume the night
30 With a swift and silver glance,
Through these gates to play with a pearly ray,
And lightly here to dance!

C. BRONTË. *February* 1, 1830.

The prisoner Murry was one of the members of the Duke of
Wellington's staff in the first story by Charlotte Brontë, *The Twelve
Adventurers*; but the cause of his imprisonment is not given in any of
the stories.

WINTER

AUTUMN has vanished with his train
Of ripened fruits and golden grain,
Now the white hoar-frost spreads the fields:
Grim winter now the sceptre wields!

5 Lowering clouds deface the sky,
Veil the solemn worlds on high;
Many a storm-portending blast
Sweeps with mournful cadence past;

And the lonely traveller
10 Now sees the tempest from afar;
Benighted on some desert moor,
He hears the distant, sullen roar

Sent by the Spirit of the Storm;
　　From the dark bosom of a cloud
15　　It floats, and sounds more near and loud
As in the heavens black he sees an awful form!

It rears its huge and ghastly head
Around which plays a halo red,
From out the battlements of air
20　All gilded by the moonlight fair,

Which suddenly, as if unbound,
Flings a radiance around,
Brightening, with a fitful glory,
The grim cloudy giant hoary!

25　Lost again in desert gloom,
It sinks within a vapouring tomb,
Meantime, the swift descending snow
Comes with one continuous flow,

Whitening all the earth around,
30　　From the heavens black and lowering,
　　Ceaseless and incessant pouring,
Till in its winter robe is clothed all the ground!

Dismal and death-like is the scene;
But soon, arrayed in robes of green,
35　Spring will come,—the budding hour!
And the snow-drop, humble flower,

Heralding her coming step,
From the verdant earth will peep;
While the little birds will sing
40　At the approach of gentle spring.

Soon the rose will ope her bud,
And each fair floweret of the wood:
The violet dark, the primrose pale,
The cowslip of the sweeping vale,

45   Will all unfold their fragrant leaves:
    Purple, crimson, and bright gold,—
  A wreath from meadow, waste, and wold
    Their rich, united sweets harmoniously weaves!

CHARLOTTE BRONTË, February 3, 1830.

PLEASURE

TRUE pleasure breathes not city air,
    Nor in Arts temples dwells,
In palaces and towers where
    The voice of Grandeur dwells.

5   No! Seek it where high Nature holds
    Her court 'mid stately groves,
Where she her majesty unfolds,
    And in fresh beauty moves;

Where thousand birds of sweetest song,
10   The wildly rushing storm
And hundred streams which glide along,
    Her mighty concert form!

Go where the woods in beauty sleep
    Bathed in pale Luna's light,
15   Or where among their branches sweep
    The hollow winds of night.

Go where the warbling nightingale
    In gushes rich doth sing,
Till all the lonely, quiet vale
20   With melody doth ring.

Go, sit upon a mountain steep,
    And view the prospect round;
And hills and vales, the valleys sweep,
    The far horizon's bound.

25   Then view the wide sky overhead,
     The still, deep vault of blue,
  The sun which golden light doth shed,
     The clouds of pearly hue.

  And as you gaze on this vast scene
30   Your thoughts will journey far,
  Though hundred years should roll between
     On Time's swift-passing car.

  To ages when the earth was young,
     When patriarchs, grey and old,
35   The praises of their god oft sung,
     And oft his mercies told.

  You see them with their beards of snow,
     Their robes of ample form,
  Their lives whose peaceful, gentle flow,
40   Felt seldom passion's storm.

  Then a calm, solemn pleasure steals
     Into your inmost mind;
  A quiet... your spirit feels,
     A softened stillness kind.

CHARLOTTE BRONTË. *February* 8, 1830.

HOME-SICKNESS

OF College I am tired; I wish to be at home,
  Far from the pompous tutor's voice, and the hated
    school-boy's groan.

I wish that I had freedom to walk about at will;
That I no more was troubled with my Greek and slate and
    quill.

5   I wish to see my kitten, to hear my ape rejoice,
To listen to my nightingale's or parrot's lovely voice.

And England does not suit me: it's cold and full of snow;
So different from black Africa's warm, sunny, genial glow.

I'm shivering in the day-time, and shivering all the night:
10 I'm called poor, startled, withered wretch, and miserable
    wight!

And, oh! I miss my brother, I miss his gentle smile
Which used so many long dark hours of sorrow to beguile.

I miss my dearest mother; I now no longer find
Aught half so mild as she was,—so careful and so kind.

15 Oh, I have not my father's, my noble father's arms
To guard me from all wickedness, and keep me safe from
    harms.

I hear his voice no longer; I see no more his eye
Smile on me in my misery: to whom now shall I fly?

                    C. B. C. W. *February*, 1830.

The initials 'C.W.' stand for Charles Wellesley, the supposed
school-boy author of the poem, whose home is in West Africa. In a
short unpublished story by Charlotte Brontë, dated January 16, 1830,
there is the following reference to the boy: 'He was reclining under
the shadow of an immense chestnut tree, playing upon a small Spanish
guitar, and with a nightingale perched upon his shoulder. A beautiful
grey monkey, a small silky spaniel, and a young kitten, bounded and
danced before him in the brilliant light of the uprisen moon.'

THE VISION

THE gentle showery Spring had passed away,
　　And no more breathed the fragrant air of June;
Summer had clad in glorious array
　　Each hill and plain; and now the harvest-moon
5　　Shone on the waving corn,—brown Autumn's
　　　golden boon!

In that glad time, as twilight softly crept
　　Over the earth, I wandered to a place
Where stillness reigned as if the whole world slept,—
　　For there of noise remained no wearying trace:
10　　But deepest silence sat on Nature's face.

It was a wild glen; near it frowned huge rocks
　　Which hung their dark beams o'er its stony bed;
And, in their caverned sides, faint echo mocks
　　When rolls some fragment down, with rumbling
　　　dread
15　　And horrid noise, launched from the mountain's
　　　head.

The valley now was still; a midnight calm
　　Fell on it as I sat beneath a tree
Whose leaflets glistened with the dew's mild balm
　　Wept by the evening gale so freshly free,
20　　And filling all the air with soft humidity.

'Mong the huge trees which canopied that glen
　　I saw the sky with many a bright star hung,
And through the midst alone sailed (glorious gem)
　　The moon, who still her trembling lustre flung
25　　Unchanged, as when the spheres together tuneful
　　　rung.

At intervals her light fell through the trees
　　And with mild glory silvered all the vale,
While through those branches whispered not a breeze:
　　No hollow blast did sad and mournful wail,
30　　But solemn silence walked beneath the moonbeams pale.

Yet black the gaunt rocks rose before my eyes,
　　And their black caverns filled my heart with dread;
They stood in grand relief from out the skies
　　Whose clear vaults archèd o'er each shaggy head,
35　　And from whose quivering stars a radiant light was shed.

I gazed upon this scene till slumber fell
　　Upon my eyelids; then methought I saw
On my entrancèd sight a vision swell
　　Whose glory passed the bounds of Nature's law,
40　　And filled the spirit with a mingled joy and awe!

A land was spread before me where the trees
　　Formed woods of emerald clearness, and high bowers
Through which there whispered many a murmuring breeze
　　Perfumed with incense of a hundred flowers,
45　　Watered by clouds of light that fell in fragrant showers.

I heard sweet voices, not like human sound,
　　But tuneful of articulate harmony;
I saw no shape, but oft there floated round
　　A zephyr soft, and breathing from the sky,
50　　As if some unseen form in light wings flitted by!

At length the air 'gan brighten; faint there shone
　　A rainbow path through all the expanse of blue,
And music of a soft melodious tone,
　　Subdued by distance, through heaven's wide arch flew,
55　　Falling upon the ear, calm as the twilight dew.

Louder it rose: sweet harp and timbrel clear
  Rang tunefully to many a sweeter voice;
These mingling fell upon the listening ear
  While all the echoes answered to the noise,
60   And Nature seemed united to rejoice!

Then a bright chariot glided through the air
  Attended by a glorious company
Of beings radiant surpassing fair;
  Around them rolled of light a mighty sea;
65   And now the music played with loudest melody.

And while this scene slow passed before my eyes,
  Dazzled with splendour, suddenly I woke,
And, lo! the light dawn tinged the eastern skies,
  Showing the rugged front of many a rock,
70   And faintly gilding each wide-branching oak.
                C. BRONTË. *April* 13, 1830.

FRAGMENT

NOW rolls the sounding ocean
  'Neath night's tenebrous wing:
How wild is that eternal motion,
  That sullen, slow, unceasing swing

5 Of waves and billows loudly roaring
    Under cloud-becurtained skies;
    Up the scattered foam-ball flies,
  While down the dashing torrents pouring;

And rejoicing in the storm
10 Glides, through all, the aëriel form
Of some snow-white sea-bird fair,
Borne on sleek wings light as air.

Now the dull, uncertain sound
Of rising wind moans oft around.
                May 29, 1830.

REFLECTIONS

NOW sweetly shines the golden sun,
 The howling wind is still;
The glorious light of day is flung
 O'er every vale and hill.

5 On yonder bank myself I'll rest,
 A blue stream wanders by
In whose smooth, wavy, liquid breast
 Inverted glows the sky.

The sweet, wild flowers are loosely cast
10 In wreaths and clusters round;
I'll watch the waves meandering past,
 To far-off regions bound.

I'll gaze upon the world below:
 The clear translucent sky,
15 The shrubs and trees that downward grow,
 The swift clouds sailing by.

Each shines with dim and watery gleam;
 A pale and gentle light
Encircles them with solemn beam,
20 Like glory of the night.

The willow waving o'er my head
 Waves also 'neath my feet;
Reflected in the river's bed
 The heavens and branches meet.

25 Lone drooping to the azure deep
 They seem to touch the cloud,
And there unmoved they calmly sleep,
 Not e'en by zephyrs bowed.

       C. BRONTË. *May* 31, 1830.

THE EVENING WALK
A POEM BY
THE MARQUIS OF DOURO
In Pindaric Metre
PUBLISHED

AND SOLD

BY

CAPTAIN TREE

AND ALL OTHER BOOKSELLERS IN THE CHIEF GLASS-TOWN, WELLINGTON'S G-T, PARIS, PARRY'S G-T, ROSS'S G-T, ETC., ETC.

PREFACE

The following pages are the production of my pen, not, according to a much-used scrap of cut and dried phraseology, the emanations of leisure hours, but the fruit of some days' labour. I shall not introduce them to my readers by a servile appeal to their indulgence and compassion, but, having cast them unprotected on the world, I leave them entirely at the Public's mercy to praise or condemn them as she pleases.

DOURO. *June* 28, 1830.

This book contains 71 ordinary verses of four lines each, which is 284 lines.[1]

CHARLOTTE BRONTË.

June 28, 1830.

The original manuscript of *The Evening Walk* is in the form of a very small book, with title-page and preface as above, and written in minute characters resembling the smallest of printed type.

The pseudonym of 'Douro' or 'Marquis of Douro,' first used with this poem, is appended to most of the ensuing poems written by Charlotte Brontë during the year 1830, but is usually followed by her own signature.

The 'Marquis of Douro' was the principal hero of her prose stories at that time, and his abilities as a poet are enlarged on in the story entitled *Albion and Marina*.

[1]Actually the poem contains 276 lines.

THE EVENING WALK

AN IRREGULAR POEM: BY THE MARQUIS OF DOURO

WHEN August glowed with fervid summer pride,
And noon had faded into eventide
A fresh breeze through my unclosed lattice playing
Amid a vine's young tendrils wanton straying,
5   Asked me with voice more sweet than harp or lute
Or merry dulcimer or gentle flute
To walk abroad and taste the balmy air
Which violets of the vale and lilies fair
Had filled with fragrance, as it o'er them breathed.
10 Upon the green grass in rich clusters wreathed
They lay—when the wind passed each raised its head,
And odorous perfumes softly calmly shed,
Pouring delights upon the sweeping vales
Ere twilight came their beauties bright to veil,
15 Their loveliness in sheltering leaves to fold,
While clouds of night high o'er the skies are rolled,
And shadows blacken meadow, plain and wold.

Not unheeded spoke the wind
Murmuring in my ear;
20   Soon I saw afar behind
The thunderous city[1] peer

Above its girdling green-robed hills,
Above its forests wild and high,
And the Tower,[2] which with wonder fills
Each stranger, clave the sky.

25   No mist slept on its head,
No clouds begirt it round,
And the majesty about it shed
With awe my spirit bound.

[1]Verreopolis (Glass-town) or Verdopolis.   [2]The Tower of all the Nations.

Then I turned away opprest
30 Towards the glories of the west:
I could gaze for aye
On the proud array
Of the sunset heavens at close of day;

At the radiant dyes
35 Which paint the skies
When Apollo to his haven hies,
And bathed in seas of golden light,
Diving, he leaves the world to night.

There the roses crimson blend
40 With purple bright that soft ascend
To the stainless blue
Whose heavenly hue
Robes the vault which distils translucent dew
On the thirsty earth,
45 Giving joyous birth
To signs of vegetable mirth.
And while each clear drop is lit with glory
The pearl-strewn plains to the frost looks hoary.

On splendour of the gorgeous west
50 At length I ceased to gaze:
My dazzled eyes sought in the east
The soft restoring haze
That dusky, sun-clad twilight brings
Ever on its silent wings;

55 There a belt of palest red
All the horizon circlèd;
Dimly it did wane and fade
With indistinctly melting shade
Into the cerulean sky
60 As it calmly rose on high,
Rivalling the rainbow's hue
When it blended with the blue.

Eastward I took my lonely way,
Attracted by that aspect mild;
65   And as the last transcendent ray
Of sun o'er verdant nature smiled,
I came to a pile of high, gaunt rocks,
Whose Giant plumes were the shaggy oaks
Now grimly waving;
70   And a mighty stream went howling by,
Whose voice arose to the lofty sky,
As wildly raving
It chafed its bounds of solid stone
And the desert rung with the ceaseless moan,
75   While the caverned rocks sent back the sound
Which through all that region echoed round.

A while by that impetuous flood,
Wrapped in thought, I silent stood;
Till splashed with spray
80   I turned away,
Aided by the sinking day.

Emerging from that chasm wild,
Where in solitude the rocks were piled,
I entered a grassy plain,
85   Embosomed in mountains tow'ring aloft:
It smiled with a garb of green herbage soft,
Like the emerald-circlets which fairies trace
When their morrice-dance they merrily pace.

An enormous gloom was round it cast
90   Of a frowning forest of Pine-wood vast
Which stretched o'er every mountain grey.
Densely it grew the hills along,
And even in meridian day
Night reigned those hills among.

95 For blackened there a shade
By nodding branches made;
And in the solemn twilight murk
A hundred noisome reptiles lurk;
The matted grass or bushy brake
100 Conceal the slyly creeping snake;
While hemlock rears its baleful head
Where thickest is the darkness shed.

But no loathsome creature crept
Through that flowery plain:
105 There 'mid sweets the skylark slept
Chanting in dreams the strain

Which soon the morning skies should thrill,
The air of dawn with music fill,
When on its spotted breast
110 The first light gleamed amid some cloud,
While far below in misty shroud
The earth is laid at rest.

Now above the horizon bar
The quiet moon rose o'er the world;
115 Night's banner decked with many a star
Was silently unfurled.

In one continuous sheet of light
And yellow lustre swathed,
Meek nature lay, and faintly bright
120 Her hills and trees were bathed

With floods of glory
Gushing from on high,
On rocks made hoary
By splendour of the sky.

125 The plain I wandered o'er,
Uncertain where to go,
Until I heard before
A warbling streamlet flow.

Soon I crossed the narrow brook,
130　And my onward way I took
Till I reached a haunted dell;
Down the green sides sloping fell;
'Broidering moss spread o'er each bank
'Neath my footsteps softly sank,
135　Purple violets frequent peeped
From where, with closèd buds, they slept
Nestling in their leaves!

Coming night had deepened round
On the solitary ground,
140　And the bottom of the dell,
As it far receding fell
From the fair moon's silver light
Which pierced the gathering gloom of night,
Indistinct and dark, appeared
145　Covered with a dusky veil,
Through which no fair object peered,
Star-illumined, faint and pale!

From the gloom methought I heard
Music sweet ascend
150　Like the voice of singing-bird,
Sweetly did it blend

Strain of thrush and nightingale
In one superhuman song;
Pensive as a wind-harp's wail
155　It poured the air along.

Fairies were in the hollow green,
Feasting amid wild flowers,
And the harmony came from them unseen
Passing in joy the hours.

160 I knew the trip of their little feet
   By the rustling grass far down,
   As o'er it they flew, elastic, fleet,
   Where it waved in that region lone.

   I heard the song of the elves arise,
165   And O 'twas sweetly flung
   On the breeze, as it mingled with whose sighs
   Thus, the tiny spirits sung:—

   Come fill with sparkling dew
   Each gold and crystal cup;
170   Let the clarion and the horn
   Full joyously resound.
   Lo! the lamps of eve are twinkling
   And the stars of night are up
   And the music of the night-bird
175   Is gushing all around.

   The flowers close their leaflets
   And listen to the tone
   Dull howling through those ancient trees:
   'Tis the hoarse, wild wind's moan.

180 That blast has broken from its hold
   With might of thunders roar
   O'er the trembling vault of heaven rolled
   O'er the mountain summits hoar.

   Hark! how it rushes
185   And furiously gushes
   Adown that narrow vale!
   The stern oaks bend,
   Their strong roots rend
   'Neath that triumphant gale.

190 Now, fierce tumult cease!
Loud wind rest in peace!
Restrain thy wearying
Tumultuous breath
And let a silence come
195 Frozen and fast as death!

Now stopped the merry dancing:
I heard it no more;
Yet by light moonbeams glancing,
I saw the fairies soar

200 On swift and noiseless silken wing,
The calm air gently winnowing
They swiftly rose on high,
Then slowly disappeared
And melted in the sky.

205 Now the hush of moonlight lay
On all the hills around:
And no murmuring sign of lightsome day
Pierced the still night profound.

I yet walked on unheeding
210 Over the lonely plain,
The stars of heaven reading,
Like wanderer on the main;

When sudden the sound of a torrent fell,
Loud rushing on my ear,
215 And I saw through trees a cataract swell
That roared impetuous near.

Strangely that ceaseless thunder broke
Those vast solitary woods:
Silence dead, that eloquent spoke!
220 It ever rolled its floods.

Eagles that shoot on wings athwart the sky,
 Or soar sublimely wrapt in solemn cloud;
That build their inaccessible nests on high
 'Mid oaks, whose gnarlèd trunks in homage bowed,
225 Conceal their fury and in their leafy shroud

Sleep sometimes; and the Lion doth also rest
 In forest den, couching till close of day,
Till the sun sinking in the crimson west
 Shall call him forth again to hunt for prey,
230 And for his royal food the subject beasts to slay.

Huge Behemoth shakes not for aye the ground:
 At night he lays his vast bulk under trees
Whose thick leaves lull him to repose, with sound
 Of hoarsely murmuring waters of the seas,
235 Where swell the azure waves, unswept by wind or
   breeze.

  But running brook and river
   Still rush along their way;
  They stop their courses never
   By midnight or noonday.
240 Though stars to soothe their raving
   May sweetly o'er them play,
  Yet still their green banks laving
   They hold the channelled way
  Though quiet moonlight's streaming,
245   Unmindful that still ray;
  Through emerald foliage gleaming
   They churn the silver spray.

  How weary seems that lasting task,
   Still in motion on to pour!
250 Ne'er in fixèd calm to bask
   Like mirror by the sounding shore.

Then the trees might droop unshaken
   Round the quiet bay
And the silence then might waken
255   Birds to chant their lay,

Inarticulate anthems hymning,
   Perched on slender twig and bough,
Their music o'er the surface skimming
   While the stream rests from its flow;
260 And no longer past meandering
   Doth eternal go!

When again the river glides,
   From binding chains set free,
Each majestic wavelet rides
265   Laden with melody,
Bearing its tribute waters
   Towards the boundless sea;
Then in awful billows heaving
   With its own loud harmony.

270 These were my thoughts as home my steps I turned
By clouds which sailed along the horizon warned:
I cast one last glance at the lovely moon
To see if yet in the wide heavens she shone.
Lo! curtaining mists o'er all the sky were spread
275 And weary with nightly watching she'd veiled her
   beauteous head.

              MARQUIS OF DOURO.
              C. BRONTË. *June* 28, 1830.

MORNING

LO! the light of the morning is flowing
  Through radiant portals of gold,
Which Aurora, in crimson robes glowing,
  For the horses of fire doth unfold.

5   See Apollo's burnished car
      Glorifies the East afar.
      As it draws the horizon nigher,
      As it climbs the heavens higher,
      Richer grows the amber light,
10   Fairer, more intensely bright,
      Till floods of light in splendour roll
      O'er all the earth from pole to pole.

    Hark! the birds in the green forest bowers
      Have beheld the sun's Chariot arise;
15 And the humblest, the stateliest flowers
      Are arrayed in more beautiful dyes.

    Now, while the woodland choirs are singing,
    Opening buds fresh odours flinging;
    And while Nature's tuneful voice
20 Calls on all men to rejoice,
    I cannot join the common gladness:
    'Tis to me a time of sadness:
    All these sounds of mirth impart
    Nought but sorrow to my heart.

25 But I love evening's still, quiet hour,
      The whispering twilight breeze,
    The damp dew's invisible shower
      Conglobing in drops on the trees.

Then is heard no sound or tone
30 But the night-bird singing lone;
Peacefully adown the vale
It passes on the balmy gale;
Ceases oft the pensive strain,
Solemn sinking, and again
35 Philomela sends her song
To wander the night-winds along.

While silver-robed Luna is beaming
Afar in the heavens on high,
And her bright train of planets are gleaming
40 Like gems in the dome of the sky.

From the firmament above
Down they gaze with looks of love
On the minstrel, all unheeding,
Still their ears entrancèd feeding
45 With the notes of sweetest sound
Gushing forth on all around:
Music not unfit for Heaven
But to earth in mercy given;
Thou dost charm the mourner's heart,
50 Thou dost pensive joy impart:
Peerless Queen of Harmony,
How I love thy melody!

MARQUIS OF DOURO. *August* 22, 1830.

The above poem is included in the October 1830 number of the
Second Series of the *Young Men's Magazine*, comprising six small MS.
books, measuring about 2 inches by 1¼ inches, prose and verse,
written in minute characters resembling the smallest of printed type.
The contents of these 'Magazines' appear to be the exclusive work of
Charlotte Brontë. See the volumes of *Miscellaneous and Unpublished
Works* in this edition.

YOUNG MAN NAUGHTY'S ADVENTURE

MURK was the night: nor star, nor moon,
Shone in the cloud-wrapped sky,
To break the dull, tenebrous gloom
Of the arched vault on high,

5 When Naughty, with his dog and gun,
Walked lonely o'er the moor;
True, the shooting-season had not begun,—
But poachers commence before!

The howling winds blew fierce around,
10 The rain drove in his face;
And, as Naughty heard the hollow sound,
He quickened his creeping pace.

For as each hoarse sepulchral blast
Drew slow and solemn near,
15 It seemed like spirits sailing past
To his affrighted ear.

For he was on a dreadful errand bent
To the ancient witch of the moor;
A delegate by his comrades sent
20 To consult the beldam hoar.

Now yelled the wind with more terrible din,
Now rattled the rain full fast;
And, noiselessly gliding, forms were seen,
As around his eyes he cast;

25 When a rustling sound in the heather he heard:
Starting, he turned about;
Was it a spirit? Was it a bird?
No! a hare sprang trembling out.

The shot went 'Whizz!' and the gun went 'Bang!'
30   A flash illumined the air;
Far and wide the moor with the echo rang
As down dropped the luckless hare.

He ran to the spot, and, lo! there lay
A woman on the hard heath-bed,
35   Whose soul had left its breathless clay,
For the witch of the moor was dead!

CHARLOTTE BRONTË. *October* 14, 1830.

Young Man Naughty is a character in the Angrian stories of
Charlotte and Branwell Brontë.

THE VIOLET

A POEM

WITH SEVERAL SMALLER PIECES

BY THE

MARQUIS OF DOURO

MEMBER OF THE SOCIETY OF ANTI-
QUARIANS; PRESIDENT FOR 1830 OF
THE LITERARY CLUB; HONORARY
MEMBER OF THE ACADEMY OF ARTISTS
& TREASURER TO THE SOCIETY FOR
THE SPREAD OF CLASSICAL KNOW-
LEDGE; CHIEF SECRETARY OF THE
CONFEDERATE HUNDRED FOR PRO-
MOTING GYMNASTIC EXERCISES
&C. &C. &C.

PUBLISHED

BY

SERGEANT TREE

AND SOLD

BY

ALL OTHER BOOKSELLERS IN THE
CHIEF GLASS TOWN, THE DUKE OF
WELLINGTON'S GLASS TOWN, PARIS,
PARRY'S GLASS TOWN, ROSS'S GLASS
TOWN, &C. &C. &C. &C. &C.
November the 14th, 1830.

The above is a copy of the title-page of the original manuscript in which the seven following poems are included. The MS. contains 16 pages, $3\frac{3}{4}$ inches by $2\frac{1}{4}$ inches, microscopic writing.

THE VIOLET

ONE eve, as all the radiant west,
   Far-beaming with the liquid gold
Of sunset, gilt the mountain's crest
   Girdling the sky with outlines bold,

5 And flung a broad and mellow light
   Around the rocks that rose on high,
As pillars for the throne of night
   Then shading soft the eastern sky,

I stood amid a desert vast:
10   Nor golden field nor mead was there;
No tree or grove their shadow cast
   Or shook their tresses in the air.

But one wide solemn wilderness,
   Whose aspect filled the mind with fear,
15 Showed Nature in her sternest dress
   With rugged brow and face severe.

Winds o'er that land have come and gone,
   But, voiceless and unblent with sound
Of living song or human tone,
20   They ceaseless sigh and murmur round.

Yet oft the lonely traveller hears
   A sugh[1] as of some distant stream;
And, lo! far off in gloom appears
   A mighty water's azure gleam.

25 No white sail glideth o'er its breast,
   No snowy seamew cuts the waves,
But all unburdened and at rest
   The passing surge that lone shore laves.

[1]This most expressive word is surely more worthy of being adopted into the English language than many of the foreign phrases we light on. (Note by Charlotte Brontë.)

Life in these wilds has ceased to be:
30   Not e'en the eagle's royal wing
Waves in the sky: no red-deer free
    Makes with his cry this desert ring.

My heart quaked at the silence dead,
    The utter silence reigning there;
35 An incubus, an awful dread,
    With leaden power oppressed the air.

At length a gentle breeze up-sprang:
    With low, wild moaning, on it swept;
It seemed Æolian music rang
40   As softly on the ear it crept;

And, watered by that harp-like blast,
    Thoughts rose within my spirit's cell
Of those who in long ages past
    Attuned the muse's hallowed shell:

45 Of him,[2] the Bard that swept the lyre
    Whose sounding strings were stained with gore;
Whose agèd eyes shot heavenly fire,
    Beaming beneath his forehead hoar.

All honour to that mighty one;
50   Let earth with his great praises ring;
Child of the self-illumined sun,
    How did'st thou strike the trembling string

While music like a mountain-flood
    Rolled forth as swept thy hand along,—
55 Wars, horrid wars and streaming blood
    Ensanguined deep thy martial song?

Greece, thy fair skies have flung their light
    On mightiest of this sunlit world:
Genius, enthroned in glory bright,
60   O'er thee her banner hath unfurled.

[2] Homer.

Now desolate, by time decayed,
    Thy solemn temples mouldering lie;
While black groves throw Cimmerian shade
    Beneath a still transparent sky.

65 Degenerate are thy sons, and slaves;
    Athens and Sparta are no more;
Unswept by swans, Eurotas laves
    As yet its laurel-shaded shore.

Parnassus now uplifts her head
70   Forsaken by the holy nine:
They from her heights for aye have fled,
    And now in fair Britannia shine.

If, rising from the silent tomb,
    Thy tragic bards could see thee now,
75 What solemn clouds of grief and gloom
    Would shade each spirit's lofty brow!

How would the haunted air resound
    With moanings of each shadowy lyre!
How would earth tremble at the sound,
80   And quake before the wailing dire!

He,[1] that with soft but stately tread
    Passed solemn o'er the Grecian stage,—
What tears of pity would he shed
    At sight of thy base vassalage!

85 The tender,[2] and the terrible,[3]
    Commingling each their notes of woe;—
One strain with rage divine would swell,
    The other sadly sorrowing flow.

Though fair Ausonia too hath sunk,
90   And fallen from her high estate;
Though deeply she the cup hath drunk
    Of vengeance, from the hand of Fate;

[1] Sophocles.   [2] Euripides.   [3] Æschylus.

Yet, 'mid her mighty ruins, oft
   Some beauteous flower is seen to bloom,
95 Piercing with radiance mildly soft
   Her crumbling cities' cloudy gloom.

Such, he[1] that sang Jerusalem
   In strains as sweet as ever flows
From harp of Mantua's glorious swain,[2]
100   Though heaven's own fire within him glows.

But no faint star on thee hath shone,
   O Greece! since set those orbs of light;
Each in itself a quenchless sun
   Refulgently, divinely bright!

105 And said I set? No! still they beam
   With dazzling lustre far on high,
Aye sending forth a golden gleam
   O'er azure of the vaulted sky.

And sons of Albion in the rank
110   Shine crowned with honours they have won;
For deeply of the fount they drank:
   The sacred fount of Helicon!

Hail! army of Immortals, hail!
   Oh, might I 'neath your banners march!
115 Though faint my lustre, faint and pale,—
   Scarce seen amid the glorious arch,—

Yet joy, deep joy, would fill my heart:
   'Nature, unveil thy awful face!
To me a poet's power impart,
120   Though humble be my destined place.'

'Twas thus arose my ardent prayer
   Amid the desert solitude;
It reached the 'Mighty Mother's' ear;
   She saw me where I lowly stood.

[1] Tasso.   [2] Virgil.

125 And first a voice went sweeping by
     On the wild wind that murmured round:
   From the deep bosom of the sky
     Seemed to proceed that solemn sound.

   Then shadowy vapours gathered fast
130   Which shut from view the pale moonlight;
   Swelled louder the triumphant blast,
     High-pealing with tumultuous might.

   The river's voice from distance far
     Proclaimed some prodigy was nigh;
135 Clouds veiled from sight each glimmering star,
     And waned their splendour from the sky.

   I trembled as a brighter ray,
     Unknown from whence, illumed the air,
   Transforming twilight into day,
140   As Luna's beam of silver fair.

   Now dawned upon my awe-struck eyes
     A shape more beauteous than the morn
   When, radiant with a thousand dyes,
     The pearls of night her brow adorn.

145 A woman's form the vision wore;
     Her lofty forehead touched the sky;
   Her crown, a rugged mountain hoar
     Where plume-like trees waved solemnly.

   Down fell her mantle white as snow;
150   An azure river girt her round:
   That liquid belt did circling flow
     With faint, but never-ceasing, sound.

   The heavenly and the terrene globe
     In lines of light were pictured fair
155 On foldings of her spotless robe
     Wide-floating on the ambient air.

Her dusky tresses, dark as night,
 With crescent moon and stars were bound,
As through black clouds shone out their light
160 In rays of glory beaming round.

A gracious smile illumed her face
 As throned she sate on clouds of light,
In attitude of heavenly grace,
 Beneath an arch like rainbow bright.

165 Sweet as the echoes of the hill
 At length her voice the silence broke:
In accents calm, serene, and still,
 Thus, Nature, condescending, spoke:—

'Thy prayer hath reached me where I dwell,
170 In river, or in sounding cave,
By woodland bower, by hidden dell,
 Or under ocean's foamy wave.

'Thou would'st be one of that bright band,
 The favoured children of the sky;
175 The chosen from each shore and land
 Of deathless fame and memory?

'Mortal! I grant that high request,
 (But dim thy beam, and faint thy ray),
Partake the glory of the blest,
180 Son of Apollo, king of Day!

'Laurel thy temples may not bind:
 In humbler sphere thy fate is set;
That for the more exalted mind;
 But take yon lowly violet;

185 'And press it, mortal! to thy heart,
 And wreathe the floweret round thy brow;
Oh! never from that token part
 Till death thy energies shall bow!'

Thus spake the glorious deity,
190   Then passed in dazzling light away;
The mighty sovereign of the sky
    Shone never with so bright a ray.

I plucked the violet where it grew
    Beside a stone, green moss amid;
195 Its lovely leaflets bright with dew,—
    Like modest worth, half seen, half hid.

Years have rolled o'er me since that night;
    Still doth the flower its perfume shed;
Still shall it free from withering blight
200   Till I lie with the silent dead.

MARQUIS OF DOURO.

CHARLOTTE BRONTË. *November* 10, 1830.

This poem was printed (with facsimiles of the title-page and two pages of the original manuscript) in an edition limited to twenty-five copies for private circulation only, by Mr Clement Shorter, in April 1916. Facsimiles of the same pages of the manuscript have also been given in *The Sphere*, April 22, 1916, pp. 94 and 96; and in *A Bibliography of the Writings in Prose and Verse of the Members of the Brontë Family*, 1917, p. 76, by Mr. T. J. Wise.

LINES ON SEEING THE PORTRAIT OF
——[1] PAINTED BY DE LISLE

RADIANT creature! is thy birth
Of the heavens or of the earth?
For those bright and beaming eyes
Speak the language of the skies;
5   And, methinks, upon thy tongue
Dwell the songs by angels sung!
Still and tranquil is the beam
That from those blue orbs doth stream,—
Like the azure moon-lit sky,
10   Like the lucid stars on high,—
Rays of mind are darting thence
Mild and pure intelligence.

Art thou then of spirit birth
And not a denizen of earth?
15   No! thou'rt but a child of clay,
Simply robed in white array;
Not a gem is gleaming there;
All as spotless snow so fair,
Symbol of thy angel-mind,—
20   Meek, benevolent, and kind;
Sprightly as the beauteous fawn
Springing up at break of dawn,
Graceful, bounding o'er the hills
To the music of the rills!

25   What bright hues thy cheeks adorn
Like the blushes of the morn!
How thy curled and glossy hair
Clusters o'er thy forehead fair!
How the sportive ringlets deck
30   Like golden snow thy ivory neck!

[1]Marian Hume (Marina), betrothed to the Marquis of Douro.

And thy hands so smooth and white
Folded, while the rosy light
Of a summer sunset sky
Gleams around thee gloriously,
35 All the west one crimson flood
Pouring light o'er mount and wood!

Beauteous being, most divine!
I am thine, and thou art mine!

MARQUIS OF DOURO.
CHARLOTTE BRONTË. *November* 10, 1830.

VESPER

I'LL hang my lyre amid these ancient trees,
And while the sad wind moans the chords among,
Sweet forest-music of the harp and breeze
    Shall steal the circumambient air along,
5   And I will sing meantime a low, responsive song.

What shall I sing? Wilt thou, O rising moon!
    Like a broad shield suspended in the east,
Wilt thou attend some melancholy tune
    While sleeps thy light upon the river's breast
10   Whose swelling wavelets sink when by thy beams
        caressed?

No! beauteous as thou art, thy gentle ear
    Would call my music rugged, and 'mid clouds
Thou might'st offended hide thy silver ear,
    And draw o'er heaven the dark and sombre shrouds,
15   Concealing all the hosts marshalled in radiant
        crowds!

What shall I sing then? Hark! that sudden swell
    That rose in the old forest's glimmering light,
How like the tune of some old convent-bell
    Borne to the traveller's ear at dead of night,
20   Sounding in utter silence with a tenfold might!

The rising wind hath stolen it from the strings
    Of my sweet lyre, suspended in yon tree;
And now the wild wood with rich music rings,
    And thrilling cadences, most bold and free,
25   Are pealing round with heavenly melody.

I need not sing, the armies of the skies
    Night's empress and the dryad wood-nymphs fair
Would rather list the tones that now arise
    And fill with harmony the twilight air;
30   Sweet sounds for all the winds beneath the stars to
        bear.

Then I will sit and listen: not a voice
Disturbs the unbroken silence of this hour;
No nestling bird, with faintly rustling noise,
    Raises the leaflets of the vernal bower,
35   Or bends the spray where blooms the fruit-betoken-
        ing flower.

Even the chorister of night is still!
    Sweet Philomel restrains her 'customed song;
Hushed are the murmurs of the unseen rill
    Creeping through matted grass and weeds along;
40   Silent I too will be, these solemn shades among!

MARQUIS OF DOURO.

CHARLOTTE BRONTË. *November* 11, 1830.

LINES ADDRESSED TO LADY ZENOBIA ELL-RINGTON SENT WITH MY PORTRAIT WHICH SHE HAD ASKED ME TO GIVE HER.

LADY! this worthless gift I send,
    Obeying your command;
Now, to my poor request attend,
    And give with willing hand!

5 You have an aspect passing fair,
    A form of beauteous guise,
A Juno-like, majestic air,
    And piercing, radiant eyes;

And you have locks whose jetty light
10   Is like the raven's wing;
And oh! when from your forehead bright
    Those glossy locks you fling,

How down your shoulders fair they stream,
    And down your stately neck!
15 How richly, with their dusky gleam,
    Your queen-like form they deck!

Now, from those ample treasures take
    One little sportive ring,
And I will keep it for your sake,
20   And oft its praises sing!

I'll get it bound with orient pearls,
    Enclosed in case of gold;
More I shall prize that queenly curl
    Than precious gems untold!

25 Memorial though frail yet fair
    Of one whose genius bright
Hath glorified our age with glare
    Of its unsetting light,

O'er which it gracefully did stray,
30   And bright and burnished shone,
Like the vine-tendril's wanton play
    In times long past and gone!

MARQUIS OF DOURO.

CHARLOTTE BRONTË. *November* 12, 1830.

MATIN

LONG hath earth lain beneath the dark profound
    Of silent-footed, planet-crested night:
Now from the chains of slumber soft, unbound,
    She springs from sleep to hail the glorious birth of light.

5   A solemn hush lay on her hills and woods,—
    Now, as the day approaches, fast dispelling;
For at the touch of the bright orient-floods
    Thousands of voices rise, in mingled murmurs swelling.

First the sun's glories tip the lofty hills,
10   Then roll impetuous down the dusky vale;
Sings sweet in light the pebbled crystal rill,
    And joy expands the buds or flowers that woo the gale.

Oh! I might sing of pastures, meads, and trees,
    Whose verdant hue is tinged with solar beams;
15   And I might sing of morn's fresh, bracing breeze
    That, with awakening breath, ripples the glassy streams;

And of the merry lark who soars on high,
    Aye rising in his course towards the sun;
Of his descending from the vaulted sky
20   To the expectant nest, when that sweet song is done.

These I could sing if thou[1] wert near me now,—
    Thou whom I love, my soul's most fair delight;
If the fair orbs that beam beneath thy brow
    Shed on my darkling page their ray divinely bright.

25 But no, great waters of the mighty deep,
    Howling like famished wolves, roll us between;
Oh! sad and bitter drops I mournful weep
    To think of those vast leagues of tossing billows green.

Come from the fairy valley where thou dwellest,—
30   Shady and green is Britain's favoured isle;
Come, for all gloom and sadness thou dispellest,
    And chase away my grief with one sweet sunny smile.

Methinks I see thee sitting calm and lonely
    Beneath the umbrageous elm upon the lawn;
35 And near thee but the woodland warblers only
    Singing their matin-song; and perchance some gentle
    fawn.

Or pearly dews thy footsteps may be brushing,
    Tripping as cheerful as the lambkins gay
Beside the cataract whose thunderous rushing
40   Covers its shaken banks with white-churned bells and
    spray.

Hark! Afric unto her desert sand now calls thee,
    Where the bright sun outpours his fervid beams;
Alas! the chain of love for aye enthralls me:
    My prisoned heart still pants in wild and shifting dreams.

45 I hear thy voice, I see thy figure nightly;
    Thou comest to me in midnight slumbers deep!
And through the dark thy blue eyes, glimmering brightly,
    Beam down upon my restless, spirit-haunted sleep.

             [1] Marian Hume (Marina).

Oh! but I loved to hear thy low sweet singing
50   When evening threw her quiet shades around;—
The moon, her mild light through the casement stealing,
    Seemed from the sky to list the half-angelic sound.

Thou to the scene a calmer beauty lending,
    With eyes steeped in the lingering light of song;
55 And from the harp, thy form so graceful, bending,
    Drew melting notes that stole the dusky air along.

Oh! when within thy still, retired bower
    Shall I once more hear that dear entrancing strain?
Would I could win the oft-desired hour
60   That my bereavèd heart might beat with joy again!

Oh! still I hope for thy long-wished returning:
    Come swiftly o'er the dark and raging sea!
Come, for my soul with hope deferred is burning;
    Then will I sing a song worthy of morn and thee!

MARQUIS OF DOURO.

CHARLOTTE BRONTË. *November 12, 1830.*

REFLECTIONS ON THE FATE OF
NEGLECTED GENIUS

MIGHTY winds that sing on high
  Wildly, sweetly, mournfully,
  Bear my song through heaven's dome,
  Add from your stores some sweeter tone
5 To fit it for its passage in the sky.

  None can tell the bitter anguish
  Of those lofty souls that languish,
    With grim penury still dwelling:
  Quenched by frowns their sacred fire,
10   All their powers within them swelling,
  Tortured by neglect to ire;

  And only conscious that the radiant light
    Of Genius is around them ever shed:
  What marvel if their high poetic might
15   When Hope is vanquished,
  And for the golden-haired and bright-eyed queen
  A ghastly band of brooding cares are seen.

  Genius enthroned in light!
    Dost thou for those who at thine altars kneel
20   One passing cloud of grief to dim thy radiance feel?
  Speak from thy dwelling bright!

  Hark! Came that voice from thee,
  Omnipotent and great divinity?
  No, 'twas but the breeze drew near
25 And seemed articulate to my ear!

Answer, thou that dwellest on high,
Answer from the azure sky;
Oh! this utter silence break
And do, thou unseen shadow, speak!

30 Spiritual essence, pure, divine,
Which the hearts of men enshrine,
And that sheds a holy ray
Over animated clay,

And for him in whom it dwells,
35 Whose heart with generous feelings swells,
Clear film darkness from his eye
And his vision purify
Of that dim and earthly haze
Through which less favoured mortals gaze.

40 And, oh! what strange sensations gush
To his expanding soul,
With wild and overwhelming rush,
And onward silent roll

When some fair scene of nature breaks
45 At once upon his eye,
And to his heart, though voiceless, speaks
Sweetly and solemnly.

Some huge and hoary mountain
A shade tremendous flinging o'er the land,
50 Like a dark cloud, that Nature's mighty hand
Hath piled aloft, 'cumbering the earth with gloom
And ominous blackness, as the last great day
Were hasting fast, and dreadful signs of doom,
Tokens of coming terrors, upon the great world lay.

55 These are the joys of genius; but the grief,
The sting of cold neglect, unheeding merit.—
No cheering ray, no balsam of relief,
Soothe the heart-piercing pains that rack his spirit.

Thousands on thousands pass the mourner by,
60   Nor heave a sigh, nor one kind tear-drop send
In sorrow for his woeful agony
        And for the pangs that all his bosom rend.

Far brighter burns the universal fire
        Within his breast, whom now I feebly sing,
65   Possessing but that high and soul desire,
        That after-times should with his praises ring.

And thus 'mid grief and strife he yields to death:
        Slow and solemn tolls his funeral knell,
And broken-hearted he resigns his breath:
70   Unhappy child of genius, fare-thee-well!

MARQUIS OF DOURO.

CHARLOTTE BRONTË. *November* 13, 1830.

A SERENADE

AWAKE! Awake! fair sleeper. Awake and view the
        night,
For the armies clad in diamond mail now shed abroad
        their light;
Come forth with me, fair sleeper; perchance upon our
        ears
While we walk may fall the chiming of the music of the
        spheres.

5   We will go to the huge forest and hearken to the sound,
Like the voices of a hundred streams for ever rushing
        round,—
Of nodding boughs and branches, great plumes that
        wave on high,
And hide with their thick darkness the star-bespangled
        sky.

And haply, as we tread beneath that black embowered
    shade,
10 Full on our sight may sudden burst some moon-illumined
    glade,
Where with crowns of radiant adamant and robes of ver-
    nal green
The morrice-dancing fairy train in other times was seen.

Or shall we wander by the side of ancient ocean's shore
Where the dull thundering billows are sounding ever
    more?
15 And gaze into the mighty depths whence comes that
    'wildering sound,
On the swift wings of heaven dispersing all around.

There dwell great dragons of the deep, and issuing from
    their caves
Our eyes may view them gliding amid the liquid waves
Or solemnly withdrawn into tenebrous gloom
20 With noiseless movement entering their coral shaded
    tomb.

While still, sad music rises from regions far beneath,
At which the winds hush every sound of sigh and mur-
    mured breath.
Unseen the sweet musician, but still the tones ascend,
And e'en the everlasting rocks their cloud-veil'd summits
    bend.

25 It is the maiden of the sea that sings within her cell,
Where she with gold and orient pearl in glimmering
    gloom doth dwell;
And when her monstrous form is seen swift-gliding o'er
    the deep,
The blood within the sailors' veins in frozen streams doth
    creep.

For mighty winds behind her fly and clouds are round her
    shed,
³⁰ And lurid lightning's flashings wreathe the green locks on
    her head;
But she shall bode no storm for us to rack the lucid skies—
Then, Awake! Awake! fair sleeper, and unclose thine
    azure eyes!

MARQUIS OF DOURO.

CHARLOTTE BRONTË. *November* 14, 1830.

The appearance of the mermaid is said by sailors to be a sign of
approaching tempest. I have heard many an experienced mariner
confidently assert his belief in the existence of such a creature. (Note
by Charlotte Brontë.)

SONG

T H E pearl within the shell concealed
    Oft sheds a fairer light
Than that whose beauties are revealed
    To our restricted sight.

⁵ So she who sweetly shines at home
    And seldom wanders thence,
Is of her partner's happy dome
    The blest intelligence.

The highest talents of her mind,
¹⁰   The sunlight of her heart,
Are all to illumine her home designed,
    And never thence they part.

Sung by the Marquis of Douro to Marian Hume, in the story entitled *Visits in Verreopolis*, by Lord Charles Wellesley, Vol. I, Chap. 1.
The volume was commenced by Charlotte Brontë on December 7,
1830, and finished on December 11, 1830.

THE FAIRIES' FAREWELL

THE trumpet hath sounded, its voice is gone forth
From the plains of the south to the seas of the north;
The great ocean groaned, and the firm mountains shook,
And the rivers in terror their channels forsook.
5 The proud eagle quailed in her aerial dome,
The gentle dove flew to her bowery home,
The antelope trembled as onward she sprang,
When hollow and death-like the trumpet-blast rang.

It was midnight, deep midnight, and shrouded in sleep
10 Men heard not the roar of the terror-struck deep
Nor the peal of the trumpet still sounding on high;
They saw not the flashes that brightened the sky.
All silent and tomb-like the great city lay,
And fair rose her towers in their moonlight array:
15 'Twas the Ruler of Spirits that sent forth the sound
To call his dread legions in myriads around.

They heard him, and from land and wave
The genii armies sprung:
Some came from dim green ocean cave
20 Where thousand gems are flung;

Some from the forests of the west,
'Mid dark shades wandering;
A giant host of wingéd forms
Rose round their mighty king!

25 Some from the chill and ice-bound north,
All swathed in snowy shrouds,
With the wild howl of storms came forth
Sailing in tempest-clouds.

The gentler fays in bright bands flew
From each sweet woodland dell,
30   All broidered with the violet blue,
And wild-flower's drooping bell.

A sound of harps was on the blast
Breathing faint melody;
35   A dim light was from distance cast
As their fair troops drew nigh.

And, mingling with stern giant forms,
Their tiny shapes are seen,
Bright gleaming 'mid the gloom of storms
40   Their gems and robes of green.

The Hall where they sat was the heart of the sky,
And the stars to give light stooped their lamps from on high
The noise of the host rose like thunder around,
The heavens gathered gloom at the grave sullen sound.
45   No mortal may farther the vision reveal:
Human eye cannot pierce what a spirit would seal.
The secrets of genii my tongue may not tell,
But hoarsely they murmured: 'Bright city, farewell!'
Then melted away like a dream of the night,
50   While their palace evanished in oceans of light.
Far beneath them the city lay silent and calm;
The breath of the night-wind was softer than balm
As it sighed o'er its gardens, and mourned in its bowers,
And shook the bright dew-drops from orient flowers;
55   But still as the breeze on the myrtle-groves fell,
A voice was heard wailing: 'Bright city, farewell!'
The morning rose over the far distant hill,
And yet the great city lay silent and still.
No chariot rode thunderous adown the wide street,
60   No horse of Arabia, impetuous and fleet.

The river flowed on to the foam-crested sea,
But, unburdened by vessel, its waves murmured free.
The silence is dreadful. O city, arise!
The sound is ascending the arch of the skies.
65   Mute, mute are the mighty, and chilled is their breath,
For at midnight passed o'er them the Angel of Death!
The king and the peasant, the lord and the slave,
Lie entombed in the depth of one wide solemn grave.

    Now Ruin, dæmon of the wild,
70   Her shadow round hath flung;
    And where the face of beauty smiled,
      Where sweetest music rung,

    The tiger's howl shall oft be heard
      Sounding through bower and dome,
75   And to the moon the desert-bird
      Shall make her thrilling moan.

    The murmur of the myrtle-bowers,
      The voice of waving trees,
    The fragrance of the sweet wild-flowers,
80   Shall mingle with the breeze.

    Unheard that gentle wind shall sweep
      The wide campaign of air;
    Unfelt the heavens their balm shall weep:
      The living are not there.

December 11, 1831.

The above poem was written when Charlotte Brontë had been nearly twelve months at school. She appears to have decided to write no more about fairyland, and to have written the poem for the purpose of calling her fairies and genii together in their aerial palace over the city of Verdopolis to bid them 'Good-bye!' We do not meet them again in any of her poems or stories of a later date.

OH! there is a land which the sun loves to lighten,
  Whose bowers are of myrtle, whose forests are palm,
Whose shores the pure rays of the amethyst brighten,
  Whose winds as they murmur are softer than balm.

5 The streams of that land spring in might from their foun-
    tains,
  Rush through the deep valley and o'er the vast plain,
Pass swiftly the cloud-crested, sky-girdling mountains,
  As onward, bright-bounding, they meet the wide
    main.

The boughs of the willow-tree, gracefully drooping,
10   Hang over their borders in shadowy gloom,
And on the green banks to the clear waters sloping
  Flowers bright as the rainbow eternally bloom.

There silence asserts not her solemn dominion,
  There the bird of the wilderness evermore sings,
15 Still tunes the sweet pipe, and still waves the soft pinion,
  While echo her tribute from far distance brings.

    But though fair as bright Elysian dreams
      These vernal Eden bowers,
    Yet, oh! this land hath other scenes
20   Than woods and streams and flowers.

    High hills that woo the winds of heaven
      To breathe upon them from the skies;
    Rocks tempest-shaken, thunder-riven,
      Whose cliffs like giant turrets rise.

25 Great cataracts rolling down the steep,
      Shaking the sky and steady shore;
    Rousing all nature from her sleep,
      With hoarse, rebounding, thunderous roar.

Trees shaken by the wailing blast
   Wave in the dim air mournfully;
While sullen sounds float fitful past
   Like the dull moaning of the sea.

There rubies shed their blood-red ray,
   There orient emeralds softly gleam,
There diamonds flash forth transient day
   And emulate the solar beam.

But vainly the diamond sheds light through that land
As though formed by the might of some fair wizard's
   wand;
And vainly the rivers flow forth to the sea
In brightness and beauty and sweet melody.

And the hills lift their tall stately summits on high,
And the winds are called forth from the heart of the sky;
And vainly the cataracts roll swift down the steep;—
To a murmur is softened the voice of the deep.

The bright sun in vain to this far land is given,
And the planets look forth from the windows of heaven;
The birds sing unheeded in woods fresh and green,
And the flowers grow unscented, ungathered, unseen.

The lion rules the forest and the eagle the air:
Mankind is dominionless, portionless there;
His voice never rang through those wide-spreading
   woods;
His bark never stemmed the wild rush of those floods;

His foot never trod on the green, flowery sward;
No beast of those deserts acknowledged him lord;
His hand never gathered those gems rich and rare:
Mankind is dominionless, portionless there.

December 25, **1831**.

LINES ON BEWICK

THE cloud of recent death is past away,
    But yet a shadow lingers o'er his tomb
To tell that the pale standard of decay
    Is reared triumphant o'er life's sullied bloom.

5   But now the eye bedimmed by tears may gaze
    On the fair lines his gifted pencil drew,
The tongue unfaltering speak its meed of praise
    When we behold those scenes to Nature true—

True to the common Nature that we see
10   In England's sunny fields, her hills and vales,
On the wild bosom of her storm-dark sea
    Still heaving to the wind that o'er it wails.

How many winged inhabitants of air,
    How many plume-clad floaters of the deep,
15 The mighty artist drew in forms as fair
    As those that now the skies and waters sweep;

From the great eagle, with his lightning eye,
    His tyrant glance, his talons dyed in blood,
To the sweet breather-forth of melody,
20   The gentle merry minstrel of the wood.

Each in his attitude of native grace
    Looks on the gazer life-like, free and bold,
And if the rocks be his abiding place
    Far off appears the winged marauder's hold.

25 But if the little builder rears his nest
    In the still shadow of green tranquil trees,
And singing sweetly 'mid the silence blest
    Sits a meet emblem of untroubled peace,

'A change comes o'er the spirit of our dream,'—
30   Woods wave around in crested majesty;
We almost feel the joyous sunshine's beam
    And hear the breath of the sweet south go by.

Our childhood's days return again in thought,
    We wander in a land of love and light,
35 And mingled memories, joy—and sorrow—fraught
    Gush on our hearts with overwhelming might.

Sweet flowers seem gleaming 'mid the tangled grass
    Sparkling with spray-drops from the rushing rill,
And as these fleeting visions fade and pass
40   Perchance some pensive tears our eyes may fill.

These soon are wiped away, again we turn
    With fresh delight to the enchanted page
Where pictured thoughts that breathe and speak and
        burn
    Still please alike our youth and riper age.

45 There rises some lone rock all wet with surge
    And dashing billows glimmering in the light
Of a wan moon, whose silent rays emerge
    From clouds that veil their lustre, cold and bright.

And there 'mongst reeds upon a river's side
50   A wild bird sits, and brooding o'er her nest
Still guards the priceless gems, her joy and pride,
    Now ripening 'neath her hope-enlivened breast.

We turn the page: before the expectant eye
    A traveller stands lone on some desert heath;
55 The glorious sun is passing from the sky
    While fall his farewell rays on all beneath;

O'er the far hills a purple veil seems flung,
    Dim herald of the coming shades of night;
E'en now Diana's lamp aloft is hung,
60   Drinking full radiance from the fount of light.

Oh, when the solemn wind of midnight sighs,
   Where will the lonely traveller lay his head?
Beneath the tester of the star-bright skies
   On the wild moor he'll find a dreary bed.

65 Now we behold a marble Naiad placed
   Beside a fountain on her sculptured throne,
Her bending form with simplest beauty graced,
   Her white robes gathered in a snowy zone.

She from a polished vase pours forth a stream
70   Of sparkling water to the waves below
Which roll in light and music, while the gleam
   Of sunshine flings through shade a golden glow.

A hundred fairer scenes these leaves reveal;
   But there are tongues that injure while they praise:
75 I cannot speak the rapture that I feel
   When on the work of such a mind I gaze.

Then farewell, Bewick, genius' favoured son,
   Death's sleep is on thee, all thy woes are past;
From earth departed, life and labour done,
80   Eternal peace and rest are thine at last.
                 C. BRONTË. *November* 27, 1832.

This poem was first printed under the tentative title of 'Lines on the Celebrated Bewick' in *The Times Literary Supplement*, January 4, 1907.

LAMENT

O HYLE! thy waves are like Babylon's streams
 When the daughters of Zion hung o'er them in woe;
When the sad exiles wept in their desolate dreams,
 And sighed for the sound of their calm Kedron's flow.

5 The palms are all withered that shadowed thy shore,
 The breezes that kiss thee through sepulchres sweep:
For the plume of the Ethiop, the lance of the Moor
 All under the sods of the battle-field sleep.

O Hylle! that moonlight shines colder on thee
10 Than afar off it shines on the sad lake of graves
And drear as the voice of its wild waters be
 'Tis joy to the sound of thy desolate waves.

O Hylle! thy children are scattered afar;
 All gone is their glory, all faded their fame;
15 Crushed is their banner-staff, vanished their star,
 Unburied their ashes, forgotten their name.

February 12, 1833.

The spelling of the name Hyle or Hylle is given as it appears in the MS.

DEATH OF LORD ROWAN

FAIR forms of glistening marble stand around
　　Whose fixed and sightless eyeballs chill the soul
As they stand cold and silent, while a sound
　　Is heard without of the deep thunder's roll;
5　And wild, swift wind-blasts sweep the moonless sky,
　　Now with a far-off wail, now howling sternly nigh.

Stretched on that couch, I see an old man's form,
　　Whose head is hoary with a century's snow;
He shudders while he lists the sullen storm;
10　　And the cold death-sweats trickle from his brow,
As his high palace echoes to a yell
Loud as a hundred tempests' mightiest swell.

There lies Lord Rowan, all his eyes' dark light
　　Quenched in the lapse of time; his raven hair,
15　Which once in grapelike clusters, thick and bright,
　　Hung o'er his temples, now so wan and bare,
Falls down in meagre locks of hoary grey
Which turn to silver where the torch-beams play.

A cloud of costliest incense fills the room;
20　　The wealth of nations shines resplendent round;
But shadowy horrors cast o'er him their gloom,
　　And near his death-bed fiendish whispers sound,
Calling his soul with awful summonings
To stand ere morn before the King of Kings.

25　Now that dark contract, which in years gone by
　　He sealed with solemn oaths, weighs on his breast
A fiery burden, that eternally
　　Will shut his spirit from the haven of rest,
And claim it where the wicked ceaseless cry,
30　And where the pangs of torture never die.

He hath lived long the terrible, the feared
　Of all that journey on the sounding sea;
And long hath in the storm of battle reared
　His blood-red pirate flag triumphantly.
35 His hand is known to all the sons of men
　O'er hill and plain and far-off mountain-glen.

And ever it was rumoured through the land
　That he was guarded by a spirit's might;
For still a shield, borne by some unseen hand,
40　Hovered around him in the raging fight;
And still, when fiercest tempests swept the sea,
His stately ship sailed on, unscathed and free.

But now he feels the ghastly King draw nigh;
　The life-blood turns to ice in every vein,
45 As through the black night sounds that solemn cry
　Rising above the howling storm again.
Strongly he struggles: Death will have his prey,
And 'mid responsive shrieks his spirit bursts away.

　　　　CHARLOTTE BRONTË. *March* 26, 1833.

LORD EDWARD AND HIS BRIDE

THE night fell down all calm and still,
　The moon shone out o'er vale and hill,
　　Stars trembled in the sky;
Then forth into that sad pale light
5　There came a gentle lady bright,
　With veil and cymar spotless white,
　　Fair brow and dark blue eye.

Her lover sailed on the mighty deep,
　The ocean wild and stern;
10　And now she walks to pray and weep
　For his swift and safe return.
Full oft she pauses as the breeze

Moans wildly through those giant trees,
    As startled at the tone;
15 The sounds it waked were like the sigh
Of spirit's voice through midnight sky,
So soft, so sad, so dreamily
    That wandering wind swept on.

And ever as she listened
20   Unbidden thoughts would rise,
Till the pearly teardrops glistened
    All in her starlike eyes.

She saw her love's proud battleship
Tossed wildly on the storm-dark deep,
25 By the roused wind's destroying sweep,
    A wrecked and shattered hull;
And as the red-bolt burst its shroud
And glanced in fire o'er sea and cloud,
She heard a peal break deep and loud,
30   Then sink to echoes dull.

And as that thunder died away,
She saw amid the rushing spray
    Her Edward's eagle-plume.
While thus that deadly scene she wrought
35 And viewed in the deep realms of thought
    His soul's appalling doom,

A voice through all the forest rang:
Up like a deer the lady sprang—
    "'Tis he! 'tis he!' she cried;
40 And ere another moment's space
In Time's unresting course found place,
By Heaven! and by our Lady's grace!
    Lord Edward clasped his bride.

Included in an unpublished story entitled 'The Green Dwarf,' by
Lord Charles Albert Florian Wellesley, commenced by Charlotte
Brontë on July 10, 1833, and finished on September 2, 1833.

THE HAUNTED TOWER

OH! who has broke the stilly hush
    Which hung around the spirits' tower?
What strange wild tones and voices rush
    Through the lone silence of their bower!

5 Who bade the builder's hammer ring
    Through chambers dedicate to gloom?
Who dared his household gods to bring
    Where wander dwellers of the tomb?

    O thou who lists the spirits' song!
10   O thou who broke the spirits' rest!
Long shall their terrors deep and strong
    Wake torture in thy guilty breast.

I bid thee by the spectral light
    Of the wan moon that sails the sky,
15 And by the sunshine glad and bright
    When dim night's loving spectres fly;

I bid thee quit these haunted halls
    Ere morn emits one golden ray.
Haste! leave to us our ruined walls,
20   And speed thee on a brighter way.

Included in an unpublished short story entitled 'Brushwood Hall,' one of a series of pieces in a manuscript entitled 'Arthuriana, or Odds and Ends, being a Miscellaneous Collection of Pieces in Prose and Verse,' by Lord Charles A. F. Wellesley, commenced by Charlotte Brontë on September 27, 1833, and finished on November 20, 1833. The story in which the poem appears was completed on October 1, 1833.

The three poems which follow are also included in the same manuscript.

THE RED CROSS KNIGHT

TO the desert sands of Palestine,
   To the kingdoms of the East,
For love of the Cross and the Holy Shrine,
   For hope of heavenly rest,
5 In the old dark times of faintest light
Aye wandered forth each Red Cross Knight.

Warmed by the Palmer's strange wild tale,
   Warmed by the Minstrel's song,
They took plumed helm and coat of mail
10   And sabre keenly strong;
Then left, O high and gallant band!
For unknown shores their own sweet land.

The Cross was still their guiding-star,
   Their weapon and their shield;
15 In vain the lance and scymitar
   Opposing squadrons wield!
For still victorious from the fight
Came back each noble Red Cross Knight.

In vain shrill pipe and timbrels' swell
20   Rose from the turbaned host,
For still the bloody Infidel
   The wreath of conquest lost;
And still that garland's hallowed light
Crowned gloriously each Red Cross Knight.

.   .   .   .

25 The Lion King of Christendom
   Sleeps where his fathers rest;
And ne'er again did battle-hum
   Sound from the calling East;
And on Britannia's Island-shore
30 The Red Cross Knight was seen no more.

Six hundred circles of our earth
   Moved round the God of Light,
When, lo! a great and glorious birth
   Broke forth on Afric's night.—
35 Now flow, my strain, more swiftly flow:
Drink inspiration's spirit-glow.

For Gifford is thy wondrous theme:
   The bravest, best of men;
Whose life has been one martial dream
40   Against the Saracen;
Reviver of the holy sign
Which whelmed with slaughter Palestine.

Hail, great Crusader! lift the Cross!
   Call to thy banners' shade!
45 And, heedless of all earthly loss,
   Through blood, through carnage wade;
Led by that high and heavenly gem,
The living star of Bethlehem.

Wade to the city of renown,
50   Wring Zion from her foe;
Win for thyself a radiant crown,
   For him eternal woe;
Then shall earth's mightiest bless thy name
And yield to thee the palm of Fame.

October 2, 1833.

MEMORY

WHEN the dead in their cold graves are lying
      Asleep, to wake never again;
When past are their smiles and their sighing,
      Oh! why should their memories remain?

5   Though sunshine and spring may have lightened
            The wild flowers that blow on their graves;
      Though summer their tombstones have brightened,
            And autumn have pall'd them with leaves;

      Though winter have wildly bewailed them
10   With her dirge-wind as sad as a knell;
      Though the shroud of her snow-wreath have veiled
            them,
            Still how deep in our bosoms they dwell!

      The shadow and sun-sparkle vanish,
            The cloud and the light flee away;
15   But man from his heart may not banish
            The thoughts that are torment to stay.

      The reflection departs from the river
            When the tree that hung o'er is cut down,
      But on Memory's calm current for ever
20   The shade without substance is thrown.

      When quenched is the glow of the ember,
            When the life-fire ceases to burn,
      Oh! why should the spirit remember?
            Oh! why should the parted return?

25 Because that the fire is *still* shining,
   Because that the lamp is still bright;
  While the body in dust is reclining
   The soul lives in glory and light.

October 2, 1833.

This poem was first printed (with several slight variations in the text and minus the fifth and seventh stanzas) in *Scribner's Monthly*, May 1871, in an article entitled 'Reminiscences of Charlotte Brontë,' by A Schoolfellow (Miss Ellen Nussey). The complete poem was first printed in the *Cornhill Magazine*, February 1893. A later version of the same poem was printed in *Saul and Other Poems*, 1913, pp. 12-14, for Mr. T. J. Wise, in an edition limited to thirty copies for private circulation only. This was from a MS. dated August 2, 1835, the principal variation from the text as printed above being in the last stanza, as follows:

   Because that the fire is yet shining,
    Because still the ember is bright;
   While the flesh is in darkness reclining
    The soul wakes to glory and light.

LINES WRITTEN BESIDE A FOUNTAIN

DEAR is the hour when, freed from toils and care,
  I wander where this lonely fount is singing,
And listen to the sounds which fill the air,
   From its sweet waters springing.

5 Oh! who can tell how welcome is that hour,
  How deeply tranquil, how divinely blest?
None but the wearied know the hallowed power
   Of one sweet pause of rest.

My burning brow, pressed to the cool green grass,
10 Freshened with spray-drops from the murmuring well,
What strange wild musings through my spirit pass—
   What transient fancies swell.

High soars my soul from its chilled earthy bed—
I hear the harmonious gates of heaven unfold—
15   I see around me all the silent dead:
     Great ones who lived of old!

.   .   .   .

But these bright shadows fade full soon away:
The wood, with all its twilight shade, returns;
Again the fount springs in the moon's dim ray—
20   Again the night-breeze mourns.

O God of Heaven! What now is Earth to me—
What all the power, the grandeur, she can give?
But for the joys of sweet tranquillity
     I care not now to live.

25   Aye! by this lonely fount on this hushed night
I would amid untroubled silence die,
Expire in stilly darkness—wake to light
     And heavenly melody!

C.B. *October* 7th, **1833.**

RICHARD CŒUR DE LION AND BLONDEL

THE blush, the light, the gorgeous glow of eve
 Waned from the radiant chambers of the west;
Now, twilight's robe, dim, orient shadows weave;
 One star gleams faintly lustrous in the east;
5 Far down it shines on the blue Danube's breast,
As calmly, wavelessly, its waters glide
 On to the appointed region of their rest,
The sea, profound and hoary waste, and wide,
Whose blackening billows swell in ever restless pride.

10 High o'er the river rose a rocky hill
 With barren sides, precipitous and steep;
There 'gainst the sunset heavens, serene and still,
 Frowned the dark turrets of a feudal keep.
 The folded flag hung in the air asleep;
The breathless beauty of the summer night
15 Gave not that Austrian standard to the sweep
Of freshening zephyr, or wild storm-blasts' might;
But motionless it drooped, in eve's soft, dying light.

In that stern fortress there were arch and tower
 And iron-wrought lattice, narrow, deep-embayed,
20 Where the gloom gathered thick as night's mid hour,
 And round about it hung a chilling shade
 Which told of dungeons where the light ne'er played,
Of prison walls, of fetter-bolt and chain;
 Of captives, 'neath a tyrant's durance laid,
25 Never to view the sun's bright face again,
Never to breathe the air of free, wild hill and plain.

The moon had risen a host of stars among,
   When to the embattled castle walls drew nigh
A wandering minstrel; from his shoulder hung
30   A harp, sweet instrument of melody.
   He paused awhile beneath the turret high,
Then took his harp and all the sweet chords swept,
   Till the sound swelled beneath the silent sky,
And holiest music on the charmed air crept,
35 Waked from the magic strings, where till that hour
   they slept.

Oh, how that wild strain o'er the river swelled
   And mingled with its gentle murmuring!
From the true fount of song divine it welled:
   Music's own simple, undefilèd spring,
40   Notes rose and died, such as the wild birds sing
In the lone wood, or the far lonelier sky.
   Oh! none but Blondel, but the minstrel-king,
Could waken such transcendent melody,
Sweet as a fairy's lute, soft as a passing sigh.

45   The strain he sang was some antique romance,
   Some long-forgotten song of other years,
Born in the cloudless clime of sunny France,
   Where earth in vernal loveliness appears;
   Where the bright grape distils its purple tears,
50 And clear streams flow, and dim blue hills arise,—
   A gleaming crown of snow each mountain wears
And there are cities 'neath her starry skies
As fair as ever blest with beauty mortal eyes.

BLONDEL'S SONG

THE moonlight sleeps low on the hills of Provence,
    The stars are all tracking their paths in the sky:
How softly and brightly their golden orbs glance
    Where the long shining waves of the silver Rhone lie!

5   The towers of de Courcy rise high in the beam
        From sky to earth trembling, so lustrous and pale;
    Around them there dwells the deep hush of a dream,
        And stilled is the murmur of river and gale.

There are groves in the moonlight all sparkling with dew;
10   There are dim garden-paths round that Castle of Pride,
Where the bud of the rose and the hyacinth blue
    Close their leaves to the balm of the moist eventide.

And long is the alley, dark, bowery, and dim,
    Where sits a white form 'neath a tall chestnut tree
15   Which waves its broad branches all darkling and grim
    O'er the young rose of Courcy, sweet Anna Marie.

And who kneels beside her? A warrior in mail;
    On his helm there's a plume, in his hand there's a lance;
And why does the cheek of the lady turn pale?
    Why weeps in her beauty the Flower of Provence?

20   She weeps for her lover: this night are they met
        To breathe a farewell 'neath love's own holy star;
    For to-morrow the crest of the young Lavalette
        Will float highest and first in the van of the war.

Thus far sang Blondel, when a sudden tone
25   Of quivering harp-strings on his ear upsprung;
It sounded like an echo of his own,
    So faintly that mysterious music rung,
    So sweet it floated those dark towers among
And seemed to issue from their topmost height.
30   Then there were words in measured cadence sung,—
Now soft and low, then with a master's might
Poured forth that varying strain upon the stilly night.

Who sings? The minstrel knows there is but one
    Whose voice has music half so rich and deep,
35 Whose hand can summon from the harp a tune
    So thrilling that it calls from latent sleep
    Heroic thoughts, dims eyes, that seldom weep,
With tears of ecstasy, and fires the breast,
    Till listening warriors from their chargers leap,
40 Assume the glittering helm and nodding crest,
Unsheathe the ready sword, and lay the lance in rest.

But not of war nor of the battle blast
    Sung now the kingly harper. No, his strain
Was mournful as a dream of days long past;
45   At times it swelled, but quickly died again.
    And, oh! the sadness of that wild refrain
Suited full well with the lone, solemn hour:
    Too sad for joy, too exquisite for pain,
It touched the heart, subdued the spirit's power,
50 Blent with the Danube's moan, and wailed around the
      tower.

RICHARD'S SONG

THRICE the great fadeless lights of heaven,
 The moon, and the eternal sun,
As God's unchanging law was given,
 Have each their course appointed run.
5 Three times the Earth her mighty way
  Hath measured o'er a shoreless sea,
While hopeless still from day to day
  I've sat in lone captivity
Listening the wind and river's moan,
10 Wakening my wild harp's solemn tone,
  And longing to be free.

Blondel! my heart seems cold and dead,
 My soul has lost its ancient might;
The sun of chivalry is fled,
15 And dark despair's unholy night
Above me closes still and deep,
 While wearily each lapsing day
Leads onward to the last long sleep:
 The hour when all shall pass away,
20 When King and Captive, Lord and Slave,
Must rest unparted in the grave
 A mass of soulless clay.

Oh! long I've listened to the sound
 Of winter's blast and summer's breeze,
25 As their sweet voices sung around
  Through echoing caves and wind-waved trees;
And long I've viewed from prison-bars

Sunset and dawn, and night and noon;
Watched the uprising of the stars;
30 Seen the calm advent of the moon.
But blast and breeze, and stars and sun,
All vainly swept, all vainly shone,—
  I filled a living tomb!

God of my fathers! Can it be?
35 Must I, the chosen of Thy might,
Whose name alone brought victory,
  Whose battle-cry was, 'God my Right!'
Closed in a tyrant's dungeon-cell
  Wear out the remnant of my life,
40 And never hear again the swell
  Of high and hot and glorious strife,
Where trumpets peal and bugles sing,
And minstrels sweep the martial string,
  And wars and fame are rife?

45 No, Blondel! thou wert sent by Heaven
  Thy King, thy Lion-King to free:
To thee the high command was given
  To rescue from captivity!
Haste from the tyrant Austrian's hold,
50 Cross rapidly the rolling sea,
And go, where dwell the brave, the bold,
  By stream and hill and greenwood tree:
Minstrel, let Merry England ring
With tidings of her Lion-King,
55 And bring back liberty!

Such was the lay the Monarch Minstrel sang.
  A few bright moons waned from the silent heaven,
And Albion with a shout of triumph rang
  As once again her worshipped King was given
60   Back to her breast, his bonds asunder riven.
And the sweet Empress of the subject sea
  Sent up her hymn of gratitude to Heaven.
Through all her coasts she hailed him crowned and free,
The champion of God's hosts, the pride of liberty!

CHARLOTTE BRONTË. *December* 27, 1833.
Haworth, nr. Bradford.

On a high rock near the village of Dürrenstein or Diernstein, in Lower Austria, on the left bank of the Danube, are still to be seen the ruins of the castle in which Richard the First of England was imprisoned on his return from the Holy Land.

The poem makes it appear that Richard was imprisoned for three years, but this is not in accordance with historical records. Hume, the historian, says: 'King Richard was captured, by the Duke of Austria, in November 1192; and early in 1193 was transferred to the Emperor; who confined him in the castle of Diernstein, in Lower Austria. He was liberated towards the end of January 1194; and landed at Sandwich on the 12th of March.'

DEATH OF DARIUS CODOMANNUS[1]

THE muffled clash of arms is past, as if it ne'er had been;
 The lightning scymitar has sheathed its terrors bright
    and keen:
Once bright, *once* keen, dark spots of blood bedim its lustre
    now;
And the sharpness of the tempered edge is dulled by many a
    blow.

5   Dark windings of the valley's bed!
          Deep gorges of the hill!
        Bear further off that hurried tread
        Which wakes your echoes low and dead:
          It fails, and all is still.

10   Seems now as if no voice, no sound,
        Had ever rung or moaned around,
        Save perhaps some lone bird's plaintive song
        Dying those wild, vast woods among
        Unanswered, for there lingers there
15   No joyous denizen of air.

        And that one wanderer, flitting by,
        Vainly for sweet response might sigh,—
        Vainly might hope for some far strain
        To greet his warbled call again.

20   The breeze alone—shrill, dirge-like, sad—
        Borne down those huge hills, cedar-clad;
        Deep hid in gloom, the river's rush
        Pouring unseen through reed and bush;
        And (sign of utter solitude)
25   Strange sounds of alien rill and wood:

[1]Darius Codomannus was the last King of Persia of the Achæmenian dynasty.
He reigned from 336 B.C. to 331 B.C.

Woods that are murmuring far away;
Rills that glide off in foam and spray
Through mistlike distance, dim and grey;
No other sounds erewhile were heard
30 Responsive to the lonely bird.

But now there *is* another tone,—
Faint as the river's faintest moan;
Low as the west-wind's softest sigh
Breathed sweet from an unclouded sky;

35 Sad as the last note's calm decay
Ere the wild warbler flits away;
Yet, heard through all, those tones belong
Neither to stream nor wood nor song.

They speak of life, they bear a thrill
40   Not native to the wordless grove;
The whispered echoes of the hill,
The gushing waters of the rill
       Have no such power to move.

And there *is* life: a human form
45   Lies prostrate in the vale
Like a reft victim of the storm,—
       Fallen, bleeding, cold and pale;

A stately form, though blighted now,—
For grandeur dwells upon his brow;
50 And light shines in his lifted eye
Which looks on death unfearingly;
And o'er him rests that placid grace—
Sign of high blood and noble race.

The forehead bears a diadem
55 Burning with many an orient gem
       Stained ruddy now in blood.

The starry robe, the flashing ring,
The pearls in bright and braided string,
All speak of Persia's slaughtered king
60   Stretched dying by the flood.

Let not the glass be shaken,—
Life's sands are ebbing low;
Let no loud winds awaken,—
The tide is past its flow.

65 The swords that gleamed around him
Are reddened with his gore;
The traitor-hands that bound him
Will never bind him more.

All Iran[1] has forsaken
70   The god to whom she kneeled:
This word no more can waken
Life on the battle-field.

Not one of all the glorious host
That bowed to Mithras'[2] beam
75 Ere Persia's crown was won and lost
By Issus'[3] fatal stream;

Not one, who by the Granicus[4]
Poured forth their lives in blood;
Not one, who on Arbela's[5] plain
80   In serried phalanx stood;

---

[1]Persia occupies the western part of the plateau of Iran.

[2]Mithras, the god of light, identified with the sun, was one of the three principal gods of the ancient Persians.

[3]Issus, an ancient city in south-east Cilicia. In a neighbouring valley Darius Codomannus was defeated by Alexander in November 333 B.C.

[4] Granicus is the name of a river in Asia Minor. It was there that Alexander gained a victory over the Persians in 334 B.C.

[5]Arbela, a city in Assyria, was the headquarters of Darius Codomannus before he was finally defeated by Alexander on October 1, 331 B.C. The battle was not fought on 'Arbela's plain,' but near the village of Gaugamela, about forty-five miles west of Arbela.

Not one remains to watch him now;
Not one to wipe his death-damp brow;
A monarch left without a throne:
Pomp, might, dominion,—all are gone!

85 A son bereaved, a childless sire,
A king slain in the traitor's ire;
On the dark streamlet's wild bank lying
Behold Darius, lone and dying!

Where are now his farewell dreams
90 Fading fast as daylight's beams?
Oh! where rests the monarch's heart
Now, when life and glory part?

Sees he with that glazing eye
Susa's[1] gorgeous majesty;
95 All the light of regal halls
Where the gushing fountain falls;

All that rich and radiant ring
Once the guard of Asia's king;
Gardens bright where flower and tree
100 Waved in airs of Araby?

Whither wings his spirit now?
Whither do his last thoughts flow?
All his mighty empire lies
Round him as he droops and dies:

105 Ancient Egypt's storied pride,
With the dark Nile's ponderous tide;
India rich in pearl and gem,
Hallowed by the Ganges' stream;

[1]Susa, chief city of the province of Susiana in ancient Persia, was a favourite residence of the Persian kings.

Syria with her tideless sea
110   Ever sleeping placidly;
Desert lands where wandering dwell
Ishmael's sons invincible;

Fallen Palmyra, ruined Tyre
Where the Grecians' flood of ire
115   Burst so full and fierce and strong,
Rolled so dark and deep along,

That no voice was left to tell
How their sovereign-city fell:
As the prophet-doom was spoken,
120   'Her robe is rent, her sceptre broken'!

Israel's God is conqueror now
Crown and plume have left her brow;
She rests silent by the sea,
And so shall rest eternally.

125   Oh! not to these the monarch turns;
    Not to glories passed away:
Remembrance in his spirit burns,
    But not of power's decay.

A voice still whispers in his ear
130   Of one his word betrayed;
And, shadow-like, there lingers near
    A form that will not fade;

The warning words of one who died,
That victim to a tyrant's pride,—
135   The Athenian voice of prophecy:
'King! my Avenger's step draws nigh;
The twilight of thy day is closing
And clouds are on its fall reposing;
I hear the distant tempest sighing
140   In muttered murmurs, faint and dying;

Asia with sound of arms is shaken,
But who will to the conflict waken?
On rolls the foe in living thunder
Insatiate for the dazzling plunder!

145 'The steelèd bands of Macedon,
The hosts of Ammon's haughty son,[1]
Shall crush thy pomp, shall spurn thy gems,
Shall dye with blood thine Empire's streams;
From Iran's throne its sovereign hurl,
150 And Mithras' gorgeous standard furl;
For ever furl: the sacred fire
Shall never more to Heaven aspire;
Its light shall fade, its flames shall die:
They own not Immortality.
155 Another Altar shall arise
Beneath the bright earth's cloudless skies.
King of the Earth! thy course is run:
Remember me and Macedon!'

Thus, boldly, Charidemus spoke,
160 Then sank beneath the tyrant's stroke;
But his last voice to Heaven ascends,
And Heaven to hear its accent bends!

From the dark tomb Darius gave
There comes no murmur of a slave:
165 The hallowed blood of liberty
Sends from the dust its thrilling cry;
Makes to the gods its stern appeal,
And summons Grecia's sons of steel!

They come! They come! A measured tread
170 Heavy and clanking, deep and dread,
Breaks up the hush, profoundly dead,
Of that wild rocky vale;

[1]When Alexander the Great conquered Egypt in 332 B.C. he was crowned King, for which purpose (as the Pharaohs were held to be sons of the god Ammon) he visited the oracle Ammon in the Libyan desert, and was acknowledged son of the god.

And gleaming lance, and flashing shield,
Their blood-gilt light and glitter yield,
175   And plumes are on the gale!

Onward they come, a noble host!
Now in the deepening valley lost;
Now through the wood-glade glancing seen:
All mailed and burnished, bright and sheen.

180 At length around the king they pour,
Of Grecia's hosts the pride and power.
Darius lifts again his eye;
He sees not now the placid sky:
For the green-wood and lonely glen
185 He views a throng of steel-armed men.

The hum and clash swell stern and loud,
And o'er him many a form is bowed,
And many an eye of eagle-light
Meets piercingly his failing sight.

190 Tall warriors on their lances leaning,
Plume-shadowed brows of darkest meaning,
    Surround the dying king;
Their shapes before his vision swim
Ghost-like and wandering, faint and dim;
195 Their voice sounds like a sacred hymn:
    Low, solemn, murmuring.

One kneels beside and props his head,
And from the river's crystal bed
    Sprinkles his ghastly brow;
200 The cool clear water, as it falls,
A moment sight and speech recalls:
    Darius knew his foe!

He clasped his hands, and raised his eyes
Bright with forgiveness to the skies;
205 He blessed his conqueror in that hour;
He prayed for added might and power

To follow Asia's alien lord
And strengthen his resistless sword!

Statira's[1] shade is near him now:
210 She lightens thus his kingly brow,
And with her calm and holy smiles
Her lord and captor reconciles!

But soon that gentle shade is gone,
And Vengeance lingers there alone:
215 A sudden gloom falls round the king;
Stern thoughts within his bosom spring.

The rebel-satrap and his band:
Men of unhallowed heart and hand,
Before their slaughtered monarch rise:
220 His curse falls on them ere he dies;—

'Soldiers of Greece and Macedon!
For the dark deed by Bessus[2] done
I leave revenge to Ammon's son:
He before whom all Persia fell—
225 The glorious! the Invincible!
The lord of Cyrus'[3] solemn throne:
The crowned in haughty Babylon!—
I charge him by his power and pride
To think how Iran's monarch died;
230 To turn the traitor's blood-stained sword
Back to the bosom of its lord!
A bitter draught he gave his king:
His lips shall drain the same dark spring.
Warriors! I may not longer stay
235 For Mithras calls my soul away!'

[1]Statira, wife of Darius, was captured by Alexander after the battle of Issus, 333 B.C., and was treated by him with honour and humanity.
[2]Bessus was a satrap of Bactria, under Darius Codomannus. He seized Darius soon after the battle of Gaugamela (Arbela), 331 B.C., and carried him off. Being pursued by Alexander, he murdered Darius. He was soon betrayed to Alexander, who had him executed, 328 B.C.
[3]Cyrus the Great, founder of the Persian Empire.

He said; his pale lips ceased to quiver;
His soul soared to its awful Giver;
The host stood round all hushed and still
While dirge-like murmured breeze and rill.

CHARLOTTE BRONTË. *May 2, 1834.*

STANZAS

ON THE FATE OF HENRY PERCY

'Lieutenant Henry Percy, it is well known, took a voyage to the South Sea Islands on board the *Mermaid*—Commander: Captain Steighton.

'He was drowned off Otaheite. I have heard strange reports respecting the manner of his death, many of them from undeniably authentic sources. To give the reader some insight as to their nature, I need only say they tend to fix another crime of the darkest dye in the character of his terrible father.[1] Steighton was a minion of the elder Percy's. Men say he served him but too well in the matter now before our notice.'

CHARLOTTE BRONTË.

ON THE FATE OF HENRY PERCY

THE tropic twilight falls, the deep is still;
  All turmoils of the busy day are past;
From the calm lands no voice sounds deep or shrill;
  No murmur from the world of waters vast,
5   Save its own ceaseless sound that breeze or blast
Now chafes not into dull or thundering moan.
  The faintest gleam of eve is o'er it cast;
And, oh! how sweet, how holy is the tone
That swells from each green wave, then trembling
    dies alone!

[1] Alexander Percy, Earl of Northangerland, and Prime Minister of Angria.

10 There's not a boat upon the darkened billow,
 There's not an oar dips in the moonlight main;
Each islander rests on his happy pillow,
 Each swift canoe has sought its home again;
 And neither ringing shout nor trembling strain
15 Comes from the shore to break the green sea's rest:
 All earth lies hushed to watch the glorious wane
Of that bright sunset from her burning breast;
To see the light of heaven die dim and soft and blest.

Fair southern islands! they are sweetly sleeping,
20 While the stars gather in their heaven above,
While sky-breathed airs the deep dark woods are
  sweeping
 In gales too low to wake the slumbering dove;
 Almost too faint to bend the palmy grove.
Intenser purple grows that kindling dome,
25 And brighter flash those orbs of light and love:
Sweet tropic islands! ye are beauty's home;
Oh! who from your bright shores to colder lands
  would roam?

Midnight is near: that bark upon the water
 Has furled her sails and set her watch on deck;
30 She rides at anchor, Neptune's noblest daughter;
 The very waves seem subject to her beck;
 They dare not dash her glory to a wreck!
How the cool foam curls round her mighty bows
 As fair as braided pearls on beauty's neck!
35 How the wild wave more softly gliding flows
Where that proud ocean-queen far down her shadow
  throws!

A wondrous stranger! from afar appearing,
 Long has she walked the path that leaves no track;
And her brave crew, a thousand hazards daring,
40 Still scorned to turn their noble vessel back.
 No heart fell cold, no hand grew faint and slack,

As on with heaven above and waves beneath,
   And round a wild horizon, densely black,
They stretched before the trade-gales' fiery breath;
45   Looked full of joy to hope, and fearlessly to death!

Now all is tranquil: they have gained their bourne,
   The fair blest island of the stormless sea,—
Those happy shores where man may cease to mourn,
   Where all is peace and bliss and harmony;
50   Gardens of many a wondrous flower and tree;
Homes of strange birds with wings of rainbow light;
   Shapes formed by nature in her fantasie,
Glowing and fresh and fair and Eden-bright;—
But these were now unseen, beneath the veil of night.

55   And one within that anchored bark is sleeping:
   The youngest, fairest, bravest of her crew.
Oh! how the stars his brow with light are steeping,
   The sails to his lone berth they tremble through.
He sleeps on deck, and many a pearl of dew
60   Gleams in his light hair as unroofed he lies,
   And from the abyss of pure deep speckless blue
A sweet gale round him wildly sings and sighs;
A dirge comes to the ear, so sad each cadence dies.

Would he might waken! some sad dream is on him;
65   How heavily the breath flows from his breast!
Some unseen influence strangely dwells upon him,
   Some mournful memory will not let him rest.
Whate'er it was he calms: the unwelcome guest
Has passed away with all its mystery;
70   And now, his clasped hands to his bosom pressed,
He turns his fair face to the solemn sky,
His forehead woos again the low breeze wandering by.

Yes! he has dreamed of one now far away,
   His own sweet Florence,[1] she who was his bride
75 Ere thirteen summer suns had flung their ray
   With gentlest glow on her youth's springing pride.
   Oh! often had he wandered by her side
Through woodland walks and alleys dimly bright,
   Too happy to discern how fast the tide
80 Of time was lapsing into shadowy night,
How swift the gloaming veiled each parting ray of
    light.

And now he saw her in a lofty chamber
   Solemn and grandly vast; he knew it well;
And as a light stole down from lamps of amber
85   The veil of years and distance sundered fell.
   Faintly there tolled her father's castle-bell:
It spoke the midnight hour; then all was hushed;
   Round on the panels pictured visions swell
Where forms of buried beauty voiceless blushed,
90 And the rich silent light more softly o'er them gushed.

Calm, tenderly, and pure the moon was shining;
   Through one vast window its white lustre streamed;
On her it fell, her loveliness refining
   To beauty such as mortal never dreamed.
95   Her blue eyes looked to heaven: how bright they
    beamed!
How their deep zones caught glory from the sky!
   And as the long fringe trembling o'er them gleamed
Their lucid light was almost mystery:
They shone like mirrored stars that glassed in dark
    waves lie!

[1]Florence Marian Hume (usually called Marian), who became the wife of the Marquis of Douro, afterwards King of Angria (Zamorna).

100　Henry! she looks to heaven through that vast sea,
　　　That boundless ocean decked with isles of light:
　　Are her thoughts travelling to their home in thee?
　　　　Wake[?] they remembered from the radiance bright
　　　That fills her eye? A touch of love's own might
105　Has surely clothed her in such living grace;
　　　　'Tis not the calm serenity of night
　　That brings the blood so swiftly to her face
　　Like the clear flush of wine seen through a crystal vase.

　　Yes, it is love, but not such love as thine:
110　　Not that pure, young affection of the breast
　　That used to breathe of peace and bliss divine,
　　　And o'er her white brow fling a shade of rest.
　　　Oft with his hand in hers in transport pressed
　　Henry has watched that calm fall on her cheek,
115　　And while his own heart felt most deeply blest
　　Has wished a blush of bashfulness to break:
　　What seemed to him too still, too sisterly, too meek.

　　She's not alone—there's one[1] beside her bending:
　　　Is it a friend? The form is dark and high,—
120　A magic to the solemn chamber lending.
　　　Flashes through darkness that refulgent eye—
　　　Its fixed gaze calls that blush and wakes that sigh,
　　And well might timid maiden shrink and quail,
　　　For never yet a shape on earth passed by
125　So like a spirit in a mortal veil:
　　The cheek that glows for it will soon turn deadly pale.

　　At once the chamber fades in slow decay,
　　　The lights are quenched that erst so softly shone,
　　The dream revolves, the vast hall melts away,
130　　And gleaming arch and golden lamp are gone,
　　　And all is dim and imageless and lone.

[1]Zamorna.

But trees are rustling in the darkened air,
   And mossy grass the pavement springs upon,
And for the vanished taper's dazzling glare
135   There dawns a gentle gleam—faint, mellow, mildly fair.

Now o'er the scene a mighty wood is sweeping,
   And long deep glades on through it glimmering go;
Rays of the moon the spectral boughs are steeping:
   They wave in winds whose voice sounds wild and low;
140   And from far off a river's dreary flow
Swells ceaseless, though the gale at times be still;
   And though the strange sighs, wandering to and fro
Like spirit's wailings, cease the heart to thrill,
Yet the swift waves rush on of that unpausing rill.

145   The maiden and the shape stand in the lustre
   Flung from the sky on that star-silvered glade;
Those mighty arching trees that round them cluster
   The flood of glory with their shadows braid;
   And when a sudden wind among them played
150   They swung like giant phantoms on the grass:
   All their boughs trembled, all their foliage swayed.
Ghosts, such as they, in cloudy gloom might pass
Amid the gleaming pomp of some dread wizard's glass!

The maiden weeps: clear moonlit tears are sparkling
155   Upon her cheeks; fast from her eyes they gush.
She looks to *him*: his brow grows strangely darkling;
   His cheek is shadowed with a sudden flush
   Of earnest, eager triumph: that rich blush
Fades not before her mute and sad appeal.
160   Now passion's waves of conflict o'er her rush:
The sob, the tear, the pallid brow reveal
How wildly strong the love her heart and spirit feel.

Oh! Henry knows his Florence loves *him* not;
   Not as he would be loved, not as his bride;
165   Then youthful tenderness is all forgot,
   All vanished in the rapid burning tide

That flows resistless from those eyes of pride
Flashing into her heart so fixedly.
    The voice of that strange vision by her side
170   Brings with its sweet, deep music other joy
Than that which erewhile woke to bless her fair-haired boy.

    The token of their love is on her finger:
       A golden circlet like a ring of light;
    And round her small, sweet lip there seems to linger
175   Some saddening touch of memory's holy might.
      The tears, too, glancing as the lamps of night
From their clear sources are not tears of bliss;
     But almost ere they tremble into sight
Her stately lover dries them with a kiss,
180   And soothes her spirit's awe with some proud warm caress.

    Sudden a voice comes to the dreamer's ear
      Mournful and sadly murmured, low and dread;
    At first it wailed far off, then whispered near:
      Percy! thy Marian deems her bridegroom dead;
185   Lover she mourns not: when the rumour spread
She strove to quench the joy that filled her breast.
      Yes! when she heard that the unfathomed bed
Of the wild sea was by her Henry pressed
She wept that she should feel so deeply, truly blest!

190   And, Percy! she shall be thy rival's bride;
      She from his hands shall take the marriage-wreath,
    And, standing at the altar, side by side,
      Each unto each resolves of faith shall breathe—
      Oaths of eternal fealty till death;
195   And hill and plain shall with that bridal ring;
      Breezes shall waft it with their balmiest breath;
Minstrels shall raise the song and strike the string;
And wide the fires of joy like beacon-lights shall spring.

Full glad shall be her life, in bright halls dwelling,
200   Beneath the awful light of those loved eyes,
The fount of perfect bliss for ever swelling,—
    Deep, fathomless, exhaustless in the skies,—
    Shall, sparkling to her very lips, arise.
Yet there are warnings of an early end:[1]
205   There breathes afar a dreary sound of sighs,
And cold the tears of lonely woe descend:
Shades of untimely death, how silently ye blend!

Percy! thy love so strong, so unreturned,
    Shall be avenged on earth: her time is brief;
210 The radiant form for whom her spirit burned
    Shall smile awhile, then leave her bowed with grief.
    The reaper's sickle shall cut down the sheaf
While the young corn is budding fresh and green;
    She shall be gathered like a springing leaf;
215 One year, and that fair plant is no more seen;
Few e'en shall know where once its sunny place has been.

            And never from that vision woke
                The journeyer of the deep:
            Ere the pale light of morning broke
220   He slept his final sleep.

            The coral banks of those far isles
                Now pillow Percy's head;
            Their blessed moon for ever smiles
                Above his lonely bed.

225   And many a spicy zephyr sings
                Sweet from those radiant skies;
            And many a bright bird waves its wings
                Around where Henry lies.

            No more his rayless eyeballs shine,
230   No more his curls are fair;
            For tangled seaweeds wet with brine
                Are garlanding his hair.

But how he died no tongue can tell:
   No eye was there to see;
235 Yet the winds that were his requiem knell
   They moaned him mournfully.

Some say the decks were red with blood
   And wet with trampling feet;
It recks not: he sleeps in the secret flood
240   With surge for his winding-sheet.

Dark were the rumours and faintly spoken
   That came to his native shore,
Less by speech, than by sign and token,
   The crew these rumours bore.

245 There was no sound of wail and weeping
   Heard in his own proud home
When the whisper came that he was sleeping
   Beneath the green sea-foam.

His father's brow first lit, then darkled,
250   He smiled a demon's smile
And in his piercing eye there sparkled
   A glimpse of hell the while.

Henry! thy name still lives in story,
   Where the Percies' dark woods swell,
255 And it will live, till time grows hoary,
   A talisman, a spell!

And where wild Wansbeck's waves are foaming
   In Grassmere's lonely vale,
At the dim, still hour of solemn gloaming
260   I oft have heard thy tale.

The peasant o'er his calm hearth bending
   Will speak of Percy's fame,
The name of Lady Florence blending
   Young sailor! with thy name.

265 Thy dreaded sire! thine awful father!
Of him they seldom speak,
For then the clouds of horror gather,
And words of mystery break.

Thy rival! every spirit thrills
270 When that proud name is heard,
And light each flashing eye-ball fills
As at a battle-word.

But not of hatred, not of scorn—
They see him in his gorgeous morn,
275 Their country's living sword;
And wild and wicked though he be,
Though his sun rises stormily,
He is their own young Lord!

Yet Henry rest! his name can never
280 Ring through thy tomb profound,
And thou may'st sleep unmoved for ever
By that enkindling sound.

CHARLOTTE BRONTË. *June* 15, 1834.

This poem is contained in a manuscript entitled 'Corner Dishes:
Being a small collection of Mixed and Unsubstantiated Trifles in
Prose and Verse. By Lord Charles Albert Florian Wellesley.'

A NATIONAL ODE FOR THE ANGRIANS

THE sun is on the Calabar, the dawn is quenched in day,
  The stars of night are vanishing, her shadows flee
    away;

The sandy plains of Etrei flash back arising light,
And the wild wastes of Northangerland gleam bright as
    heaven is bright.

5 Zamorna lifts her fruitful hills like Eden's to the sky,
And fair as Enna's fields of flowers her golden prairies lie;

And Angria calls from mount and vale, from wood and
    heather-dell,
A song of joy and thankfulness on rushing winds to swell.

For Romalla has put his robe of regal purple on,
10 And from the crags of Pendlebrow[1] the russet garb is gone;

And Boulsworth off his giant sides rolls down the vapours
    dim;
And Hawkscliffe's bright and bowery glades uplift their
    matin hymn.

The ancient hills of Sydenham have never felt the glow
Of such a dawn as that which burns their blushing summits
    now.

15 The fields and woods of Edwardston are full of song and
    dew;
Olympia's waves glance clear along their wandering line
    of blue.

Green Arundel has caught the ray upspringing from the
    East;
Guadima rolls exultingly with sunshine on its breast.

[1]Pendle Hill and Boulsworth Hill—two prominent hills near Haworth.

All Angria through her provinces to arms and glory cries:
20 Her sun is up and she has heard her battle-shout, 'Arise!'

My Kingdom's gallant gentlemen are gathered like a host:
With such a bold and noble band was never conflict lost!

For they would fight till the red blood burst in sweat-drops
    from their brow,
And never to the victor's yoke their lion-souls would bow.

25 Enara on the Douro's banks his serfs is gathering;
From hut and hall on the highland heath the sons of Warner
    spring;

And Howard o'er his breezy moors the bugle-blast has
    blown:
O Leopard! swift are the ready feet that answer to that tone.

The Gor-cock quailed at the summons shrill unconquered
    Agar sent;
30 A living whirlwind crossed the tracks that marked the
    withered bent;

Proud Moray called from the Calabar his vassals to the fight;
And the Lord of Southwood joyously has raised the flag of
    light.

Segovia's dark, Italian eye is lit with high-born pride;
The Chevalier of Arundel has bade his horsemen ride;

35 Young Stuart in the ranks of war uplifts his lofty plume;
And Roslyn like a red-deer bounds from the depths of
    mountain-gloom;

And Seymour's heir has heard a voice come from the
    ancient dead:
At once the ancestral dauntlessness through all his veins
    was shed.

But the sullen flag of Percy swells most proudly to the
    breeze
40 As haughtily the folds unfurl as if they swept the seas!

Patrician Pirate! On each side his blighting glance is flung:
The silent scorn that curls his lip can never know a tongue!

Upon his melancholy brow a melancholy shade,
Like snow-wreaths on Aornu's slope, eternally is laid.

45 But the son of that tremendous sire amid the throng
        appears,—
His second self unpetrified by the chill lapse of years:

A form of noblest energy, most sternly beautiful;
A scymitar whose tempered edge no time can ever dull;

A sword unflushed, a quenchless flame, a fixed and radiant
        star;
50 A noble steed caparisoned which snuffs the fight afar!

The glory of his youthful brow, the light of his blue eye,
Will flash upon the battle's verge like arrows of the sky.

With such a host, with such a train, what hand can stop our
        path?
Who can withstand the torrent's strength when it shall roll
        in wrath?

55 Lift, lift the scarlet banner up! Fling all its folds abroad,
And let its blood-red lustre fall on Afric's blasted sod:

For gore shall run where it has been, and blighted bones
        shall lie
Wherever the sun standard swelled against the stormy sky.

And when our battle-trumpets sound, and when our bugles
        sing,
60 The vulture from its distant rock shall spread its glancing
        wing;

And the gaunt wolf at that signal cry shall gallop to the
        feast:
A table in the wilderness we'll spread for bird and beast.

We'll sheath not the avenging sword till earth and sea and
    skies
Through all God's mighty universe shout back, 'Arise!
    Arise!'

65 Till Angria reigns Lord Paramount wherever human
      tongue
The 'Slaves' Lament,' the 'Emperor's Hymn,' in woe or
    bliss hath sung!

ARTHUR AUGUSTUS ADRIAN WELLESLEY.

C. BRONTË. July 17, 1834.

At the time this 'national ode' was written Charlotte and Branwell
Brontë had been writing about Angria (first calling it 'The Country of
the Genii') for more than five years. They chose the, at that time, little-
known region which is drained by the Calabar River, east of the Niger
delta, in West Africa, for the situation of their country, which grew in
their imagination until, at the time now reached, it had seven provinces: Zamorna, Edwardston, Sydenham, Northangerland, Arundel,
Howard, and Warner, with the rivers Olympia, Guadima, Calabar,
and Douro. Most of the persons mentioned in the poem are much-
written-about characters in their early stories. The supposed writer of
the poem is their early hero, the Marquis of Douro, now the Duke of
Zamorna, and King of Angria, who is usually referred to simply as
Zamorna. The derivation of the name 'Zamorna' has puzzled several
writers on Brontë subjects. Miss May Sinclair, in her entertaining and
admirable book, *The Three Brontës*, writes of 'that one fantastic name
"Zamorna."' It was obtained by the addition of one letter to 'Zam-
ora,' the name of a province in Spain, and also of a small city on the
Douro River.

SAUL

(1 Samuel xvii, 2—And Saul and the men of Israel were gathered together, and pitched by the valley of Elah, and set the battle in array against the Philistines.)

'NEATH the palms in Elah's valley
   Saul with all his thousands lay;
Israel's mightiest nobles rally
    Round their own anointed stay.
5   This has been a battle-day,
And the host lie wearily
    On the field of conflict won,
Where their slaughtered foemen be,
    Spear and target stretched upon.

10   Saul within his purple tent
    Seeks for rest, and seeks in vain;
Still a voice of sad lament
    Mingles with the trumpet-strain
    Sounding o'er that war-like plain.
15   And the spirit of the King
    Darkens with a cloud of woe,
Thicker, denser, gathering
    As the rapid moments flow.

'Abner,' thus the monarch said,
20   'God has left me desolate;
All my heart is cold and dead,
    Crushed amid my royal state;
Samuel bid me ever mourn,
    Crown and Kingdom from me rent;
25 Saul is not a man to turn;
    Israel's strength can ne'er repent.

'Abner, is it day's declining
   Brings this hour of darkness on?
As the evening sun is shining
30   Then I feel most sad and lone.
   Lo! its beams are almost gone;
How their kindled glories burn
   All along our tented field!
Spear and helm their flash return,—
35   Back it beams from lance and shield.

'Palm and cedar catch the lustre
   Shining on them, bright and sheen;
Where those woods of olives cluster,
   Light has lit their fadeless green.
40   Those far hills are gem-like seen
Sparkling through the crimsoned air,
   All with roseate light imbued;
Abner! never scene so fair
   Smiled on Monarch's solitude.

45 'Once I could have smiled again,
   Full of hope, and young and free;
Now its beauty turns to bane
   And my spirit wearily
   Shrinks that sight of bliss to see;
50 It hath no communion now
   With a fair and sunny sky;
Nature's calm and stormless brow
   Waken in me no sympathy.

'Oh! methinks were heaven scowling,
55   Were those green hills black and hoar,
Were the winds and billows howling
   Dashed against a sullen shore,
   Dark and cheerless evermore,—
I should feel less full of woe,
60   Full of God-cursed misery,
Than when breezes soft and low
   Whisper round me peacefully;

'Than when eve and twilight meet,
   Dawning star and setting sun,
65 All that Earth has, calm and sweet,
   Resting her bright plains upon,
   Toil and strife and battle done;
Silent dews around me weeping,
   Gleaming on the warrior's brow,
70 The weary warrior, hushed and sleeping
   By his conquered foe.

'But I'll cease my bootless sighing:
   Bid the son of Jesse come;
Let his music, soft and dying,
75   Win my spirit from her gloom,—
   Call her exiled sunshine home:
He has many a sacred air,
   Many a song of holiness
That perchance may soothing bear,
80   Even to me, one hour of bliss.'

       C. BRONTË. *October* 7, 1834.

LAMENT

LAMENT for the Martyr who dies for his faith,
  Who prays for his foes with his failing breath,
Who sees, as he looks to the kindling sky,
God and His Captain, the Saviour, nigh;
5 Who sees the mighty recompense,
  When soul is conquering flesh and sense;
Sees heaven and all its angels bright,
At the very end of his mortal fight,
At the black close of that agony
10 Which sets the impatient spirit free;
Then, as in Christ he sinks to sleep,
Weep for the Dying Martyr, weep.

And the soldier, laid on the battle-plain
    Alone at the close of night, alone,
15 The passing off of some war-like strain
    Blent with his latest moan;
His thoughts all for his father-land,
His feeble heart, his unnerved hand
Still quiveringly upraised to wield
20 Once more his bright sword on the field,
While wakes his fainting energy
To gain her yet one victory;
As he lies bleeding, cold and low,
As life's red tide is ebbing slow,
25 Lament for fallen bravery.

For the son of wisdom, the holy sage,
Full of knowledge, and hoar with age,
Him who had walked through the times of night,
    As if on his path a secret light
30 Lustrous and pure and silent fell;
To all, save himself, invisible,
A secret ray from Heaven's own shrine
Poured on that spirit half divine,
And making a single Isle of light
35 In the wide blank ocean of Pagan night;
Lament for him as you see him laid
Waiting for Death on the Dungeon bed,
The sickly lamp beside him burning,
    Its dim ray falling on sorrow and gloom;
40 Around him his sad disciples mourning,
    As they watch for the hour of awful doom;
And he, by coming death unshaken,
    As if that slumber would soon be o'er,
As if all freshened he should waken
45   And see the light of morn once more.

Ay, on the sage's, the soldier's bier
I could drop many a pitying tear,
And as the martyr sinks to sleep
I could in love, in sorrow weep.

.   .   .

(Unfinished).

C. Brontë. *November* 28, 1834.

Included in a manuscript entitled 'The Scrap-Book: A Mingling of Many Things,' compiled by Lord C. A. F. Wellesley, completed by Charlotte Brontë, on March 17, 1835. The manuscript is in the British Museum.

This Lament for martyr, soldier and sage was printed in *The Cornhill Magazine*, August 1916, pp. 147-148, with an introductory note by Dr. G. E. MacLean from which the following paragraph is taken:

'The obvious allusion in the first twelve lines is to the protomartyr of Christianity. The stanza upon the "son of wisdom" refers to Socrates, the protomartyr of Paganism. The lament for the soldier, "laid on the battle-plain," is set like a gem between three stanzas and flashes out her conception of the true patriot and hero. She ranks the dying common soldier

"His thoughts all for his fatherland,"

with St. Stephen and Socrates, a trinity of martyrs of faith, of patriotism, and of philosophy.'

RETROSPECTION

WE wove a web in childhood,
    A web of sunny air;
We dug a spring in infancy
Of water pure and fair;

5   We sowed in youth a mustard seed,
    We cut an almond rod;
We are now grown up to riper age—
    Are they withered in the sod?

Are they blighted, failed and faded,
10   Are they mouldered back to clay?
For life is darkly shaded;
    And its joys fleet fast away.

Faded! the web is still of air,
  But how its folds are spread,
15 And from its tints of crimson clear
  How deep a glow is shed.
The light of an Italian sky
Where clouds of sunset lingering lie
  Is not more ruby-red.

20 But the spring was under a mossy stone,
  Its jet may gush no more.
Hark! sceptic bid thy doubts be gone,
  Is that a feeble roar
Rushing around thee? Lo! the tide
25 Of waves where armèd fleets may ride
Sinking and swelling, frowns and smiles
An ocean with a thousand isles
  And scarce a glimpse of shore.

The mustard-seed in distant land
30   Bends down a mighty tree,
The dry unbudding almond-wand
  Has touched eternity.
There came a second miracle
Such as on Aaron's sceptre fell,
35 And sapless grew like life from heath,
Bud, bloom and fruit in mingling wreath
All twined the shrivelled off-shoot round
As flowers lie on the lone grave-mound.

Dream that stole o'er us in the time
40 When life was in its vernal clime,
Dream that still faster o'er us steals
  As the mild star of spring declining
The advent of that day reveals,
  That glows in Sirius' fiery shining:

45 Oh! as thou swellest, and as the scenes
 Cover this cold world's darkest features,
Stronger each change my spirit weans
 To bow before thy god-like creatures.

When I sat 'neath a strange roof-tree
50 With nought I knew or loved round me,
Oh how my heart shrank back to thee,
Then I felt how fast thy ties had bound me.

That hour, that bleak hour when the day
 Closed in the cold autumn's gloaming,
55 When the clouds hung so bleak and drear and grey
 And a bitter wind through their folds was roaming.
There shone no fire on the cheerless hearth,
 In the chamber there gleamed no taper's twinkle.
Within, neither sight nor sound of mirth,
60 Without, but the blast, and the sleet's chill sprinkle.

Then sadly I longed for my own dear home
 For a sight of the old familiar faces,
I drew near the casement and sat in its gloom
 And looked forth on the tempest's desolate traces.

65 Ever anon that wolfish breeze
 The dead leaves and sere from their boughs was
  shaking,
And I gazed on the hills through the leafless trees
 And felt as if my heart was breaking.

Where was I ere an hour had passed:
70 Still listening to that dreary blast,
Still in that mirthless lifeless room,
Cramped, chilled, and deadened by its gloom?

No! thanks to that bright darling dream,
Its power had shot one kindling gleam,
75 Its voice had sent one wakening cry,
And bade me lay my sorrows by,

And called me earnestly to come,
And borne me to my moorland home.
I heard no more the senseless sound
80 Of task and chat that hummed around,
I saw no more that grisly night
Closing the day's sepulchral light.

The vision's spell had deepened o'er me:
Its lands, its scenes were spread before me,
85 In one short hour a hundred homes
Had roofed me with their lordly domes,
And I had sat by fires whose light
Flashed wide o'er halls of regal height,
And I had seen them come and go
90 Whose forms gave radiance to the glow,
And I had heard the matted floor
Of ante-room and corridor
Shake to some half-remembered tread
Whose haughty firmness woke even dread,
95 As through the curtained portal strode
Some spurred and fur-wrapped Demi-God,
Whose ride through that tempestuous night
    Had added somewhat of a frown
To brows that shadowed eyes of light
100   Fit to flash fire from Scythian crown,
Till sweet salute from lady gay
Chased that unconscious scowl away;
And then the savage fur-cap doffed,
    The Georgian mantle laid aside,
105 The satrap stretched on cushion soft,
    His loved and chosen by his side,
That hand, that in its horseman's glove
    Looked fit for nought but bridle rein,
Caresses now its lady-love
110   With fingers white that show no stain
They got in hot and jarring strife,
When hate or honour warred with life,—

Nought redder than the roseate ring
That glitters fit for Eastern King.

115 In one proud household where the sound
Of life and stir ring highest round,
Hall within hall burned starry bright
And light gave birth to richer light,
Grandly its social tone seemed strung,
120 Wildly its keen excitement rung,
And hundreds 'mid its splendours free,
Moved with unfettered liberty,
Not gathered to a lordly feast,
But each a self-invited guest:
125 It was the kingly custom there
That each at will the house should share.

I saw the master not alone,
He crossed me in a vast saloon,
Just seen then sudden vanishing
130 As laughingly he joined the ring
That closed around a dazzling fire,
And listened to a trembling lyre.
He was in light and licensed mood,
Fierce gaiety had warmed his blood,
135 Kindled his dark and brilliant eye
And toned his lips' full melody.

I saw him take a little child
    That stretched its arms and called his name.
It was his own, and half he smiled
140   As the small eager creature came
Nestling upon his stately breast,
    And its fair curls and forehead laying
To what but formed a fevered nest—
    Its father's cheek where curls were straying
145 Thicker and darker on a bloom
Whose hectic brightness boded doom.

He kissed it and a deeper blush
Rose to the already crimson flush,
And a wild sadness flung its grace
150 Over his grand and Roman face.
The little, heedless, lovely thing
Lulled on the bosom of a King,
Its fingers 'mid his thick locks twining,
Pleased with their rich and wreathed shining,
155 Dreamed not what thoughts his soul were haunting
Nor why his heart so high was panting.

I went out in a summer night,
 My path lay o'er a lonesome waste,
Slumbering and still in clear moon-light,
160 A noble road was o'er it traced.
Far as the eye of man could see
 No shade upon its surface stirred,
All slept in mute tranquillity,
 Unbroke by step or wind or word.

165 That waste had been a battle-plain,
  Head-stones were reared in the waving fern.
There they had buried the gallant slain
  That dust to its own dust might return,
And one black marble monument
170 Rose where the heather was rank and deep,
Its base was hid with the bracken and bent,
  Its sides were bare to the night-wind's sweep.

A Victory carved in polished stone,
 Her trumpet to her cold lips held,
175 And strange it seemed as she stood alone
That not a single note was blown,
  That not a whisper swelled.

It was Camilia's ancient field,
     I knew the desert well,
180 For traced around a sculptured shield
     These words the summer moon revealed:
     'Here brave Macarthy fell!
     The men of Keswick leading on.
     Their first, their best, their noblest one,
185   He did his duty well.'

I now heard the far clatter of hoofs on the hard and milk-white road, the great highway that turns in a bend from Free-Town, and stretches on to the West. Two horsemen rode slowly up in the moonlight and leaving the path struck deep into the moor, galloping through heather to their chargers' breasts.

'Hah!' said one of them as he flung himself from his steed and walked forward to the monument; 'Hah! Edward, here's my kinsman's tomb. Now for the bugle sound! He must have his requiem or he will trouble me. The bell tolled for him in Alderwood on the eve of the conflict. I heard it myself, and though then but a very little child I remember well how my mother trembled as she sat in the drawing-room of the manor house and listened while that unaccountable and supernatural sound was booming so horribly through the woods. Edward begin.'

Never shall I, Charlotte Brontë, forget what a voice of wild and wailing music now came thrillingly to my mind's—almost to my body's —ear; nor how distinctly I, sitting in the school-room at Roe-head, saw the Duke of Zamorna leaning against that obelisk, with the mute marble Victory above him, the fern waving at his feet, his black horse turned loose grazing among the heather, the moonlight so mild and so exquisitely tranquil, sleeping upon that vast and vacant road, and the African sky quivering and shaking with stars expanded above all. I was quite gone. I had really utterly forgot where I was and all the gloom and cheerlessness of my situation. I felt myself breathing quick and short as I beheld the Duke lifting up his sable crest which undulated as the plume of a hearse waves to the wind, and knew that that music which seems as mournfully triumphant as the scriptural verse

     'Oh Grave where is thy sting;
     Oh Death where is thy victory'

was exciting him and quickening his ever rapid pulse.

'Miss Brontë, what are you thinking about?' said a voice that dissipated all the charm, and Miss Lister thrust her little rough black head into my face! 'Sic transit' &c.

                         C. BRONTË, Decr. 19th. *Haworth*, 1835.

THE WOUNDED STAG

PASSING amid the deepest shade
   Of the wood's sombre heart,
Last night I saw a wounded deer
   Laid lonely and apart.

5 Such light as pierced the crowded boughs
   (Light scattered, scant, and dim),
Passed through the fern that formed his couch,
   And centred full on him.

Pain trembled in his weary limbs,
10   Pain filled his patient eye;
Pain-crushed amid the shadowy fern
   His branchy crown did lie.

Where were his comrades? where his mate?
   All from his death-bed gone!
15 And he, thus struck and desolate,
   Suffered and bled alone.

Did he feel what a man might feel,
   Friend-left and sore distrest?
Did Pain's keen dart, and Grief's sharp sting
20   Strive in his mangled breast?

Did longing for affection lost
   Barb every deadly dart;
Love unrepaid, and Faith betrayed,—
   Did these torment his heart?

25 No! leave to man his proper doom!
  These are the pangs that rise
  Around the bed of state and gloom,
  Where Adam's offspring dies!

Mrs. Gaskell included this poem in her *Life of Charlotte Brontë*
1857, vol. i, pp. 97-98, where she says: 'Though the date of the
following poem is a little uncertain . . . It must have been written
before 1833, but how much earlier there are no means of determining.'
Mrs. Gaskell does not give any reason for her statement that the poem
must have been written before 1833. The original manuscript of the
poem is included with several other poems in a small manuscript book
entitled: 'The Wounded Stag and Other Poems.' The book is signed
C. Brontë, and is dated January 19, 1836.

TURN not now for comfort here;
  The lamps are quenched, the moors are gone;
Cold and lonely, dim and drear,
  Void are now those hills of stone.

5 Sadly sighing, Anvale woods
  Whisper peace to my decay;
Fir-tree over pine-tree broods
  Dark and high and piled away.

Gone are all who saw my glory
10 Fill on festal nights the trees
Distant lit, now silver hoary,
  Bowed they to the freshening breeze.

They are dead who heard at night
  Woods and winds and waters sound,
15 Where my casements cast their light
  Red upon the snow-piled ground.

Some from afar in foreign regions,
  Some from drear suffering—wild unrest,
All light on land and winged legions
20 Fill the old woods and parent nest.

[1836]

MEMENTOS

ARRANGING in long-locked drawers, and shelves
  Of cabinets shut up for years,
What a strange task we've set ourselves!
  How still the lonely room appears!

5 And is this chamber just the same
    As when the last Ancestress died,
  As when that rumoured deed of shame
    Tarnished the baron's crested pride?
  Yes, all round looks cold and white
10 As it looked Forty years ago,
  When stretched in state that solemn night
    She lay as pale and cold as snow.
  A generation's passed since then
  And leaves have fallen and bloomed again,
15   Many, O! many a time
  In this wild woodland place, that sees
  Such constant change of flowers and trees
    And hears th' unaltered chime
  Of one Church-bell—a mile away
20 Tolled every hour of every day.
  But you are young and scarcely know
  How things went forty years ago.
  I was by when you were born
  Early one soft and pleasant morn
25   Of a mild day in spring.
  You were a pretty child and grew
  Like a young rose-bud washed with dew.
    How oft I used to sing
  Beside your cradle while you slept,
30 And never western zephyr crept
  To softer cheek or brighter curls
  Or rosier lips, enclosing pearls

Than yours young lady—but a tear
Rises as if you grieved to hear
35 Of those first days—your after fate
Has left you somewhat desolate.

Open that casket—look how bright
Those bracelets glitter in the light.
The jewels have not lost a ray
40 Of lustre since her wedding day.
But look upon that pearly chain
How black lies time's discolouring stain
I've seen that in her daughter's hair,
Sweet sylvan flower so soft and fair,
45 Ere either she or it had faded
To years which since have deeply shaded
The shine of each. You saw the hour
That trampled that unspotted flower.
The sacred marble hides her place
50   In aisles and chancels sanctified.
That's a fair form whose sculptured face
    Smiles on the line which tells she died.
Her picture as you well may see
Is now hung in the gallery,
55 Looks bright in sun and sad in gloom
Like all which fill that haunted room.

That little ring which lies among
    Those tangled chains, I found one day
On yonder toilet—She was young
60   Who left it in her girlish play
    Ere she went bright in hope away,
Almost a child but still a bride.
Her name was high, her lands were wide,
A scion of this noble line,
65 And flushed with all its radiant shine
Of pure but passing beauty, made
    Like all her ancestry

To be in moulds sepulchral laid
   Before maturity.
70 I stood a moment by that chair
   The morn she went away;
The room was freshened with the air
   Of early summer day;
Her white dress on that toilet laid
75   Hung soft as silver cloud,
Fresh flowers that but too soon would fade
   Were strewn as o'er a shroud;
The mirror where her hair she drest
   Clear, dark, and silent gave
80 Each object from its placid breast
   Like stream unstirred by wave.
She was not there the room was lone;
   Down in the open hall
Was many a hurrying step and tone
85   And many a hasty call.
The carriage stood with harnessed steeds
   Beside the gates flung wide.
O'er all the manor's woods and meads
   The word was 'mount and ride!'

90 And as I stood and watched the gloom
   And sunshine check the wall,
I heard her in a distant room
   Singing farewell to all,—
A wild, half-sad, half-playful strain
95   Which closed at every line,
'O! shall I e'er come back again
   To these old haunts of mine?'
She never did—the winter snow
   Lay white on every glade;
100 It melted and each aged bough
   In April sunshine swayed.
Then she, too, closed her gentle eyes
   Serene on all below,

And she, too, watched those golden skies
105   In dreary glimpses go.
And now she has no other home
     Than those monastic piles,
With crypt beneath—and arch or dome
     Above their darkened aisles.

110   This graven seal was his whose hand,
     As fire-side tales have said,
One moonless night, by secret light
     With guiltless blood was red.
Years lapsed—and then they found him laid,
115   When crime for wrath was ripe,
Dead, with the suicidal blade
     Clutched in his desperate gripe.
'Twas on the threshold of that hut,
     Where now my age decays,
120   The fierce axe struck his giant root
     And lopped his bloody days.
You know the spot, where three vast trees
     Entwine their arms on high
And moan to every passing breeze
125   This voice 'We saw him die!'
Blackened and mouldering rest his bones
     Where holier ashes lie,
But doubt not that his Spirit groans
     In Hell's eternity!

This long and hitherto unpublished version of Charlotte Brontë's poem 'Mementos' is written at the end of a prose MS. written *c*. December 1836, describing the Return of Zamorna. For the poem as printed by Charlotte, see p. 8.

CHARGE ON THE ENEMY

CHARGE on the enemy
    Victory leads.
Capture their battery,
Footmen or cavalry,
5   He shall be conqueror
    Fastest who speeds.

Think not of danger now,
    Enter the breach.
Dream not of cannon-ball,
10   Mount by the shattered wall,
Soon shall their banner-staff
    Bend to your reach.

War is an ecstasy
    Risk is wild
15   What though their battlements
    Stand like a rock.

.   .   .   .

[*January*, 1837]

THE RING

THIS ring of gold, with one small curl
    Of chestnut hair beset with pearl;
This ring and ringlet bright reveal
What time and tears would fain conceal.
5   Time might have touched with his decay
    And hid with his green moss the scene,
And tears might long have washed away
    The traces of where that thought has been.
But this, my mystic amulet,
10   Revives the picture when it fades,
Heightens the lights I would forget
    And deepens the declining shades.

Though quite alone and knowing well
That none on earth now think of me,
15   How to the summons of that spell
Answers the voice of memory!
And what delusive hopes it brings
Fanning me with their rainbow wings.
I stood in that habitual mood
20   Of anxious thought I feel all day,
Watching the starlight solitude
That round my forest mansion lay.
I looked into the deep, dark wood
Down a dim path soon lost in gloom,
25   Then from the window where I stood
Glanced round upon my firelit room.
I thought of phantoms, for so still
Was all in the dim, flashing glimmer,
There crept a kind of winter's chill
30   Over my flesh to watch the shimmer
Of shapeless shadows o'er the walls,
And o'er the high and gilded ceiling,
And o'er the draperies dark as palls
Festooned apart, and now revealing
35   Through the clear panes, gigantic trees
Waving their plumes against a heaven
Glorious with stars, a summer breeze
That movement to their boughs had given,
And then it swept the slips between
40   Of dewy lawn, and stirred the flowers
And down the alleys calm and green
Went singing to remoter bowers.
Well, as I stood a thousand dreams
Into my restless mind came thronging
45   With quick and strange and varying gleams,
With wild regret and wilder longing.
I felt impatient that my life
Was so unmarked, unloved and fated
While on the world's turmoil and strife

50 I gazed with interest never sated,
    While all day long my heart and eye
  Traversed a hundred regions over
    In city domes, neath open sky,
  Wandered and watched a viewless rover—
55   Viewless yet anxious on the fate
  Of battles, and of armies pondering,
    Resting at many a lordly gate
  That oped not to relieve my wandering,
    And turning desolate away,
60 Knowing that none would now remember,
    The friend of one brief summer day
  Forgotten in her life's November.

  This ring then as I moved my hand
    Flashed suddenly, a star uplighting
65 Its clear dark stone, and like a wand
    The sounding chords of memory smiting,
  A full, soft, deep, but fitful tone
    By that mysterious harp was uttered.
  It sounded as I sat alone
70   As if a hidden spectre muttered.
  It called back such a sweet remembrance,
    It placed so fair a scene before me,
  I longed to shake off time's encumbrance,
    To check the years that had flowed o'er me
75 And roll them back and see again
    The moonlight on that glorious region,
  That broad, unbounded green champaigne
    With here and there a scattered legion
  Of trees from the great pathless wood
80   Like plumy tropic headlands stretching
  Over the deep green, quiet flood
    Of verdure to the horizon reaching.
  I stood in a low fronted door
    One of the antique range of arches

85 Pierced in the Hall front towering o'er
   The noble, fertile, Western Marches
And that was in my early youth
   Before by sin and sorrow shaded
I gazed on Love and life and truth
90   Through mists all dim, in hues all faded.
I lived in an heroic band
   Heroic spirits round me moving
And thought took my humble stand
   Beneath them. I looked up with loving,
95 A kind of loving, though a sense
   Of vassal awe, blent with the feeling
My sires had died in their defence
   And I to tread their path was willing.
Could I be otherwise when eyes
100   So dark so radiant smiled on me,
Smiled in their haughtiness like skies
   Of midnight starlit suddenly.
Soon, O noble Idol, I have given
   My last at thy exacting shrine,
105 And thou hast lavished an earthly heaven
   Upon me in thy love divine.

True, it is past, and all is vanished
Into forgetfulness, with thee.

A softened look, a kindly word,
110   An epithet of gentleness
Would thrill me like a subtle sword
   And urgently my heart would press
To show by answering gratitude
   My deep devotedness of spirit,
115 The fervour almost wild and rude
   My fathers gave me to inherit.

That eve when he by chance had found me
   At the threshold of the door alone
Watching the wide expanse around me
120   Of park and wood beneath the moon.

He spoke and at his princely bidding
  I sat down humbly at his feet.
He asked me and, his anger dreading,
  I sang a ballad wild and sweet.—
125 Wild, sweet, and full of Western fire
  I know not how the words flowed forth
But I felt the night my heart inspire
  And the glory of the moonlit earth,
And I *felt*, though I dared not look and see,
130 Who stood half bending over me,
And there was a vague strange sense of wrong
That he stood so near and gazed so long,
And I would not that any beside had seen
His eagle eye and his smiling mien,
135 And felt a kind of troubled joy
That the shade was so deep in that solemn sky,
That the close veil of ivy clustering near
Had shut out the moonbeam broad and clear,
And yet there was terror in that delight,
140 And a burning dread of the lonely night—
I would have given life to be away
And out in the pure and sunny day.

[May, 1837]

THE HARP

NO harp on earth can breathe a tone
  In unison with thoughts like mine.
It is the night descending lone;
  It is the winds that wildly pine
5 Among the trees, and seem to tell
  Of all things sorrowful and drear,
'Tis these that weave so strange a spell
  Of causeless sorrow, aimless fear.
I sat and played in solitude
10   A hundred old, sweet   ¹ airs;

¹Space in MS.

Their spirit all my heart imbued
   Till it was even touched to tears.
I turned to wipe the drops away,
   My glance unthinking met the sky:
15 So drear it looked, so cold, so grey.

[May, 1837]

THE LONELY LADY

S H E was alone that evening—and alone
   She had been all that heavenly summer day.
She scarce had seen a face, or heard a tone
   And quietly the hours had slipped away,
5 Their passage through the silence hardly known
   Save when the clock with silver chime did say
The number of the hour, and all in peace
Listened to hear its own vibration cease.

Wearied with airy task, with tracing flowers
10   Of snow on lace, with singing hymn or song
With trying all her harp's symphonious powers
   By striking full its quivering strings along,
And drawing out deep chords, and shaking showers
   Of brilliant sound, from shell and wires among,
15 Wearied with reading books, weary with weeping,
Heart-sick of Life, she sought for death in sleeping.

She lay down on her couch—but could she sleep?
   Could she forget existence in a dream
That blotting out reality might sweep
20   Over her weariness, the healing stream
Of hope and hope's fruition?—Lo the deep
   And amber glow of that departing beam
Shot from that blood-red sun—points to her brow
Straight like a silent index, mark it now

25 Kindling her perfect features, bringing bloom
    Into the living marble, smooth and bright
As sculptured effigy on hallowed tomb
    Glimmering amid the dimmed and solemn light
Native to Gothic pile—so wan, so white
30 In shadow gleamed that face, in rosy flush
Of setting sun, rich with a living blush.

Up rose the lonely lady, and her eyes
    Instinctive raised their fringe of raven shade
And fixed upon those vast and glorious skies
35   Their lustre that in death alone might fade.
Skies fired with crimson clouds, burning with dyes
    Intense as blood—they arched above and rayed
The firmament with broad and vivid beams
That seemed to bend towards her all their gleams.

40 It was the arc of battle, leagues away
    In the direction of that setting sun
An army saw that livid summer day
    Closing their serried ranks and squared upon,
Saw it with awe, so deeply was the ray,
45   The last ray tinged with blood—so wild it shone,
So strange the semblance gory, burning, given
To pool and stream and sea by that red heaven.

                               [*May*, 1837]

IT is not at an hour like this
    We would remember those we love,
As the far hills commingling kiss
    That grey and sunless heaven above,
5 All dim and chill, a time of tears
And dying hopes and gathering fears.

But I am lone, and so art thou,
    And leagues of land between us lie;
And though we moaned expiring now,
10   One could not watch the other die;
And till corruption's work was done,
Neither could gaze his idol on.

And well I know this cloudy close,
  Sealing a long, dark day of gloom,
15 Will bring o'er that soft brow's repose
  A token of untimely doom;
And it will droop in heart-felt pain,
As though it ne'er might rise again.

All pale that cheek; no fervent glow
20 Of longing, watching, waiting love,—
No swell of that white breast to show
  How pants in hope my suffering dove;
But one hand on the other laid,
She sits and weeps in twilight's shade.

[*May*, 1837]

MY DREAMS

AGAIN I find myself alone, and ever
  The same voice like an oracle begins
Its vague and mystic strain, forgetting never
  Reproaches for a hundred hidden sins,
5 And setting mournful penances in sight,
Terrors and tears for many a watchful night.

Fast change the scenes upon me all the same,
  In hue and drift the regions of a land
Peopled with phantoms, and how dark their aim
10 As each dim guest lifts up its shadowy hand
And parts its veil to shew one withering look,
That mortal eye may scarce unblighted brook.

I try to find a pleasant path to guide
  To fairer scenes—but still they end in gloom;
15 The wilderness will open dark and wide
  As the sole vista to a vale of bloom,
Of rose and elm and verdure—as these fade
Their sere leaves fall on yonder sandy shade.

My dreams, the Gods of my religion, linger
20   In foreign lands, each sundered from his own,
And there has passed a cold destroying finger
    O'er every image, and each sacred tone
Sounds low and at a distance, sometimes dying
Like an uncertain sob, or smothered sighing.

25 Sea-locked, a cliff surrounded, or afar
    Asleep upon a fountain's marble brim—
Asleep in heart, though yonder early star,
    The first that lit its taper soft and dim
By the great shrine of heaven, has fixed his eye
30 Unsmiling though unsealed on that blue sky.

Left by the sun, as he is left by hope:
    Bowed in dark, placid cloudlessness above,
As silent as the Island's palmy slope,
    All beach untrodden, all unpeopled grove,
35 A spot to catch each moonbeam as it smiled
Towards that thankless deep so wide and wild.

Thankless he too looks up, no grateful bliss
    Stirs him to feel the twilight-breeze diffuse
Its balm that bears in every spicy kiss
40   The mingled breath of southern flowers and dews,
Cool and delicious as the fountain's spray
Showered on the shining pavement where he lay.

                       [*May*, 1837]

DREAM of the West! the moor was wild;
    Its glens the blue Guardina ploughed;
An August sunset, rich and mild,
    Over the heath in amber glowed.

5 Dream of the West! two thousand miles
    Between me and the Gambia spread.
Land of the sun! transcendent smiles
    Like thine, his orb departing shed.

Birthplace of gods! thy forests proud
10 Hung in the air their sea-green piles.
Eden of earth! the sunset cloud
 Portrayed thee in its golden isles.

Now what shall tell the scene and sound
 I wrought from eve's voluptuous gale,
15 Singing of bright and hallowed ground
 Where wild wood moans from wilder vale?

Linked with the name of every land
 Some thought will rise, some scene unfold,—
The bending wood, the barren sand,
20 The lake, the Nile, the dreary wold.

Speak of the North! A lonely moor
 Silent and dark and trackless swells;
The waves of some wild streamlet pour
 Hurriedly through its ferny dells.

25 Profoundly still the twilight air,
 Lifeless the landscape; so we deem,
Till like a phantom gliding near
 A stag bends down to drink the stream.

And far away a mountain zone,
30 A cold white waste of snow-drifts lies,
And one star, large and soft and lone,
 Silently lights the unclouded skies.

Speak of the South! A sun-bright sea
 Washes a land of vines and flowers,
35 Where lowly huts lie pleasantly
 In the green arms of guardian bowers.

WHEN THOU SLEEPEST

WHEN thou sleepest, lulled in night,
    Art thou lost in vacancy?
Does no silent inward light,
    Softly breaking, fall on thee?
5 Does no dream on quiet wing
    Float a moment 'mid that ray,
Touch some answering mental string,
    Wake a note and pass away?

When thou watchest, as the hours
10   Mute and blind are speeding on,
O'er that rayless path, where lowers
    Muffled midnight, black and lone;
Comes there nothing hovering near,
    Thought or half reality,
15 Whispering marvels in thine ear,
    Every word a mystery?

Chanting low an ancient lay,
    Every plaintive note a spell,
Clearing memory's clouds away,
20   Showing scenes thy heart loves well?
Songs forgot, in childhood sung,
    Airs in youth beloved and known,
Whispered by that airy tongue,
    Once again are made thine own.

25 Be it dream in haunted sleep,
    Be it thought in vigil lone,
Drink'st thou not a rapture deep
    From the feeling, 'tis thine own?
All thine own; thou need'st not tell
30   What bright form thy slumber blest;—
All thine own; remember well
    Night and shade were round thy rest.

Nothing looked upon thy bed,
   Save the lonely watch-light's gleam;
35 Not a whisper, not a tread
   Scared thy spirit's glorious dream;
Sometimes, when the midnight gale
   Breathed a moan and then was still,
Seemed the spell of thought to fail,
40   Checked by one ecstatic thrill;

Felt as all external things,
   Robed in moonlight, smote thine eye;
Then thy spirit's waiting wings
   Quivered, trembled, spread to fly;
45 Then the aspirer wildly swelling
   Looked, where 'mid transcendency
Star to star was mutely telling
   Heaven's resolve and fate's decree.

Oh! it longed for holier fire
50   Than this spark in earthly shrine;
Oh! it soared, and higher, higher,
   Sought to reach a home divine.
Hopeless quest! soon weak and weary
   Flagged the pinion, drooped the plume,
55 And again in sadness dreary
   Came the baffled wanderer home.

And again it turned for soothing
   To the unfinished, broken dream;
While, the ruffled current smoothing,
60   Thought rolled on her startled stream.
I have felt this cherished feeling,
   Sweet and known to none but me;
Still I felt it nightly healing
   Each dark day's despondency.

THE trees by the casement are moistened with dew;
 The first star has risen o'er that long ridge of heath,
And it smiles from the verge of that sky's boundless blue
 Through the green garden-bowers on the still walks
  beneath.

5 She stood by the casement and looked at the sky;
 It was cloudless as summer and breezeless as June.
She thought, as a bird to its nest fluttered by,
 Of her home, and she murmured a soft Western tune.

There was no one to hear it, the Hall in repose
10 Lay vacant and dark, save where firelight was thrown,
Where broad mirror gleamed and where high pillar rose
 Round the lady still singing her vesper alone.

  Sweetly died both words and air.
   It was over, and her face
15 Told by its soft shade of care
   Thought had stolen to music's place.
  Canst thou tell by that dark eye
   Lifted, and that suffering brow
  Fair yet clouded what thoughts lie
20   In that lady's bosom now?

  Thou may'st feel but never can words
   Tell their rise, their aim, their flow,
  Who the course of wandering birds
   Through the trackless skies may know.
25 Lo! she smiles, in solitude,
   Twilight grief, she smiles again.
  She has hope, some flowers are strewed
   O'er her path though drenched in rain.

Through a dim, uncertain track
30   Long her pilgrimage hath lain;
Fleeting sunshine, shadows black,
    Transient pleasure, lingering pain;
No keen grief, few floods of tears,
    Distant hope to call her on,
35   Still each day that hope appears
    Fainter promised, farther flown.

Sad existence! O she feels
    All its misery even now. . . .
                       [unfinished]

HE could not sleep!—the couch of war,
    Simple and rough beneath him spread,
Scared sleep away, and scattered far
    The balm its influence might have shed.

5   He could not sleep! his temples, pressed
    To the hard pillow, throbbed with pain;
The belt around his noble breast
    His heart's wild pulse could scarce restrain.

And stretched in feverish unrest
10   Awake the great commander lay;
In vain the cooling night-wind kissed
    His brow with its reviving play,

As through the open window streaming
    All the fresh scents of night it shed,
15   And mingled with the moonlight, beaming
    In broad clear lustre round his bed.

Out in the night Cirhala's water
    Lifted its voice of swollen floods;
On its wild shores the bands of slaughter
20   Lay camped amid its savage woods.

Beneath the lonely Auberge's shelter
  The Duke's rough couch that night was spread;
The sods of battle round him welter
  In noble blood that morning shed;

25 And, gorged with prey, and now declining
  From all the fire of glory won,
Watchful and fierce he lies repining
  O'er what may never be undone.

                [*May*, 1837]

DIVING

LOOK into thought and say what dost thou see;
  Dive, be not fearful how dark the waves flow;
Sing through the surge, and bring pearls up to me;
  Deeper, ay, deeper; the fairest lie low.

5 'I have dived, I have sought them, but none have I found;
  In the gloom that closed o'er me no form floated by;
As I sank through the void depths, so black and profound,
  How dim died the sun and how far hung the sky!

'What had I given to hear the soft sweep
10 Of a breeze bearing life through that vast realm of death!
Thoughts were untroubled and dreams were asleep:
  The spirit lay dreadless and hopeless beneath.'

                [*May*, 1837]

I SCARCE would let that restless eye
  Which haunts my solitude behold
The secret which its smothered sigh
  And every silent tear unfold.

5 If it were near, and if its beam
  Fell on me from a human brow,
I would awake from that wild dream
  Which spell-binds every talent now.

The voice of Pride should sometimes speak
10   When softer feelings enervate
And bind the heart; that bondsmaid break
    Its self-locked chain, ere yet too late.

Passion has surged itself to rest,
    And calms from hope descending tell
15 How soft she comes, a golden guest
    To shine where tears of darkness fell!

                         [*May*, 1837]

A slightly different version of this poem is contained in another MS. It runs as follows:

I scarce would let that restless eye
    Which haunts my solitude behold
The secret which each smothered sigh
    And every silent tear unfold.

5   If it were near, and if its beam
    Fell on me from a human brow,
I would awake from that long false dream
    Which spell-binds every talent now.

Why does not Reason firmly speak
10   And Pride thrust foolish Grief apart?
Why does not courage rise and break
    The chains whose rust corrodes my heart?

Long may I weep—long cry for aid
    They answer not—no impulse stirs
15 No strength will to the rescue come.

IS this my tomb, this humble stone
    Above this narrow mound?
Is this my resting place, so lone,
    So green, so quiet round?
5   Not even a stately tree to shade
    The sunbeam from my bed,
Not even a flower in tribute laid
    As sacred to the dead.

I look along those evening hills,
10   As mute as earth may be,
I hear not even the voice of rills—
     Not even a cloud I see.
How long is it since human tread
     Was heard on that dim track
15 Which, through the shadowy valleys led,
     Winds far, and farther back?

And was I not a lady once,
     My home a princely hall?
And did not hundreds make response
20   Whene'er I deigned to call?
Methinks, as in a doubtful dream,
     That dwelling proud I see
Where I caught first the early beam
     Of being's day's spring face.

25 Methinks the flash is round me still
     Of mirrors broad and bright;
Methinks I see the torches fill
     My chambers with their light,
And o'er my limbs the draperies flow
30   All gloss and silken shine,
On my cold brow the jewels glow
     As bright as festal wine.

Who then disrobed that worshipped form?
     Who wound this winding sheet?
35 Who turned the blood that ran so warm
     To Winter's frozen sleet?
O can it be that many a sun
     Has set, as that sets now,
Since last its fervid lustre shone
40   Upon my living brow?

Have all the wild dark clouds of night
Each eve for years drawn on
While I interred so far from light
Have slumbered thus alone?
45 Has this green mound been wet with rain—
Such rain as storms distil
When the wind's high and warning strain
Swells loud on sunless hill?

And I have slept where roughest hind
50 Had shuddered to pass by,
And no dread did my spirit find
In all that snow-racked sky,
Though shook the iron-rails around
As, swept by deepened breeze,
55 They gave a strange and hollow sound
That living veins might freeze.

O was that music like my own?—
Such as I used to play
When soft and clear and holy shone
60 The summer moon's first ray,
And saw me lingering still to feel
The influence of that sky?
O words may not the peace reveal
That filled its concave high,

65 As rose and bower how far beneath
Hung down o'ercharged with dew,
And sighed their sweet and fragrant breath
To every gale that blew
The hour for music, but in vain,
70 Each ancient stanza rose
To lips that could not with their strain
Break Earth's and Heaven's repose.

Yet first a note and then a line
  The fettered tongue would say,
75 And then the whole rich song divine
  Found free a gushing way.
Past, lost, forgotten, I am here,
  They dug my chamber deep,
I know no hope, I feel no fear,
80   I sleep—how calm I sleep!

June 4, **1837**.

THE PILGRIMAGE

WHY should we ever mourn as those
  Whose 'star of hope' has ceased to smile?
How dark soe'er succeeding woes,
  Be still and wait and trust the while.

5 A time will come when future years
  Their veil of softening haze shall fling
Over that mournful vale of tears
  Which saw thy weary wandering.

Wild, rough, and desolate the way
10   To every pilgrim here below;
All rough the path, all dim and grey
  The lonely wastes through which we go.

But think of Beulah's bowers, the home
  That waits thee when this path is trod,
15 Lying all free from clouds and gloom,
  Celestial in the smile of God.

One stream to cross, one sable flood,
  Silent, unsounded, deep and dim:
It blights the flesh, it chills the blood;
20   But, deathless spirit! trust in Him;

For on the shore of Heaven, that lies
　　So sweet, so fair, so bathed in light,
Angels are waiting; lift thine eyes,
　　Behold them where they walk in white!

25　A little while, an hour of pain,
　　One struggle more, one gasp for breath,
And it is over; ne'er again
　　Shall sin or sorrow, hell or death,

Prevail o'er him; he passed away
30　　A shade, a flower, a cloud from earth;
On glory look, forget decay,
　　And know in Heaven an angel's birth.

This poem was found at the end of an untitled manuscript completed by Charlotte Brontë on June 29, 1837.

WATCHING AND WISHING

OH, would I were the golden light
　　That shines around thee now,
As slumber shades the spotless white
　　Of that unclouded brow!
5　It watches through each changeful dream
　　Thy features' varied play;
It meets thy waking eyes' soft gleam
　　By dawn—by opening day.

Oh, would I were the crimson veil
10　　Above thy couch of snow,
To dye that cheek so soft, so pale,
　　With my reflected glow!
Oh, would I were the cord of gold
　　Whose tassel set with pearls
15　Just meets the silken covering's fold,
　　And rests upon thy curls.

Dishevelled in thy rosy sleep,
  And shading soft thy dreams;
Across their bright and raven sweep
20   The golden tassel gleams!
I would be anything for thee,
  My love—my radiant love—
A flower, a bird, for sympathy,
  A watchful star above.

This poem was first published by Thackeray in *The Cornhill Magazine*, December 1860. It has no title in the author's MS., where it appears as a serenade chanted by a young man who is 'exalted to the seventh heaven by the united influence of wine and love.' His advances are not reciprocated, and he is rather severely chastised for his foolishness. In the same MS. (which purports to be a record of events in Angria four or five years previous to the date of writing) appear also the following poem, and the poem 'Regret' (*see* p. 45). The MS. was completed by Charlotte Brontë on July 21, 1837.

MARIAN

BUT a recollection now,
  But a dream is she;
Not of earth the rays that glow
  Round her memory.

5 'Tis not now her youthful face,
  Nor her soft blue eye,
Wakes again the fading trace
  Of fondness ere it die.

Those are dim, and those are cold,
10   Sealed and mute and hid;
Open not the grave-sheet's fold,
  Nor lift the coffin-lid.

If you wish to think again
  Of her who loved and died,
15 Oh! look upward to the plain
  Of heaven expanding wide.

When all calm the early moon
   Looks over tower or stream,
And the unclouded heaven has grown
20   O'erwhelming in its beam;

Then though thou an exile be,
   Though far from hope and home,
Oh! seek her angel memory
   In that deep solemn dome.

25 Not hers alone, for mingled dreams
   Will come if thou but gaze
Along dim hills and wandering streams
   To that pure source of rays.

I have stood thus when not a sound
30   Arose and none was by;
And in the impending heaven I found
   A whole world's mystery.

Many like her depart, but still
   That glorious moon will rise,
35 And in her radiant rising fill
   With hope divine the skies;

And every tree at such an hour,
   And every bud and leaf,
So sweetly silvered, take the power
40   To staunch the wounds of grief;

And each blue mount that sleeps in gold
   Is but a step to heaven,
Whose glorious realms seem nearer rolled
   To meet the summer even.

45 But now farewell to all awhile,
   A lingering fond adieu
To happy dreams, to midnight's smile,
   To skies of cloudless blue!
Farewell! farewell! a pleasant isle
50 Cresting life's sea with sunlit pile,
   I leave bright thoughts in you.

C. BRONTË. July 21, 1837.

A SINGLE word—a magic spring
   That touched, revealed a world,
A tone from one sweet trembling string
   That deepest feelings stirred.

5 I cannot tell and none can tell
   How flashed the mighty stream
At once, as on the vision fell
   Its silent, written name.

The Calabar! The Calabar!
10   The sacred land it laves,
I little thought, so lone, so far
   To hear its rolling waves.

To see and hear them in their course
   As clear, as they who stand[1]
15 And watch the unbridled torrent force
   Its way through Angria's land.

How many summer nights of balm
   Have given those walls their glow?
And still their soft and golden calm
20   Alas saw only woe.

[1]The following are variant lines in the MS. :
> As clear as they who oft at eve
> Here from the lattice dim
> Looked forth where Adrian's towers receive

The eye with sleepless day-dreams dim,
　　The cheek with vigils pale,
On the rolling water gaze
　　As it sweeps beneath that sky
25 Where the sun's descending rays
　　In the path of twilight die.

All is warm, and dim and calm,
　　All in heaven is mellow blue,
And there falls a sacred calm
30　　On the earth with summer's dew.

Through the flowers, and shining leaves
　　From her lofty bower she bends
Where the rose a curtain weaves
　　And the vine a shadow lends.
35 From the turret still and grim,
　　Looks she now, far gazing down
Where a mossy walk winds dim
　　And a wood is thickly grown.[1]

How sadly her speaking eye
40　　Still looks down the castle slope,
Though the moon is lifted high
　　Like the golden lamp of hope.
As she leans her long black curls
　　On the glossy ivy lie,
45 With the strings of lucid pearls
　　That their splendid clusters tie.

As she leans the moon's full beam
　　Softly lights her cheek and brow,
And though fair as angel's dream
50　　She is pale as marble now.
Through checquering leaf and flower
　　That ray her chamber shows,
And no dark Sultana's bower
　　With such fairy splendour glows.

[1]These last four lines are cancelled in the MS.

55 In that mirror's mystic gleam,
       With its massive mouldings round,
    There is shadowed like a dream
       Yonder hill's aërial bound,
    And soft green woods, and skies
60   With a moon of milder light,
    And more shadowy stars that rise
       But to gem a dimmer night.

    Scarce imagined, ere' tis gone!
       O bright dream a moment stay!
65 Though so sweet, so calm, and lone,
       It is fading fast away.
    I scarce saw thee by the light
       Of the moon that filled thy cell,
    Ere thy form was wrapt in night
70   O thou lovely sentinel!

    And thy vigil never more
       In that watch-tower came again,
    For the sands on Fancy's shore
       Lost the trace in stormy rain.

                    November 17, 1837.

GODS OF THE OLD MYTHOLOGY

GODS of the old mythology, arise in gloom and storm;
   Adramalec,[1] bow down thy head; Nergal,[2] dark fiend,
      thy form;—
The giant sons of Anakim bowed lowest at thy shrine,
And thy temple rose in Argob, with its hallowed groves of
      vine;
5 And there was eastern incense burnt, and there were
      garments spread,
With the fine gold decked and broidered, and tinged with
      radiant red,—

[1]?Adrammelech, a god of Sepharvaim.
[2]Nergal, the Assyrian god of warfare and of death and the grave.

With the radiant red of furnace-flames that through the
    shadow shone,
As the full moon, when on Sinai's top, her rising light is
    thrown.
Baal of Chaldæa, dread god of the sun,
10 Come from the towers of thy proud Babylon,
From the groves where the green palms of Media grow,
Where flowers of Assyria all fragrantly blow;
Where the waves of Euphrates glide deep as the sea
Washing the gnarled roots of Lebanon's tree.
15 Ashtaroth, curse of the Ammonites,[1] rise
Decked with the beauty and light of the skies,
Let stars be thy crown and let mists round thee curl
Light as the gossamer, pure as the pearl.
Semele, soft vision, come glowing and brightly,
20 Come in a shell, like the Greek Aphrodite,
Come in the billowy rush of the foam,
From thy gold house in Elysium, roam
Where the bright purple blooms of glory
Picture forth thy goddess-story.
25 Come from thy blood-lit furnaces, most terrible and dread—
From thy most black and bloody flames, god Moloch,[2] lift
    thy head,
Where the wild wail of infant lungs shrieks horribly alone,
And the fearful yelping of their tongues sounds like a
    demon's groan.
There, their heart-riven mothers haste with burdened arms
    raised up,
30 And offer in their agony to thee thy gory cup.
O Dagon![3] from thy threshold roll on thy fishy train
And fall upon thy face and hands and break thy neck again:
Enormous wretch, most beastly fiend, plague of the
    Philistine!

[1] Probably 'Sidonians' is meant.
[2] Moloch, the deity of the Ammonites, to whom it was the custom to sacrifice human victims.
[3] Dagon, the god of the Philistines, half man or woman and half fish.

O'er the locked Ark I bid thee come with its Cherubim
    divine.
35 And Belial[1] loathsome, where art thou? Dost hear my
    rampant voice?
I mean to be obeyed, man, when I make such a noise.
My harp is screeching, ringing out, with a wild fevered
    moan,
And my lyre, like a sparrow with a sore throat, has a most
    unearthly tone.
A bottle of brandy is in me, and my spirit is up on high,
40 And I'll make every man amongst ye pay the piper ere I die;
And as for thee, thou scoundrel, thou brimstone sulphur-
    ous Mammon,[2]
Let's have no more of thee nor of thy villainous gammon.
I'll be with you with a salt-whip most horrible for aye,
And I'll lash you till your hair turns as black as mine is grey.
45 You shall dwell in the red range while I blow the coals full
    fast,
And I'll make you feel the fury of a rushing furnace-blast,
Leap down the sweating rocks and the murderous caves of
    the pit,
And stamp with your hooves and lash with your tails and
    fire and fury spit.
I'll be at you in a jiffy as fast as I can run,
50 But I'm riding now on the horns of the moon and the back
    of the burning sun,
The wind is rushing before me and the clouds in a hand-
    gallop go,
And they are getting it properly when they fly a stiver too
    slow,
For the weed-slimy lands of the earth send up such a stink
    to me
That I'm fain to go on in my mad career, and soon shall I be
    with ye.

[1]Belial, or Satan, the spirit of evil.
[2]Mammon, the god or spirit of the world.

55 I'm a noble fellow, flames I spew, I shall eat them up if I'm
    spared;
I'm going to the pit of sulphur blue, and my name is
    Thomas Aird.[1]

An incorrect transcript of this poem was printed in New York in
1902, in an edition limited to one hundred and ten copies for private
circulation only.

YET sleep my lord and know
    One true heart beats for thee,
That neither pain nor want nor woe
    Can taint with treachery.

5 If in this lonely wood
    A host now sought thy life,
How freely would I pour my blood
    To shield thee in the strife.

Whitened and cold thy brow
10 And wetted thy young cheek.
                    [unfinished 1838]

LONG, long ago—before the weight of pain
    Made life a weary burden—I would dream
Of such a time as this—and now again
    Comes Memory with that faint and doubtful gleam,
5 Her faded taper yields, and shows how vain
    Is Hope—Anticipation—checked the stream
I thought would flow for ever—

I ask no more—for all that earth can give
    I see around me gathered—soft and bright,
10 Beauty arises, wooing me to live
    And never quit these scenes of placid light,
    Half-shrouded—half revealing through the night.

[1] One of the early writers in *Blackwood's Magazine.*

As midnight veils and hides in shade
    This vast and domed saloon,
15 As all those clouds in piles arrayed,
    Have screened the unsullied moon,
So thou my Lord hast been to me
    A cloud that darkened life.

O'er hill and wood—the evening bells
20   Their holy tone diffuse.
That sound of peaceful starlight tells,
    And summer's falling dews,
Silent, and golden shines that star
    In blue unclouded space.

            [unfinished *January*, 1838]

WHAT does she dream of, lingering all alone
    On the vast terrace, o'er that stream impending?
Through all the dim, still night no life-like tone
    With the soft rush of wind and wave is blending.
5 Her fairy step upon the marble falls
With startling echo through those silent halls.

Chill is the night, though glorious, and she folds
    Her robe upon her breast to meet that blast
Coming down from the barren Northern wolds.
10   There, how she shuddered as the breeze blew past
And died on yonder track of foam, with shiver
Of giant reed and flag fringing the river.

Full, brilliant shines the moon—lifted on high
    O'er noble land and nobler river flowing,
15 Through parting hills that swell upon that sky
    Still with the hue of dying daylight glowing,
Swell with their plumy woods and dewy glades,
Opening to moonlight in the deepest shades.

Turn lady to thy halls, for singing shrill
20   Again the gust descends—again the river
Frets into foam—I see thy dark eyes fill
    With large and bitter tears—thy sweet lips quiver.

                    [January, 1838]

THE voice of Lowood speaks subdued
    In the deep, shadowy solitude.
Inured to loneliness—I know
No gloom in that communing low
5 Of tree with tree, and gale with gale,
Telling to each a plaintive tale.

Unhonoured, little thought of now,
    I come to rest my weary head
Where leafy branch and ivied bough
10   Their canopy of calm will spread,
And dreams will dawn like angels bright
From the long vista's tender light.

Have many lived as I have lived,
    Existence but a reverie,
15 Born all for kindness yet bereaved
    Of human smiles and sympathy,
Passing through scenes of grandeur high,
    And doomed with noble hearts to dwell,
Burning with love, yet forced to sigh
20   That none will mark that passion swell?
Yes one, by fiery glimpses oft
    The cloud enkindling changed to flame,
Then sun and balm immingling soft
    To melt the frozen winter came,
25 And even I have tasted joy
Pure, bright from heaven without alloy.

Yet strange it seems—that born to be
A being all unchained and free,
With powers of bliss all self contained—

              [unfinished *January*, 1838]

THE DEATH OF LORD HARTFORD

'OH, let me be alone,' he said,
   And he was left alone.
None wished to stay—a sense of dread
   Came with that hollow tone.
5 Upon his couch he rose to see
   If through the chamber wide
There shone an eye to watch how he
   Could yield to pain his pride.

No, all was still—before his bed
10   A lofty arch disclosed
How gloomily the sky was spread
   With clouds where storms reposed,
Unwilling still to break, but full
   Of awful days to be,
15 When that high concave dense and dull
   Should burst convulsively.

The light that touched the sufferer's brow
   Was brassy, faint and wan,
Yet showed it well what sense of woe
20   Worked in that dying man.
He looked forth on the dreary sky
   And back he sank again,
But not to sleep or faint, his eye
   Showed strength still strove with pain.

25 He spoke, for burning fever wrought
   So wildly in his brain
He knew not whether voice or thought
   Took up the phrenzied strain.
He spoke aloud, his vision wild
30   Seemed something to pourtray,

And as the phantom waned, he smiled
And beckoned it to stay.[1]

Be mine for evermore, I go
Where none shall watch us rove.
35 O heal this anguish, soothe this woe
And then my true heart prove.
Shall I not by the cane-brake find
Some home, some rest for thee,
Where haply on thy breast reclined
40 My future heaven shall be?

These are my father's halls, but here
I feel I may not stay.
I grieve not so these arms may bear
Mine Idol too away;
45 And thou wilt go, that heavenly smile
Forgives and grants me more
Than hours and months and years of toil
And fondness can restore.

O is it Fever brings that form
50 So near my dying bed,
And waves that hand so soft and warm
Above my throbbing head?
Is it delirium shews her now
With pitying[2] aspect nigh,
55 With dark curls o'er her snow-white brow,
With love in that deep eye?

Hollow and vapour-like it seems,
I see but cannot feel,
Like glorious thoughts, like golden dreams
60 Which youth and hope reveal.

[1] The following are variant lines in the MS.
He gazed on space then strangely smiled
And bid the phantom stay.
[2] Alternative word 'hallowed.'

But I must wake, I know she said
   She never loved but one,
And all my adoration paid
   In fire she seemed to shun.

65 Again if raised from this death-bed
   I'll peril life to try
If she for whom I fought and bled
   Will let me hopeless die;
And if an angel's voice divine
70   From God should bid me tell
In what bright heaven of glorious shine
   My spirit longed to dwell,

I'd say let it be shadowy night,
   On earth let stars look down,
75 And let her lips in their dim light
   Confess her heart my own.
Be it in black and frozen wild,
   Be it in lonely wood,
So she but loved and cheered and smiled
80   I'll buy such bliss with blood.

The white lips of the dying man
   Turned whiter still, and he
With up-turned eyes and aspect wan
   Seemed stricken with agony.
85 He felt himself alone, he knew
   All the cold lonely room around.

.   .   .   .

[January, 1838]

In an untitled MS. by Charlotte Brontë dated January 17, 1838,
Lord Hartford was shot by Zamorna for making love to his mistress,
Mina Laury. A portion of this story was published in *The Twelve
Adventurers and Other Stories* under the title 'Mina Laury' II.

SIESTA

'TIS the siesta's languid hour;
    The sun burns fierce and strong;
Softly the bird in Helen's bower
    Soothes her light sleep with song.
5 Of tropic isles and groves it sings—
    She dreams of mountains grey
Where the lone heron folds its wings
    By streams—how far away!

Fain would that weary bird return
10   Over the sea's white foam;
Gladly would Helen cease to mourn
    Safe in her mountain home.
Serene the summer-roses breathe
    Their fragrance through her bower;
15 In sleep she roams where summer heath
    Waves in the winds its flower.

Deeply the lowland river flows,
    She hears it in her dreams.
She thinks the fall of winter snows
20   Have swelled her native streams.
All in meridian light she lies,
    Faint in this burning noon;
To her it seems that evening skies
    Disclose a rising moon.

25 No sound is in her garden heard
    Save the soft hum of bees;
Scarcely a blossom's leaf is stirred,
    So softly swells the breeze.
That silence sinks too on her sleep,
30   But there the sleep of night
Glides on with dews and shadows deep
    Over a hill's dim height.

The bird is flown—her dream is gone;
   Moon, hills and shadows wane,
35 And Helen lies awake, alone;
   She fain would sleep again.
No, lady, rise—the time of sleep
   For thee has glided by.
Wake now and watch the transient sweep
40   Of clouds across the sky.

Sit by the dial-plate, as oft
   Thy weary wont has been,
And mark the sunshine passing soft
   Each shadowed hour between;
45 And wait for night, for sunset yearn,
   Then long again for day;
Thus shalt thou wait and watch and mourn
   Till life is past away!

            C. BRONTË. *July* 7, 1838.

A VALENTINE

A ROLAND for your Oliver
   We think you've justly earned;
You sent us such a valentine,
   Your gift is now returned.

5 We cannot write or talk like you;
   We're plain folks every one;
You've played a clever jest on us,
   We thank you for the fun.

Believe us when we frankly say
10   (Our words, though blunt, are true),
At home, abroad, by night or day,
   We all wish well to you.

And never may a cloud come o'er
The sunshine of your mind;
15 Kind friends, warm hearts, and happy hours
Through life, we trust, you'll find.

Where'er you go, however far
In future years you stray,
There shall not want our earnest prayer
20 To speed you on your way.

A stranger and a pilgrim here
We know you sojourn now;
But brighter hopes, with brighter wreaths,
Are doomed to bind your brow.

25 Not always in these lonely hills
Your humble lot shall lie;
The oracle of fate foretells
A worthier destiny.

And though her words are veiled in gloom,
30 Though clouded her decree,
Yet doubt not that a juster doom
She keeps in store for thee.

Then cast hope's anchor near the shore,
'Twill hold your vessel fast,
35 And fear not for the tide's deep roar,
And dread not for the blast.

For though this station now seems near,
'Mid land-locked creeks to be,
The helmsman soon his ship will steer
40 Out to the wide blue sea.

Well officered and staunchly manned,
    Well built to meet the blast;
With favouring winds the bark must land
    On glorious shores at last.

CHARLOTTE BRONTË. *February*, 1840.

This 'valentine' is supposed to have been sent to the Rev. William
Weightman, M.A., at that time curate of Haworth, who had sent a
valentine to each of the Brontë sisters. In a letter written to her friend,
Ellen Nussey, a year later, Charlotte Brontë says: 'I dare say you have
received a valentine this year from our bonny-faced friend the curate
of Haworth. I got a precious specimen a few days before I left home,
but I know better how to treat it than I did those we received a year
ago.'

NAPOLEON

Translated from the French of Henri Auguste Barbier.

O CORSICAN! thou of the stern contour!
    Thy France, how fair was she
When the broad ardent sun of Messidor[1]
    At length beheld her free!
5 Like a young horse unbroke to servitude,
    Bridle she scorned and rein:
Still on her hot flanks smoked the recent blood
    Of kings on scaffolds slain.

Proudly her free hoof struck the ancient soil;
10   Insult by word or deed
She knew not: never hand of outrage vile
    Had pressed on that wild steed;
Never had her deep flanks the saddle borne
    Or harness of the foe:
15 All virgin she, her heavy mane unshorn
    Wantoned in vagrant flow.

[1] The tenth month of the calendar of the first French Republic, from June 19 to
July 18.

The eye of fire, set in her slender head,
　　Shot forth a tameless ray;
Reared up erect, the whole world she dismayed
20　　With her shrill savage neigh.
Napoleon came: he marked her noble strain,
　　Her blood, her mettle bold:
Grasping the thick locks of her gipsy mane
　　His hand took steadfast hold.
　　　　·　　　·　　　·　　　·[1]

25　O'er flesh, like clay, galloped the goaded horse,
　　Breast deep in blood and tears;
She trampled generations in her course
　　For fifteen bloody years.
For fifteen years of carnage, woe, and wrath,
30　　O'er prostrate lands she rode,
And still she wore not out the endless path
　　Her hoof of iron trode.

Weary at last of ever onward hasting,
　　Finding no resting place,
35　Weary of grinding earth, of wildly wasting,
　　Like dust, the human race;
With limbs unnerved, staggering at every pace,
　　Weak as if death were near,
She prayed the Corsican a moment's grace:
40　　Tyrant! he would not hear.

Closer he pressed her with his vigorous thigh;
　　In rage her teeth he broke,
Hard drew the bit, stifled the piercing cry
　　That quickened torture woke.
45　Once more she rose; at length, one battle-day,
　　Prone to the field she fell:
Unhorsed, unhelmed, her haughty rider lay
　　Crushed, on a heap of shell!

March, 1843.

[1]The fourth stanza is omitted: it has been left in an unfinished state in the MS.

MASTER AND PUPIL

I GAVE, at first, attention close;
  Then interest warm ensued;
From interest, as improvement rose,
  Succeeded gratitude.

5 Obedience was no effort soon,
    And labour was no pain;
  If tired, a word, a glance alone
    Would give me strength again.

  From others of the studious band
10   Ere long he singled me;
  But only by more close demand
    And sterner urgency.

  The task he from another took,
    From me he did reject;
15 He would no slight omission brook,
    And suffer no defect.

  If my companions went astray,
    He scarce their wanderings blamed;
  If I but faltered in the way,
20   His anger fiercely flamed.

  When sickness stayed awhile my course,
    He seemed impatient still,
  Because his pupil's flagging force
    Could not obey his will.

25 One day when summoned to the bed
    Where pain and I did strive,
  I heard him, as he bent his head,
    Say, 'God, she must revive!'

I felt his hand, with gentle stress,
30   A moment laid on mine,
And wished to mark my consciousness
    By some responsive sign.

But powerless then to speak or move,
    I only felt, within,
35   The sense of Hope, the strength of Love,
    Their healing work begin.

And as he from the room withdrew,
    My heart his steps pursued;
I longed to prove, by efforts new,
40   My speechless gratitude.

When once again I took my place,
    Long vacant, in the class,
Th' unfrequent smile across his face
    Did for one moment pass.

45   The lessons done; the signal made
    Of glad release and play,
He, as he passed, an instant stayed,
    One kindly word to say.

'Jane, till to-morrow you are free
50   From tedious task and rule;
This afternoon I must not see
    That yet pale face in school.

'Seek in the garden-shades a seat,
    Far from the playground din;
55   The sun is warm, the air is sweet:
    Stay till I call you in.'

A long and pleasant afternoon
    I passed in those green bowers;
All silent, tranquil, and alone
60   With birds, and bees, and flowers.

Yet, when my master's voice I heard
    Call, from the window, 'Jane!'
I entered, joyful, at the word,
    The busy house again.

65 He, in the hall, paced up and down;
    He paused as I passed by;
His forehead stern relaxed its frown;
    He raised his deep-set eye.

'Not quite so pale,' he murmured low.
70   'Now, Jane, go rest awhile,'
And as I smiled his smoothened brow
    Returned as glad a smile.

My perfect health restored, he took
    His mien austere again;
75 And, as before, he would not brook
    The slightest fault from Jane.

The longest task, the hardest theme
    Fell to my share as erst,
And still I toiled to place my name
80   In every study first.

He yet begrudged and stinted praise,
    But I had learnt to read
The secret meaning of his face,
    And that was my best meed.

85 Even when his hasty temper spoke
    In tones that sorrow stirred,
My grief was lulled as soon as woke
    By some relenting word.

And when he lent some precious book,
90   Or gave some fragrant flower,
I did not quail to Envy's look,
    Upheld by Pleasure's power.

At last our school ranks took their ground,
  The hard-fought field I won;
95 The prize, a laurel-wreath, was bound
  My throbbing forehead on.

Low at my master's knee I bent,
  The offered crown to meet;
Its green leaves through my temples sent
100 A thrill as wild as sweet.

The strong pulse of Ambition struck
  In every vein I owned;
At the same instant, bleeding broke
  A secret, inward wound.

105 The hour of triumph was to me
  The hour of sorrow sore;
A day hence I must cross the sea,
  Ne'er to recross it more.

An hour hence, in my master's room,
110 I with him sat alone,
And told him what a dreary gloom
  O'er joy had parting thrown.

He little said; the time was brief,
  The ship was soon to sail;
115 And while I sobbed in bitter grief
  My master but looked pale.

They called in haste: he bade me go,
  Then snatched me back again;
He held me fast and murmured low,
120 'Why will they part us, Jane?

'Were you not happy in my care?
  Did I not faithful prove?
Will others to my darling bear
  As true, as deep a love?

125 'O God, watch o'er my foster-child!
    Oh, guard her gentle head!
When winds are high and tempests wild
    Protection round her spread!

    'They call again: leave then my breast;
130   Quit thy true shelter, Jane;
But when deceived, repulsed, opprest,
    Come home to me again!'

The original draft of the above poem is in an exercise-book used by Charlotte Brontë in Brussels, 1843. It contains two rejected stanzas, the tenth and eleventh, as follows:

    It was a genial summer day,
      The sun the lattice lit;
    Bees humming in the ardent ray
      O'er garden beds did flit.

    A gentle breeze, as fresh as sweet,
      In through the window blew;
    I, weary of the schoolroom heat,
      Aside the curtain drew.

The remainder of the MS. differs from the printed version in only two words: 'returning' for 'responsive' in the eighth stanza; and 'trees' for 'bees' in the fifteenth stanza.

THE Autumn day its course has run,
    The Autumn evening falls,
Already risen the Autumn moon
    Gleams quiet on these walls;

5   And twilight to my lonely house
    A silent guest is come:
In mask of gloom, through every room
    She passes dusk and dumb.

Her veil is spread, her shadows shed
10   O'er stair and chamber void,
And now I feel her presence steal
Even to my lone fireside.

Sit, silent Nun—sit here and be
Comrade and confidante to me.

This and the following poem were written by Charlotte Brontë in
her German exercise book used at Brussels in May 1843.

EARLY wrapt in slumber deep
    Rest the serving-men;
Master, dame, and hand-maid sleep
    Sound, at Bonny glen.

5   Time's dark stream, in yonder vales,
    Glides with shadowed flow;
O'er each latticed window falls
    A drapery, sweeping low.

While, within the house, is spread
10   Shade o'er weary eyes,
Screenless, in his out-door shed,
    A little herd-boy lies.[1]

Splendid light from summer moon
    Falls on each green tree;
15 Soft as twilight, clear as noon,
    Smiles each dewy lea.

Water in the clear brook flows
    Fast, with trembling brightness;
By its side, the causeway shews
20   A track of silver whiteness.

[1]Variant in MS.: 'The little shepherd lies.'

ON THE DEATH OF
EMILY JANE BRONTË

MY darling, thou wilt never know
The grinding agony of woe
That we have borne for thee.
Thus may we consolation tear
5   E'en from the depth of our despair
And wasting misery.

The nightly anguish thou art spared
When all the crushing truth is bared
To the awakening mind,
10   When the galled heart is pierced with grief,
Till wildly it implores relief,
But small relief can find.

Nor know'st thou what it is to lie
Looking forth with streaming eye
15   On life's lone wilderness.
'Weary, weary, dark and drear,
How shall I the journey bear,
The burden and distress?'

Then since thou art spared such pain
20   We will not wish thee here again;
He that lives must mourn.
God help us through our misery
And give us rest and joy with thee
When we reach our bourne!

December 24, 1848.

Emily Jane Brontë died on December 19, 1848.

ON THE DEATH OF ANNE BRONTË

THERE'S little joy in life for me,
 And little terror in the grave;
I've lived the parting hour to see
Of one I would have died to save.

5   Calmly to watch the failing breath,
     Wishing each sigh might be the last;
Longing to see the shade of death
O'er those belovèd features cast.

The cloud, the stillness that must part
10   The darling of my life from me;
And then to thank God from my heart,
To thank Him well and fervently;

Although I knew that we had lost
The hope and glory of our life;
15 And now, benighted, tempest-tossed,
Must bear alone the weary strife.

June **21, 1849.**

Anne Brontë died at Scarborough on May 28, 1849, four days after leaving home with her only remaining sister. Charlotte Brontë returned home to Haworth Parsonage on June 21, 1849, the day on which the poem appears to have been written. Facsimiles of the manuscripts containing the two preceding poems were printed in *Woman at Home*, December 1896; and in *A Bibliography of the Writings in Prose and Verse of the Members of the Brontë Family*, by Thomas J. Wise, 1917, p. 199.

Undated Poems

REASON

UNLOVED I love, unwept I weep,
    Grief I restrain, hope I repress;
Vain is this anguish, fixed and deep,
    Vainer desires or means[1] of bliss.

5   My life is cold, love's fire being dead;
    That fire self-kindled, self-consumed;
What living warmth erewhile it shed,
    Now to how drear extinction doomed!

Devoid of charm how could I dream
10 My unasked love would e'er return?
What fate, what influence lit the flame
    I still feel inly, deeply burn?

Alas! there are those who should not love;
    I to this dreary band belong;
15 This knowing let me henceforth prove
    Too wise to list delusion's song.

No, Syren! Beauty is not mine;
    Affection's joy I ne'er shall know;
Lonely will be my life's decline,
20 Even as my youth is lonely now.

Come Reason—Science—Learning—Thought—
    To you my heart I dedicate;
I have a faithful subject brought:
    Faithful because most desolate.

[1] ?dreams.

25 Fear not a wandering, feeble mind:
    Stern Sovereign, it is all your own
To crush, to cheer, to loose, to bind;
    Unclaimed, unshared, it seeks your throne.

Soft may the breeze of summer blow,
30   Sweetly its sun in valleys shine;
All earth around with love may glow,—
    No warmth shall reach this heart of mine.

Vain boast and false! Even now the fire
    Though smothered, slacked, repelled, is burning
35 At my life's source; and stronger, higher,
    Waxes the spirit's trampled yearning.

It wakes but to be crushed again:
    Faint I will not, nor yield to sorrow;
Conflict and force will quell the brain;
40   Doubt not I shall be strong to-morrow.

Have I not fled that I may conquer?
    Crost the dark sea in firmest faith
That I at last might plant my anchor
    Where love cannot prevail to death?

HE saw my heart's woe, discovered my soul's anguish,
    How in fever, in thirst, in atrophy it pined;
Knew he could heal, yet looked and let it languish,—
    To its moans spirit-deaf, to its pangs spirit-blind.

5 But once a year he heard a whisper low and dreary
    Appealing for aid, entreating some reply;
Only when sick, soul-worn, and torture-weary,
    Breathed I that prayer, heaved I that sigh.

He was mute as is the grave, he stood stirless as a tower;
10   At last I looked up, and saw I prayed to stone:
I asked help of that which to help had no power,
    I sought love where love was utterly unknown.

Idolater I kneeled to an idol cut in rock!
    I might have slashed my flesh and drawn my heart's best
        blood:
15 The Granite God had felt no tenderness, no shock;
    My Baal had not seen nor heard nor understood.

In dark remorse I rose; I rose in darker shame;
    Self-condemned I withdrew to an exile from my kind;
A solitude I sought where mortal never came,
20   Hoping in its wilds forgetfulness to find.

Now, Heaven, heal the wound which I still deeply feel;
    Thy glorious hosts look not in scorn on our poor race;
Thy King eternal doth no iron judgment deal
    On suffering worms who seek forgiveness, comfort, grace.

25 He gave our hearts to love: He will not love despise,
    E'en if the gift be lost, as mine was long ago;
He will forgive the fault, will bid the offender rise,
    Wash out with dews of bliss the fiery brand of woe;

And give a sheltered place beneath the unsullied throne,
30   Whence the soul redeemed may mark Time's fleeting
        course round earth;
And know its trials overpast, its sufferings gone,
    And feel the peril past of Death's immortal birth.

EVENTIDE

THE house was still, the room was still,
    'Twas eventide in June;
A caged canary to the sun
    Then setting, trilled a tune.

5   A free bird on the lilac-bush
        Outside the lattice heard;
He listened long—there came a hush,
        He dropped an answering word.

ON the bright scenes around them spread,
　Lit tenderly with those mild rays,
　The last the dying sun had shed;

The park with its broad slopes of green,
5　　Where now the mighty shadows lay,
Of tower and turret, kindling sheen
　　With amber-light on stone-work grey;
For the Ducal Castle, like a screen,
　　Stood against the farewell's level ray
10　Shot still from that refulgent West
　　O'er Lismore's tower and Gambia's wood,
Kindling the Elver's azure breast
　　Till it ran like a red stream of blood.

All this was fair, but not to me,
15　And, oh! my heart sank heavily
When, from the casement, arched and tall,
That dimly lit that Norman Hall,
I looked far down . . .

　　　　.　　　.　　　.　　　.

I can speak no more, as, in fancy,
20　I am farther out on this sullen sea;
Darker waves of its waters come,
Driving me faster from peace and home.
Never a beacon burns on the deep;
The fires are out, and the watchers asleep;
25　And the wild race of the swelling main,
The foam-wreaths bursting and foaming again,
The scream of the sea-birds, the deep-toned blast,
The billows that roll ceaseless past,
Ay, the thoughts of an evil heart,

30   The croak of a conscience not yet cured,
      The visions that will not depart,
        Are worse than all that man has endured
      On the most troubled sea that ever
      Made the strongest vessel quiver.

These stanzas are dated January 17, 183— (?), the last figure
being undecipherable.   They are written in pencil inside the cover
of Charlotte Brontë's French Grammar (*Grammatical Exercises in
English and French*, by Mr. Porny, London, 1810) in her handwriting.

A FRAGMENT

Overcome with that delightful sensation of lassitude which the
perfect repose of nature in the stillness of such an evening occasions,
I dropped the oars, and, falling listlessly back, allowed my light-
winged pinnace to float as chance might lead. For about an hour I lay
thus, gazing on the calm water and unclouded sky above me, from
which breathed a sweet balminess that scarcely fanned my temples.
At length my boat lay perfectly motionless, and I raised myself and
found that, as if soul-taught, it had wafted itself into a little willow-
fringed fairy bay. Disembarking, I fastened it to a decayed larch, and,
following a pleasant path embroidered with moss and wild flowers, I
presently entered the twilight shadow of a wood. Ere I emerged from
the darkness of its impending boughs the moon and Hesperus had set
their watch in Heaven. The soft light which fell from them, and was
reflected from the calm fading glories of the west, showed me that I
was now in a wild, winding glen embosomed in lofty precipitous falls
barren of all ornament save the purple heath flower. A chill wind now
rose, and as it sighed around or murmured mournfully in the heart of
the forest, a sudden burst of sweet sad music mingled with its wailing.
I looked up, and saw by the clear moonlight a figure clad in white
sitting on an overhanging cliff, and bending over a harp with whose
tones this sorrowful strain was blent:

L O! stretched beneath the clustering palm
    The stately noble lies;
  Around him dwells a holy calm
    Breathed softly from the skies.

5 The zephyrs fan with sweet caress
  Recumbent majesty,
And loud winds of the wilderness
  All silently pass by.

The lion from his desert lair
10 Comes forth to fierce foray,
His red eyes fired by hunger glare
  In eager search for prey.

He spies him in his dreamless sleep
  All on the moonlit ground,
15 And away as with a whirlwind sweep
  Behold the monster bound.

For holy, holy is thy rest
  Though in the desert laid:
A spirit's spell is o'er thee cast
20 Amid that palmy shade.

Oh, clouds come o'er that vision bright,
  And soft it fades away,
The witchery of memory's might
  Inviting still its stay.

25 But vainly; where my warrior slept
  The cold sad moonbeams lie;
And where Sabean odours wept
  The winds of midnight sigh.

But while bewildered ocean spreads
30 Afar her thundering plain;
And while the light of Heaven sheds
  Still splendour on the main;

I'll ne'er forget that stately form,
  That eye's entrancing light,
35 Whence oft the wildest passion's storm
  Flashed forth in sudden might;

Or in whose dark orbs lustre lay
  Borne from the worlds of thought;
But brightest shone that wondrous ray
40 From holy regions brought;

Where spirits of the favoured few
  Alone may ever dwell;
Where clearer than Parnassian dew
  A hundred fountains well;

45 The fountains sweet of poesy,
  That nectar of the sky,
Where wreaths of immortality
  In hallowed beauty lie.

But, lo! Diana's silver bow
50 Hath quitted human ken;
And the chill night-winds coldly blow
  Adown this lonely glen.

Oh, happy may his slumber be
  This night, in lands afar,
55 Beneath the desert plantain-tree,
  Beneath the silver star;

Or in his gorgeous Indian home
  On slave-surrounded bed,
All underneath some solemn dome
60 Whence lamps their glories shed.

His dreams are of some other world,
  His mighty soul is free;
His spirit's pinions all unfurled
  Rise high in radiancy.

The MS. of this 'Fragment' is unsigned and undated. There are four pages measuring 2½ inches by 3½ inches in microscopic writing, and the contents are attributed to 'Brontë (Emily?)' in an Auction Sale Catalogue dated June 19, 1914; but the subject, style, and writing are too much like the work of Charlotte Brontë at fourteen and fifteen years of age for there to be any doubt as to authorship.

THE ROSE[1]

ON its bending stalk a bonny flower
 In a yeoman's home-close grew:
It had gathered beauty from sunshine and shower,
 From moonlight and silent dew;
5 Till the tufted leaves of the garden-bower,
 Like a star it sparkled through.

It was a little budding rose,
 Round, like a fairy globe;
And shyly did its leaves unclose,
10 Hid in their mossy robe;
But sweet was the slight and spicy smell
It breathed from its heart invisible.

Keenly his flower the yeoman guarded:
 He watched it grow both day and night;
15 From the frost, from the wind, from the storm he
  warded
 That flush of roseate light;
And ever it glistened bonnilie
Under the shade of the old roof-tree.

The morning sunshine had called him forth;
20 His garden was full of dew,
And green light slept on the happy earth,
 And the sky was calm and blue,
The yeoman looked for his lovely flower:
There were leaves, but no buds, in the sheltering
 bower.

25 The rose was borne to another land,
 And grew in another bed;
It was cultured by another hand,
 And it sprung and flourishèd;

[1]Printed as Emily's in *The Complete Poems of Emily Jane Brontë*, 1923.

And fair it budded day by day
30 Beneath a new sun's cheering ray.

But long lies the dew on its crimson leaves:
    It almost looks like tears:
The flower for the yeoman's home-close grieves
    Amid a King's parterres.
35 Little moss-rose, cease to weep;
Let regret and sorrow sleep.

The rose is blasted, withered, blighted:
    Its root has felt a worm;
And like a heart beloved and slighted,
40   Failed, faded, shrunk its form.
Bud of beauty, bonnie flower,
I stole thee from thy natal bower.

I was the worm that withered thee;
    Thy tears of dew all fell for me:
45 Leaf and stalk and rose are gone;
Exile earth they died upon.
Yes, that last breath of balmy scent
With alien breezes sadly blent.

MORNING

MORNING was in its freshness still,
    Noon yet far off with all its stir,
Cool early shade, calm leisure fill
    The silent hall and summer room.
5 Two hours I yet may number ere
Full glaring day brings tumult near
And lets intensive labour, care,
Disturb my humble home.

Two hours!—how shall they speed with me,
10   In measured task, toil self-assigned?
No, eager claim for liberty
    Some sense now urges in my mind
Through Fancy's realm of imagery
    Some strange delight in ranging free;
15 Some joy that will not prisoned be,
    Brisk as the western wind.

It hurries back and brings the Past
    Sweetly before my soul;
It wings its way like rapid blast
20   To the far Future's goal.
Pleasant the thoughts its pinions chase,
And bright though vague the dreamy place
Where tends its winged and ardent race
    Farther than Ocean's roll.

25 Each pleasant passage in my life
    I now live o'er again.
I pass the weary hours of strife,
    Forget the scenes of pain.
What scorn has said and Hate has done
30 Oblivion's veil lies dimly on,
And tears by Woe from Weakness won
    Remembrance cease to stain.

But every gift by Joy bestowed
    I count in numbers true;
35 And every hour that smoothly flowed
    This hour does well renew;
And if Love's whisper ever yet
My ear like note of music met,
This summer wind seems to repeat
40   The tones with cadence due.

'Tis bitter sometimes to recall
    Illusions once deemed fair,
But in this golden moment all
    Doth fairy gilding wear;
45 And fond and fast the pulses beat
Departed Passion's shade to greet,
Rising in transient vision sweet
    To colour empty air.

LOST IN THE HILLS

I NOW had only to retrace
    The long and lonely road
So lately in the rainbow chase
    With fearless ardour trod.

5 Behind, I left the sunshine, now
    The evening setting sun,
Before, a storm rolled dark and low
    Some gloomy hills upon.

It came with rain—it came with wind,
10   With swollen stream it howled,
And night advancing black and blind
    In ebon horror scowled.

Lost in the hills—all painfully
    I climbed a heathy peak,
15 I sought, I longed afar to see
    My life's light's parting streak.

The West was black as if no day
    Had ever lingered there,
As if no red, expiring ray
20   Had tinged the enkindled air.

And morning's portals could not lie
    Where yon dark orient spread:
The funeral North—the black dark sky
    Alike mourned for the dead.

ALFRED THE GREAT

LOOK, wife, the clouds are full of snow,
A few large flakes already fall,
A cold north wind begins to blow,
While hills will soon be piled o'er all.
5 Haste we before the drifts are deep
To house the kine and fold the sheep.

I come—the sheep are scattered wide,
Ere all are safe the night will close.
I led them up to Russets' side
10 Where green the winter grass still grows.
Stranger, beside the hearth remain,
Keep guard till we return again.

Take heed, unclose the door to none.
A Dane might knock—a wolf might howl,
15 For always after set of sun
Things strange and fierce these forests prowl.
Stay thou within and watch the bread
And keep the hearth with fuel fed.

The herdsman and his wife are gone,
20 Their passive guest remains alone,
He draws his oaken buffet near
The wood-fire burning red and clear.

Docile he turns the barley-cake
Placed on the heated stone to bake.
25 He brings more wood and seems with care
To tend the simple evening fare.
This done he folds his arms again
And thoughts disturbed resume their train.

'''Tis Christmas-eve—I mark the date'
30   (Thus did he self-communing say)
'Here lone I sit—before me Fate
    Arrested, seems her course to stay,
And having done her worst, to stand
With blade depressed and weary hand.

35   'Her stony gaze is on my eyes,
    Her dark-bent brow confronts my own.
She seems to ask—"Who yet defies
    Disaster that so deep has gone?
What heart beneath my blunted knife
40   Still quivers with the throb of life?"''[1]

His efforts one by one defeated,
    His arms disgraced—his friends dismayed,
His troops to mountain holds retreated,
    Vanquished or sold, refuse him aid,
45   And he lives still, and still he dares
To search for hope 'mongst myriad fears.

[1]Variant lines:
    Retains the throb of life
    Still strong and glowing beats with life?
      bounds with strength and glows with life.

Early in the year 878 A.D. Guthrum, King of the Danes of East Anglia, suddenly marched into Wessex. At this time Alfred was King of the West Saxons (Wessex), but he could make no effectual resistance against the attack of the Danes, and had to seek refuge in the marshes of Somersetshire. To this period belongs the well-known story of how he was left in the cottage to look after the baking, and carelessly allowed the cakes to burn.

3

OTHER POEMS OF CHARLOTTE BRONTË, NOT PREVIOUSLY PUBLISHED IN THE SHAKESPEARE HEAD EDITION

HIGH minded Frenchmen love not the Ghost,
  Who rides on the clouds of pain.
With the eye of an eagle he views your host
  And grins with delight from far.

5   For the time in his powerful mind one sees[?]
  When like a slave before him lead [?]
The kingdom of France shall bow at his knees
  To glorify him as its head.

Thou at this time his brave men do not pour[?],
10   He looks to the future with joy
When from his high embattled tower
  In his terrible might he shall cry

'Kingdom of France, I bid thee beware
  At the storm which is drawing nigh,
15   Look at the troubled shimmering [?] air,
  Look at the mirth [?] in mine eye.'

I'VE been wandering in the greenwoods,
  And 'mid flowery, smiling plains;
I've been listening to the dark floods,
  To the thrush's thrilling strains.

5   I have gathered the pale primrose,
  And the purple violet sweet;
I've been where the asphodel grows,
  And where lives the red deer fleet.

I've been to the distant mountain,
10   To the silver singing rill,
By the crystal murmuring fountain,
  And the shady, verdant hill.

I've been where the poplar is springing
From the fair enamelled ground,
15 Where the nightingale is singing
With a solemn, plaintive sound.

VERSES BY
LORD CHARLES WELLESLEY

ONCE more I view thy happy shores,
    O England bold and free,
And upon the guardian Ocean soars[?]
    Fair prospect of the sea.

5 And starlike they make gentle rest,
    Arranged in living green.
Upon the black waves' gloomy breast
    A bright gem thou art seen.

Those oft dark curtaining vapours veil
10   Thy clear cerulean sky,
And often loud winds wildly wail
    Or sorrowfully sigh

Among thy oaken forests vast,
    All robed in misty gloom,
15 Which by the lightning's fire scathed [?]
    Bend 'neath the thunder's boom.

Yet still bold hearts within thee swell;
    The brave, the free, the fierce
Inspired by the battle's knell
20   Rush forth their foes to pierce.

But Africa to me is dear,
    I love its sunny clime,
Its skies for ever blue and clear,
    And now I've done my rhyme.

MISS HUME'S DREAM

ONE summer eve as Marianne stood
In pensive melancholy mood
By lattice of her room,
Gazing with rapt and solemn eyes
5 And oft repeated mournful sighs
And face which spoke of gloom,

Towards where a towering palace
peered
'Bove a wide extending wood
Its high head statelily upreared
10 O'er tall trees stretching many a rood.

She gazed and gazed till tears 'gan
start
From deep sad fountain of her heart,
Then slowly turned away.
She sat her down to think alone
15 And by herself to mourn and moan
And weep till close of day.

Then she took a net-work veil
To 'broider graceful flowers thereon,
But, oh, her face turned deathly pale,
20 The while she laboured all alone,

To think that Arthur was not there
The mighty work with her to share,
And wind the cobweb silk
On ivory bobbins beautiful,
25 Or for her flower-vase wreaths to cull
Of lilies white as milk.

But suddenly she heard a voice
From the green shady lane below,
Which made her start up to rejoice,
30   And down the stairs she swift did go.

And when the pleasant walk she gained
Bright tears of joy her blue eyes rained,
     For *he* was standing there.
Forward she sprang, but sudden stopped.
35   From her tongue no welcome dropped.
     Arthur like empty air

Full fast before her noiseless flies
With an upraiding ghostlike look;
Fixed were his dark and lustrous eyes,
40   No sigh or murmur from him broke.

He raised his head and beckoned her.
No sound was heard, no rustling stir
     As swift he glided on,
Until they reached the churchyard gate.
45   The hour now had waxed late,
     Had set the golden sun,

The moon had risen, and many a star
Looked from the windows of the sky.
Like lamps bright beaming from afar
50   They glowed in the blue arc on high.

A hollow breeze blows over the graves,
And in the blast wildly waves
     The unmown whistling grass.
Each monument in moonlight sleeps,
55   Their sides the tall-grown rank weed
          steeps
     As on the loud winds pass.

Now the church in ruins bowed
They entered soft and silently,
And lo, enwrapped with snowy shroud
60 In the midst did form of Arthur lie.

Marianne trembling with the shock
Sent forth a loud and piercing scream,
By which the spell of midnight broke.
She raised her head; it was a dream.

HE is gone, and all grandeur has fled from the
      mountain;
All beauty departed from stream and from
      fountain;
            A dark veil is hung
         O'er the bright sky of gladness,
5   And, where birds sweetly sung,
         There's a murmur of sadness;
The wind sings with a warning tone
      Through many a shadowy tree;
I hear, in every passing moan,
10   The voice of destiny.

Then, O Lord of the Waters! the Great and
      All-seeing!
Preserve in Thy mercy his safety and being;
            May he trust in Thy might
         When the dark storm is howling,
15   And the blackness of night
         Over Heaven is scowling;
But may the sea flow glidingly
      With gentle summer waves;
And silent may all tempests lie
20   Chained in Aeolian caves!

Yet, though ere he returnest long years will have
    vanished,
Sweet hope from my bosom shall never be banished:
    I will think of the time
    When his step, lightly bounding,
25   Shall be heard on the rock
    Where the cataract is sounding;
When the banner of his father's host
    Shall be unfurled on high,
To welcome back the pride, the boast
30   Of England's chivalry!

Yet tears will flow forth while of hope I am singing;
Still Despair her dark shadow is over me flinging;
    But, when he's far away,
    I will pluck the wild flower
35   On bank and on brae
At the still, moonlight hour;
And I will twine for him a wreath
    Low in the fairy's dell;
Methought I heard the night-wind breathe
40   That solemn word: 'Farewell'.

ST. JOHN IN THE ISLAND OF PATMOS

THE holy exile lies all desolate
    In that lone island of the Grecian sea.
And does he murmur at his earthly fate,
    The doom of thraldom and captivity?

5   No. Lulled by rushing of the unquiet breeze
    And the dull solemn thunder of the deep,
Under the hanging boughs of loftiest trees
    Behold the Apostle sunk in silent sleep.

And, is that chamber dreamless, as the lone
10   Unbroken, frozen stillness of the grave?
Or is his soul on some far journey gone
    To lands beyond the wildly howling wave?

Where Zion's daughter views with tear-dimmed eye
　　Her proud all-beauteous temple's lofty form,
15 Piercing with radiant front the blue bright sky
　　And mourns with veiled brow the coming storm?

Haply his spirit lingers where the palm
　　Upspringing from the flowery verdant sod
Throws a dark solemn shade, a breezeless calm,
20 　　Over the house where he first spoke to God.

Or to his freed soul is it once more given
　　To wander in the dark, wild, wilderness,
The herald of the Lord of Earth and Heaven
　　Who came, in mercy came, to heal and bless?

25 No. From his eyes a veil is rent away,
　　The will of God is gloriously revealed;
And in the full light of eternal day
　　Jehovah's fixed decrees are all unsealed.

The armed hosts of God, in panoply,
30 　　Of splendour most insufferably bright,
Rush forth triumphant from the parting sky
　　Whose wide arch yawns before those floods of light.

He hears the voice of Archangels tell
　　The doom, the fiery, fearful doom of Earth,
35 And as the trumpets' tones still louder swell
　　On the dark world red plagues are poured forth.

At once ten thousand mighty thunders sound,
　　With one wild howl the sea yields up her dead.
A flaming whirlwind sweeps the trembling ground,
40 　　The skies are passed away in fear and dread.

All earth departs; at God's supreme behest
　　Sinners are bound in the black depths of hell.
The souls of righteous men forever rest,
　　Where Angel harps in sounds harmonious swell.

45 And now the new Jerusalem descends
    Beaming with rainbow radiance from on high;
In awe and fear the holy prophet bends
    As that bright wonder rushes on his eye.

He hears the last voice, ere Heaven's gates are sealed,
50   Proclaim that all God's works are consummate;
That unto him the Almighty hath revealed
    The unfathomed mysteries of Time and Fate.

He wakes from his wonderous trance and hears
    Faint distant warblings from the distant sky;
55 Floating like tuneful music of the spheres
    Sweet as the voice of Angel harmony
Sounding Jehovah's praise to all eternity.

JUSTINE, upon thy silent tomb the dews of evening
    weep,
Descending twilight's wings of doom around and o'er
    thee sweep,
The flowers are closed on thy grave, Justine, the
    fern-leaves bend and fade
And the fitful night-wind dies and swells as it ushers in
    the shade.

5 A lonely light in heaven smiles,—one pale star in the west;
The night-clouds rise in giant piles far along Gambia's
    breast.
I am come, and come alone, Justine, to spend one hour
    with thee,
But the turf with its flowers and fern-leaves green doth
    hide thee jealously.

'O long and still hath been thy sleep beneath that grassy
    grave:
10 Years have rolled on their billows deep, and time its
    whelming wave.'

Yet, still I do remember my young nurse ere she died,
When the gloom of dark December had quenched the
    summer's pride.

Lone lay she in the latticed room which crowns that
    turret grey;
And I used to think its death-bed gloom prophetic of
    decay
15 In the placid sunny summer eves when the light of sunset
    fell
Through the chequering play of those ivy leaves with
    smiles of sad farewell.

How did I love to climb the stair which to her chamber
    led,
That I might drop a childish tear on Justine's dying bed;
I felt she was not long for earth,—her pale cheek told
    me so;
20 She who had loved me from my birth I knew was soon
    to go.

How wearily her eye would turn to the lattice and the
    sky,
Within, a wild wish seemed to burn that yet she might not
    die,
As golden clouds went sailing on, and the sound of winds
    and trees
Came, as unto a mariner comes the deep moan of the
    seas.

25 Then her daughter, and her foster-son, she'd to her
    bosom press,
And say, with such a bitter moan, 'May God my children
    bless!'
And then I called her 'Mother', and weepingly I said
I would be Mina's brother when she was cold and dead.

That vow has since been broken,—as when lightning
    shivers trees,
30   Those words, in anguish spoken, have been scattered to
    the breeze.
'Justine, if God has given a glance of earth to thee,
Thou hast even wept in Heaven my withering crimes to
    see.'

But let me not remember those hours of darkness past,
Nor blow the dying ember to light with such a blast.
35   I do not know repentance, I cannot bend my pride
Nor deprecate my conscience even at thy cold grave side.

Life's fitful fever over, thou sleepest well, Justine
Pale flowers thine ashes cover and grass mounds ever
    green,
The fox-glove here is drooping its silent peal of bells,
40   And the shadowy yew-tree stooping of rest eternal tells.

O, might I find a dwelling but half so calm as thine,
When my life-storm stills its yelling, when my comet-fires
    decline!
But the wild, the raging, billow is a fitter home for me:
The coral for the willow; for the turf the tossing sea.

THE moon dawned slow in the dusky gloaming,
    Dimly beside it gleamed a star;
Broken they shone on the waters foaming
    Of the rapid Calabar.

5   The lustrous moon, the wailing river,
    Woke in my breast the voice of thought;
In that calm hour I blessed the Giver,—
    The Source whence ray and man were
    brought.
And while they gleamed, and while they sung,
10   I gave them life, and soul, and tongue.

I asked the river when its stream
  Rushed in resounding pride;
And a voice like whispers in a dream
  Thus solemnly replied:

15 From the caverned earth I rose,
  Mortal, like to thee;
Evermore my torrent flows
  Sounding to the sea;
Ever as thy career will close
20   In vast eternity.

I asked the rising crescent moon
  O'er what her bow was bent,
And thus the sweet response came down—
  From Heaven earthward sent:

25 Beneath my midnight wandering
  How widely lies the earth,
I view the streams meandering
  To the ocean from its birth.

I see the proud hill swelling
30   Where foot has never trod,
The snow's eternal dwelling
  Beheld alone by God.

Alike my rays are glancing
  On cities filled with life,
35 Where sounds of mirth and dancing
  And harp and song are rife.

And on the ruined tower,
  The rifted arch and dome,
The fallen and trampled bower,
40   The still, the desert home,

Where fitful winds are sighing
    Through temple's arch and hall
And slowly, calmly, dying
    With many a wild faint fall.

45 Sweet murmurs, sad, decaying
    Fill all the air with moans,
Sounds through the desert straying
    Blend mingled nameless tones.

Sounds of the palm-tree shaken,
50   Sounds of the lonely well
Whose fairy murmurs waken
    To the zephyr's softest swell.
The waving of a pinion,
    The desert wild-deer's tread,
55 Are heard in that dominion
    Of silence deep and dead.

I see beneath me spreading
    Dark visions of the slain,
For my orb its light is shedding
60   O'er many a battle-plain
Where heroes famed in story
    Their deeds of war have done,
And gained a crown of glory
    For mighty conflicts won.

65 Where sunless clouds are sweeping
    Shades of eternal gloom,
Yet my beams in peace are sleeping
    Above the warrior's tomb.
My gentlest mildest splendour
70   Is poured above that dust,
Whenceforth at last shall render
    The brave, the good, the just,

If ' mid the desert dreary
    Far far from war and strife
75 Should rest the heroic weary,
    Rest from the toil of life.
Though no shade be o'er him given,
    Though the pale sand be his shroud,
Yet above him bright in heaven
80   My silver arch is bowed.

If to the wilds denying
    That high and lofty trust,
The warrior's corpse is lying
    Amid ancestral dust,
85 Still lovelier is the lustre
    That lingers round his tomb,
And lights the trees that cluster
    Above his last dark home.

THE day is closed, that spectral sun
    Whose mighty course so strongly run
Will never die in Afric's story,
Will never lose its awful glory,
5 Dark, solemn, hidden, terrible.
For not on earth its radiance fell
From the first vision of the light
To the dread drawing on of night.
A dim eclipse before it hung,
10 A shadow o'er its disk was flung,
    A shield of gloom it passed through heaven,
    A bloody ring around it drawn.
No joy with those red beams was given,
    Earth under it looked cold and lorn.
15 That orb it sunk in death's chill river,
    It went down darkly 'mid the waves,
Whose pitchy riders [?] seemed to quiver.
    A voice rang through the world of graves

When the great sun its last light quelled
20 Where those deep stormy waters swelled,
The waves of death, when torch and plume
Saw Percy to his shrine-like tomb,
When drum to drum all muffled spoke,
When the wild wailing trumpet woke,
25 And many sounds of lovely mourning
 Came on the still hushed voiceless air,
And lamps, but not of triumph, burning
 Threw to the sky their ghastly glare,
When deep bells pealed upon the night
30 And requiem music poured its might
And holy fanes were filled with light
 Sepulchral, pale and dim,
When the pall-bearers glided by
With footsteps measured solemnly
35 To the slow funeral hymn.
Sadly they bore him to his place,
Not 'mid the fathers of his race.
 The vault was void and lone,
Arched like a palace wide and high,
40 A mansion meet for royalty
When comes the mandate, 'Monarch, die'
 To call him from his throne.
He rested by the Calabar,
His kindred dust reposed afar,
45 Where storied Gambia glides.
Trees waved above their tranquil homes,
Cloud-shadows slept upon their tombs,
Dew fell, soft sunlight came and went
As free as in the Arab's tent,
50 Winds kissed their marble sides.
And came no dream with Death's dim
  sleep
 Of all those silent graves,
Came there no memory sad and deep
 To moan of Gambia's waves,

55 No murmur of the breeze that swept
        Amid his native groves,
    No holy voice that long had slept
        To speak of ancient loves?
    Was there no strange, no haunting sound
60 That wailed his dying pillow round
    Of whispering words and gliding streams
    That o'er his soul brought wondrous gleams,
    Not like the uncertain flight of dreams,
    And not like 'wildering Memory's beams,
65   But quiet and clear and bright
    Of what was once but is no more,
    A glimpse of a retiring shore
        Fading as swift as light?
    And while it lasts each well-known place
70 The sharpened eye may clearly trace,
    As if between no sweeping sea
    Rolled on in vast solemnity,
    As if no rush of surf and foam
    Then bore the shuddering vessel home,
75 As if the dark expanse before
    Shewed 'mid the waves no other shore.
    A lone dim black unbounded line
    Which ne'er yet could man define.
    And none have yet returned to tell
80 What visions in its darkness dwell.
    No home-bound bark has crossed those
            seas
    To speak its hidden mysteries.
    Men say that sometimes wrapt in gloom
    And fraught with tidings dread of doom
85 A spectral sail has wandered back
    And noiseless ploughed its ancient track,
    But when the appointed work was done
    Had passed like mist-wreaths in the sun.
    And passed there o'er that phantom sea
90 The cherished shape of memory?

Through the dark rushing of its water
    Spoke no remembered tongue?
Maria, bright Italia's daughter,
    Wast not thy image flung
95 In all its clear and kindling light
Before the dying Percy's sight?
Long had that star sat quenched in gloom
    Long had that flower lain dead,
And long beneath the heavy tomb
100   That palm had bowed its head,
Mouldering, mouldering, silently
    Gambia's waters by
Morning, evening, vainly using,
By light's rise [?] and dusk declining.
105 Vainly on that calm grave fell,
    Faith had kissed her last farewell
[*6 illegible lines*]
One moment reappearing,
    One moment the more,
The light, the glory wearing,
110   That erst as she wore
The smile, the step, the bearing,
    All known, all loved before,
The eye so full of fire
    The brow so marked with pride.

COME now, I am alone, the day's wild riot
    Self lulled to slumber; I feel somewhat weary.
Can I not rest? All looks serene and quiet.

ALL is change—the night, the day,
  Winter, summer, cloud and sun,
Early flowers, late decay,
So the years, the ages run.
5   Beats the heart with bliss awhile,
Soon it throbs to agony;
Where a moment beamed the smile,
Soon the bitter tear shall be.
This is Nature's great decree.
10   None can 'scape it—for us all
Drops the sweet, distils the gall.
All are fettered—all are free.

LONG since, as I remember well,
    My childish eyes would weep
To read how calmly Stephen fell
    In Jesus' arms asleep.
5   Oh, could I feel that holy glow
    That brightened death for him,
I'd cease to weep that all below
    Is grown so drear and dim.

Could I but gain that lofty faith
10   Which made him bless his foes,
I'd fix my anchor, firm till death
    In hope's divine repose.
And is it now a contrite heart
    That brings me, Lord, to thee,
15   Or is but the goading smart
    Of inward agony?

And could my spirit heavenward spring
   And could I upward glance
With murderers round me thickening
20   To God, in holy trance.
And could my mangled relics cry
   'O Lord, their deed forgive,
And, Jesus Saviour, graciously
   Thy martyr's soul receive'.

25 A thousand early thoughts and dreams
   Of heaven and hope were mine,
And musings sweet by placid streams
   In childhood's vision shine.
In summer evenings mild and dim,
30   Oh, it was sweet to me
To sit and say some simple hymn
   Beneath a lonely tree.

A tree that by the garden wall
   Drooped down its graceful head
35 And oft its golden flowers let fall
   On the green grass neath it spread.
Not hid from sight and scarcely veiled.
   Was my loved seat beneath,
And still the wind around it wailed
40   I thought with softer breath,

And still the latest lingering ray
   Of sunset warmed me there,
As all the ephemerals ceased their play
   In the dimmed and dew chilled air.
45 As night closed I might hear the moan
   Of water murmuring low
Amid the stillness hushed and lone
   Past on its viewless flow.

It was a beck that far away
50   Washed many a bending tree,
Unnoticed through the busy day,
     At twilight sounding free.
I knew the valley where it flowed,
     The woods that edged its current,
55   I could recall the shady road
     That wound beside the torrent.

Tranquil the sound and sweet the thought
     Of woodland rest and shade
That saw a seaside murmur brought
60   In music from the glade.
Listening to that and feeling still
     The charm of being alone
I never thought how dim and chill
     The night was drawing on.

65   The garden all involved in gloom
     Seemed vaster than by day,
The house seemed silent as a tomb
     In outline huge and grey.
The cheering shine of firelight gleaming
70   Through the parlour window told
That while I was out in the darkness
          dreaming
     All within was bright and gold.

I never since have known such bliss
     As then came on my mind,
75   And a trace of such pure happiness
     I never again shall find.
My heart was better then than now,
     Its hopes seemed far more free,
I felt a blind but ardent glow
80   Of love for piety.

How sweetly then the strain still fell
　To Bethlehem's sacred star,
And now my heart of hearts would swell
　To those that shone afar.
85　Not long so rapt in thoughts of heaven
　　I was a child of clay
And soon by awful terrors driven
　　I almost feared to pray,

Then gloom increased; the church was nigh.
90　　Its tower with awful frown,
As I glanced upward to the sky
　　Looked like a giant down.
I thought of God and heaven no more,
　A sudden awe rushed on,
95　I wished myself by the bolted door
　　I shook as I sat alone.

I had forgotten the gloomy night
　That brooded o'er every tomb
But now with a strange and thrilling might
100　　It struck to my spirit home.
What if then from the grave were fleeting
　What the grave would again receive
To tell in the tone of a spectre's greeting
　That I had not long to live?

105　Words cannot tell of the ghastly power
　　That such thoughts then had o'er me,
I have wept when I woke in the midnight hour
　　At their grinding tyranny.
Sometimes they would come in the sunny day
110　　And haunt me unceasingly,
And no tone of pleasure could charm away
　Their nameless misery.

The books that I read all caught the tone
   Of ghostly and spectral dread,
115 And their tales would come o'er me again alone
   At night on my sleepless bed.
I read of a wizard who suffering died
   In a hut on a desert moor
On a winter's night when the hollow wind sighed
120   Through the chinks of the shuddering door.

And none but a little lonely child
   To watch his release was there,
And the sound of his ravings so strange and
     wild
   Was more than that child could bear
125 But it did not faint, it stood sick and pale
   Waiting the old man's death,
And there sounded (so ran the awful tale)
   A trump o'er the desolate heath.

And the boy as he looked to the cottage door
130   Saw it shaken and opened slow,
While a dark shade fell on the lamp-lit floor
   And he heard a sudden low.
Something passed him, a bodiless shade,
   Something stood by the bed,
135 A sign to the starkened corpse was made
   And up rose the sheeted dead.

They went, they passed like a waft of the wind
   Silent and viewless and sweeping,
And dread o'er the watcher came dizzy and blind
140   And stretched him in trance and in sleeping.
There was more of the tale, but even now
   A touch of the ancient feeling
Checked the tide of memory's flow
   With its influence cold and chilling.

145 I read of a man who just at even
    When the sun declined on high
Saw by the dying light of heaven
    His own wraith standing by.
And before another sun had brightened
150   The wood on the blue beck's verge
With his cold cheek blanched and his mute lip
        tightened
He was sleeping beneath the surge.

I read of an old man whose only daughter
    Was taken to fairy land,
155 And he used to wander along by the water
    On the beach of silver sand
And through many an endless summer's day
    Seeking her wind-bleached bones
In his dotage gathering pebbles of clay
160   From the mossy and sheltered stones,

Or the relics of lambs who years ago
    Had died of some April storm,
Sunk in the curling drifts of snow
    That untimely tempests form.
165 I read of a city that smit by the plague
    Where thousands died by the day,
And the horror I felt so strange and vague
    It was vain to chase away.

Such were my dreams in infancy.
170   I have other visions now
Which touch not the blood so painfully,
    But yet fever the blood in its flow.
When no eye is on me and all is still,
    I yet cannot feel alone;
175 When no voice speaks, yet the ear will thrill
    To a sudden and [—] tone.

When I sit in a quiet and cheerful room
   Watching the firelight play,
My thoughts will wander far from home
180   A thousand miles away.

I see an ancient and stately hall,
   I stand in the sun at its door,
And feel the soft summer shadows fall
   From the foliage that veils it o'er.

185   I step within and a vast saloon
   Lifts its vast dome for me,
Shewing from radiant skylight's dawn
   The day's resplendency.

And glorious flowers are blushing through
190   Each sash in crimson bloom,
And winds as sweet as ever blew
   Play round the royal room.

All mute and still in solitude
   Watched only by the skies
195   Where pours the sun his radiant flood
   A youthful lady lies.

And dreams she of Norwegian seas,
   The dread, the wild, the dark,
And thinks she how this balmy breeze
200   May speed the pirate's bark.
And dreads she lest the Arctic wave
   Congealed and clear and green
Has given her sire a glassy grave
   In its shrine of ice serene.

205   But she lifts her eyes and she sees around
   The painted and splendid hall,
For there flashes life through those breaths of sound
   From the forms that glow on that wall.

Glorious heads from the golden frames
210   Bend with a dreamlike smile,
Parting with snowy hand the gleams
     Of their lustrous hair awhile.

The teeth of pearl through the lips of rose
     Archly but stilly shew
215   Nothing that coral mouth can close
     Which has smiled through centuries
          so.
Glimpses of English scenery
     Northumbrian hills and halls,
And glorious plains of Italy
220   Shine on the magic walls.

And chevaliers of old English days,
     Lords of the Percy race,
With bold dark eyes of passion gaze
     On that youthful lady's face.
225   Her thoughts are changed. See her start.
     Another feeling stirs,
A longing for some kindred heart
     To blend its fire with hers.

Now dreams she that the whispering trees
230   Which heard that dome above
Reveal her future destinies
     And tell her time of love.
A hundred shadowy oracles
     Around the windows moan.
235   Is bliss the theme of that prophecy
     Which comes with so wild a tone?
We'll leave her to her haunted dreams.
     I speak not what befel.
How flowed with her life's changeful
        streams
240   I may not, dare not tell.

'Tis all delusion—yet again
   The curtain falls and shows
Another scene, as bright, as vain
   That too must coldly close.
245 'Tis all delusion, still once more
   The glancing lightning glows,
And brighter than the flash before
   Its fitful glory throws.

Succeeding fast and faster still
250   Scenes that no word can give
And gathering strength from every
     thrill
   They stir, they breathe, they live.
They live! They gather round in bands,
   They speak, I hear the tone,
255 The earnest look, the beckoning hands,
   And now I am alone.

Alone! There passed a noble line
   Alone! There thronged a race.
I saw a kindred likeness shine
260   In every haughty face.
I know their deeds, I know their fame,
   The legends wild that grace
Each ancient house, around each name
   Their mystic vigils trace.

265 I know their parks, their halls, their
     towers
   The sweet lands where they shine.
The track that leads through bowers
   To each proud gate is mine.
I've seen the dark and silent aisles
270   Where all their dead repose,
And the cold white memorial piles
   That tell their lofty woes.

The saint in stone for them must mourn,
　　The marble angel pray
275　When their proud sons and sins return
　　To man's primeval clay.
Return they must, no power can save
　　Their noblest, fairest, best.
'Tis doomed, the chill and sunless
　　　　grave
280　At last must be their rest.

They come again, such glorious forms
　　Such brows and eyes divine;
The heart exalts, the life-blood warms
　　To see, to feel their shine.
285　Oh, stay! Oh, fix! Oh, start to life,
　　Flash out reality
Methinks a strange commingling strife
　　Of dream and truth I see.

A sound of breath, making a hum
290　　Stirs the great silent band.
Some vanish, then again they come,
　　And brighter, taller stand.
Some in wide waving rich array
　　Sweep through the sterner lines,
295　And who are these? But, lo, away
　　They fade, the dream declines.

Dim the bright curls, bloodless the
　　　　cheeks,
　　Rayless the radiant eyes.
They fade like the last languid strokes
300　　Of day in twilight skies.
Even that head with awful brow,
　　Bare, cold, and white as stone,
Whose keen blue eagle eye but now
　　Flashed more than life has gone.

305 Even that Grecian bust whose glance
        From marble eyelids showed
    Promethean fire had lit the trance
        Of sculptured still repose,
    Even that pure ideal form
310   Just smiled, then passed away.
    No star dissevering clouds of storm
        Ee'r shot so brief a ray.

    Even that face which turned aside
        And shewed its high profile
315 With all the lofty lines of pride
        That western woods reveal,
    Even that full-length form which
            bowed
        Half backward in the throng
    Yet rose from the receding crowd
320   So light, so clear and strong,
    Held forth his hand which as it waved
        Showed a gleamy shine of rings,
    A flash of crimson jewels graved
        With the crests and crowns of kings.

325 Even he is gone, and all are gone,
        And wakening Reason cries
    'Thy dream is like a wild bird flown
        To summer climes and skies'.
    'Twill fitfully return again,
330   As fitfully will go.
    Each joy has its attendant pain,
        Each bliss its following woe.

    And if thou hast the solace felt
        Of Fancy's pictured play,
335 Bewail not when her visions melt,
        Like morning mists away.

Is it not well that thou canst call
   Her hallowing scenes to thee,
When haply in thy spirit all
340   Sinks chill and hopelessly.

Is it not well when severed far
   From those thou lovest to see.
That she has hung her golden star
   O'er alien hill and tree.
345 Remember those sweet evenings when
   Behind the sun's farewell
A gentle light rose up again
   And round thee calmly fell.

Remember how she sanctified
350   The moon ascending slow
And silvering pure and pale and wide
   The dewy field below.
And if it chanced, as oft has been,
   That music wandered by,
355 And from the grove of aspens green
   Stole up and sought the sky,

What hast thou felt? What soothing gush
   Of full unbroken thought?
And by the breezeless evening's hush
360   What glorious spells were wrought?
Seemed it not then that all the West
   Spread round thee in that night?
Seemed not that moon boding pure and
    blest
   Her own and her holiest light?

365 Remember those grey steps of stone
   Beneath that bowery tree
With wild green glittering ivy grown
   Around luxuriantly.

Remember how reclining there
370   One evening thou dids't see
A little dark haired child draw near
     And lie down silently.
He laid his cheek on the clustering flowers
     That grew there sweet and soft,
375   And he lifted his head to the pile of towers
     Whose dark heads frowned aloft.

And he listened to the ceaseless moan
     Of a deep stream past him flowing
And, as that child lay there alone,
380   How his little heart was glowing,
Glowing with thoughts he could not tell
     That the countless stars inspired,
And the dim night and the river's swell
     With higher beauty fired.

385   He rose up through the wild briar sprays
     Of the coppice o'er him waving.
His dark eyes looked with eager gaze
     On the stream Fort Adrian laving,
A mighty stream, broad, blue and deep,
390   Its waves in the clear sky melted.
Scarce through the gloom was seen the sweep
     Of walls where its flow they belted.

Yet he thinks he sees the far-off shine
     Of lights from his father's dwelling,
395   Where the terraced front of his halls recline
     On the river's azure swelling.

And he longs for the wing of a bird to seek
     That home o'er the rolling river.
Fain would that child repose his cheek
400   On the breast that shall greet him never,

Doomed erelong to feel the sleep
  Of a cloudy death come o'er him,
Far from the eye that shall darkly weep
  When no tear can e'er restore him,
405 Doomed on a cold and gloomy heath,
  In the arms of a noble mourner,
To breath his last and struggling breath
  On the heart of the gallant Warner.

From a stormy midnight's gloom
410   In a stormier midnight dying
The flower that showed too fair a
    bloom
  Trampled and crushed is lying.
The marble slab that Warner laid
  Above his relics telling
415 Who lies beneath and mid the shade
  Of wild moors round him swelling.
And the motto on the headstone gives
  That faith which will not perish,
'I know that my redeemer lives',
420   A blessed hope to cherish.

Dreamer, awake and close the strain.
  A summons has been spoken,
'Thou must depart', so break the chain,
  And leave the bright links broken.
425 The morn is up, then come away,
  Let dreams of night be banished.
The task, the toil, the hum of day
  Draws nigh and rest is vanished,
Haste to the field and, when the heat
430   Of afternoon is burning,
Oh, cheer thee with the prospect sweet
  Of eve again returning.

BUT once again, but once again
   I'll bid the strings awake.
Just one more strain, just one more strain
   For ancient friendship's sake

5 We must part, we must part,
   But, comrades, drop no tear.
There's a warm nook still in every heart
   To keep each image dear.

One talisman, one magic spell
10   Is sure where 'er we be,
And what will hold the prize so well
   As deathless memory.

Not far we go! Not far we go!
   And time fleets fast away,
15 And none can stop a torrent's flow,
   So none its course can stay.

Now hollow wind and movement cease,
   And let thy pibroch die.
The voice that should speak hope and peace
20   Will sadden to thy sigh.

Now flickering flame, now dying fire
   More bright, more warmly glow.
As embers quench, as sparks expire
   So sinks my song to woe.

25 There trim the lamp, there rouse the light,
   Now high their fed beams burn.
But who can whisper to the night
   'O veiled one, cease to mourn'?

From the lone moor descends that strain,
30   From glen and heathery hill,
And as I hear its voice again
    I scarce can wish it still.

The harp of heaven is turned aright,
    Now free its music flows;
35 With what a wild and wondrous might
    That sudden swell arose.

That is the touch, that is the tone,
    The old, the hallowed sound.
O, sorrowing minstrel, breathe alone
40   Thy requiem sweet, profound.

When I'm away its memory
    My heart of hearts will thrill.
'Tis the rush of sound that fills the sky
    Above my native hill.

45 'Tis the wakener of a hundred dreams
    With joy, with glory fraught.
'Tis the loosener of a thousand streams
    Of poetry, of thought.

And oft when breathes the lonely night
50   No other voice but thine.
My soul delivered to thy might
    Shall fleet to realms divine.

When fitfully thy blasts are telling
    That stars their lustre veil
55 In clouds whose misty vapours swelling
    Below the bright worlds sail,

Then on thy wings whose waft is thunder
    Then on thy wings I'll lean,
And from that strange home torn asunder
60   Wrapt in thy cloudy screen

I'll travel away, far away,
Where the dream in the darkness lies shrouded
and grey.
Time shall not chain me,
Place not restrain me,
65 Mind is not matter, soul is not clay.

And there I'll meet you, comrades,
And we'll shake hands again,
Though twenty miles between us lie
Of night and wind and rain.

70 But alas! alas! I cannot hope,
My anchor sinks away,
And riven from its faithless prop
My ship drifts out to sea.

'Tis bitterness to leave you all,
75 My heart is bound to home.
I cannot drink the cup of gall,
I was not made to roam.

I know I shall again return,
But life meantime is failing.
80 The lamp that may not always burn
Its transient light is paling.

All the sweet time of spring will be
An hour of dreamless sleeping,
A blank and vacancy to thee
85 Dark with the mists of weeping.

I will not hold those strangers dear
With whom I dwell unwilling.
My thoughts all rest on those who hear
This farewell wild and thrilling.

90   I have no subtle surface love,
      My heart's not wide nor roomy.
    No stray affection forth may rove
      Bound in exclusion gloomy.

    Just us and those we've famed in dreams,
95   Our own divine creations,
    These are my soul's unmingled themes;
      I scorn the alien nations.
    Shake hands, dark Percy! Breathe and live
      Shalt thou in nothing perish?
100   No, flesh and life and soul I'll give
      And faithfully in thee believe
    And still thy memory cherish.

    Shake hands, Zenobia, glorious form.
      Art thou a vapour, lady,
105   A rainbow traced upon the storm,
      Where the clouds lie black and shady?
    Is thy pirate husband but a name?
      Is the dust near a vision?
    Is the red Rover's fearful fame,
110   The deeps o'er which it went and came,
    Food for the world's derision?

    Are the great houses of the west
      The high clansmen of the north
    Nothing but thoughts in language dressed
115   Breathed in bright words forth?

    Must their stern words and all the glory
      Of their old and noble homes
    Pass off in mystery dim and hoary
      Like an old song or magic story,
120   Like the voice of their old domes
    Where the echo to the sound replies
      Then all in utter silence dies?

And the star I saw intensely burning
  Through the black but splendid night
125 Whose beams into itself returning
  Decked the mid heaven's solemn mourning
    With self conceived light,

Blending in red—as the sun
  But deepening only the blue gleam
130 In which a white clear orb it shone
    A gem upon the brow of doom,

I mean Zamorna! Do not say
  I speak in egotism now.
This is our last, our farewell day,
135   So here's my open unmasked brow.

I owe him something. He has held
  A lofty burning lamp to me,
Whose rays surrounding darkness quell
    And shewed he wanders, shadow free

140 And he has been a mortal king
  That ruled my thoughts right regally
And he has given a steady spring
    To what I had of poetry.

I've heard his accents sweet and stern
145   Speak words of kindled wrath to me,
When dead as dust in funeral urn
    Sank every note of melody.
And I was forced to wake again
The silent song, the slumbering strain.

150 He's moved the principle of life
  Through all I've written or sung or said,
The war-song routing to the strife,
    The life-wind wakening up the dead.

He's not the temple, but the God,
155 The idol in his marble shrine.
Our grand dream is his wide abode
 And there for me he dwells divine.

I can walk in the structure vast
 Awhile and never think of him;
160 Only at times there wanders past
 A consciousness all strange and dim
That it was his shrined divinity
Which brought me there to bow the knee.

Others as mighty rest around,
165 The great Pantheon has many a God.
But to his altar I am bound.
 For him the consecrated ground
My pilgrim steps have trod.

At times by Percy's pedestal
170 More deeply awed I worship low,
But grovelling in the dust I fall
 Where Adrian's shrine lamps dazzling glow.

It is his light, it is his star
 That leads me on resistlessly,
175 Ascending high or wandering far
 Or diving deep in sullen sea.

Now plunged amid the wild green waves
 Where storms and storm-lashed waters war
Now standing where the breaker raves
180 In wrath against the rocky bar.

Still the revolving beacon throws
 Its glory o'er the brightening sea
Whose dark floor far off burns and glows
 While reddened billows part and close.

185 Upon its surface changefully
    Gleaming and flickering liquidly.

    And art thou nothing, sea-light high;
    And thou, sublime divinity?
    Shake hands, Zamorna! God or man
190 And though thou beest incarnalined
    I vow by blessing, swear by ban
    Thy spirit is in bright flesh shrined.

    Somewhere, somewhere, all the dream
    Lives, breathes in glory. That I know
195 I feel its truth in sudden gleam
    Flashing around me, Lord, and thou,
    Thou and thy consort, living pair,
    Are not a breath of morning mist
    Not sparks that dart from reason's whirl
200 When vexed by the mind's unrest.

    Alnwick and solemn Mornington!
    And Grassmere Grange and Percy Hall!
    Your lattices now feel that sun
    Through their clear panes of crystal fall.
205 Its pallid gold on many a wall
    Under your roofs rests placidly.
    Those airs and breezes whispering call
    Answers from ancient grove and tree,
    Where in far years, in times gone by,
210 In summer evenings passed away,
    Your ancestors walked pensively
    Watching the close of twilight grey,
    Where, Duchess, thy fair mother strayed
    Dying so lone before the time
215 When the last chord of music played,
    Woodchurch called out the passing chime.
    Often the glory of that sun
    Burned on that land whose beauty none

In words may say unspeakable,
220 And round the heath couched lady fell
And, Alderwood, the summer's heat
Is in thy woods, among thy towers,
Languidly lingering, soft and sweet
Spawned by wild and hidden flowers.
225 That silver moon shone long ago
On the old porch with roses veiled
Where listening to the Wansbeck's flow
That through the twilight, falling slow
    Mournfully wailed,
230 Sat Victorine, the lily bright
Of sunset's sheet of stormy light,
    Her lonely beauty pale and still,
Pensive and saddening evermore.
What thoughts, what strains her reason felt
235 As she sits by the Norman door
With flowers and ivy shadowing o'er
And golden stars and deep blue skies
Above and stretching on before
Tall stirless trees in alley's rises
240   Deepening and deepening still,
A wood in June at even tide,
The plumy foliage all in pride
    While plants its green recesses fill
That scent each glade from side to side
245   And summer eve that breathes no chill
Is softly darkening far and wide.
Victorine, thou art not there.
With thee the leaf of life is sere
    Though in its early spring.
250 She thinks of academe's groves
Far off and waving solemnly
    Over the blue and quiet sea
Where the young Southern roves,
And watches haply now the gloom
255 Gathering on that vast marble tomb

On whose bright surface shining lies
The mirrored moon and starry skies
Lightening the high and stately towers
That soar above their classic bowers
260 And in that distant island-home
At midnight shed light o'er the foam.

Sadly the Highland baroness
Looks on that scene of awful bliss.
In kindling, vivid thought she sees
265 Lord Douro lean against the trees.
As he looks down on the mighty deep
Through all its green realms hushed in sleep
She sees his hand patrician white
Circling the bough o'er which he bends.
270 Fain would she touch those fingers white
Flashing with many a gem of light.
A touch remembrance lends
To shew her how in other times
In distant lands, in sterner climes
275 By the tall stranger's side
She wandered oft at eventide.
While that warm hand would warmly press
His own fair northern baroness
While poured his lips seductively
280 Their tones of foreign melody
And now the very agony
Of longing love thrills through her heart.
Her eyes are gazing piercingly
Where those high elms in vista part.
285 O heaven, could she, might she see
Through the leaf-chequered moonlight gliding
That form that in her memory
Is firmly even in pain abiding,
The slender boy with soft dark eyes
290 And curls upon his neck descending
Shading and where mingled lies

Sweetness and untold passion blending
And marble beauty finely wrought
Like artist's dream or sculpture wrought.

295 To hear his clear voice speak her name
With that strange smile she knew so well
'Helen', even thus the accent came.
She started, so distinct it fell
As she had heard it in the hall,
300 When suddenly he stood beside her
And when she trembled at the call
How gently would he feign to chide her.

She rose, the ivy gently waving,
   Stirred to the rustling of her dress,
305 And Wansbeck moaned its green banks laving;
   All else was utter voicelessness.
Douro six hundred miles away
Was gazing on the moonlight main
And thinking, as alone he lay,
310 Of her he ne'er should see again.
Little he dreams her lonely grave
Should greet him when he crossed the wave.
That is enough, too much; 'tis over
Helen is dead, still lives her lover
315 But no more now of the wondrous dream.
My time is pleasant holiday.
It faded like a sunny beam,
And I must here no longer stay.
May we all meet in joy again,
320 And then I'll sing a lighter strain.
This evening hear the solemn knell
'Farewell, and yet again farewell!'

AND not alone she seems she from pillared halls
To look forth on the night—so to note the sky
Bending above Fidena's moon-tipt walls
And mirrored in the flood that wanders by,
5   But where beside her in the chamber falls
The window's clear reflection broad and high
She deems another stands. That half-checked [—]
Now tells of wakened thought that know not [—]

A SINGLE word so seen at such a time
Opens a hundred corridors in the heart,
And there from every land and shore and clime
Memory has stored her gathered wealth apart.

5   A single word so soon will bring
Oppression to the heart
So waked, regrets

AND few have felt the avenging steel
Gentle [?] as now its blade I feel.

Power and glory, where are ye far?
Kindle your watchfires by this star,
5   Light there along its stormy steep.
Your lamps are quenched, your spirits sleep.
O wake each beacon, powers divine,
I've knelt before your Moloch shrine
And ever, though tost on Sorrow's wave,
10   Yet still I kneel, although the grave
Of Beauty's best and brightest daughter
Lies under this wild waste of water.

Am I like Saul? These lines of gloom
Come to me, as they came to him
15   Stealing from life its sunny bloom
And spreading shadows drear and dim.
But music would not charm me now;
Its lightest airs, its freest flow,
Its wildest swell, its softest strain
20   Would stir no life-pulse, thrill no vein.
I'll turn then to those happy hours,
When childhood plucked its earliest flowers,
Roaming the life-long summer day,
When bright they grew on bank and brae
25   But vainly; even in infancy
Life had its darkling spots for me
And times would come when sudden fell
A sadness, I knew not whence or how
[—] would all unbidden swell
30   [—] useless sorrow cloud my brow.

I NEVER sought my mother's face
    To tell my grief and make my moan,
But crept away to some lone place
    And sat until the cloud was gone.

5   But it would give so strange a tone
    Even to things inanimate.
Yes, all that then I looked upon
    Took the dark boding hue of fate.

And if I turned some storied page
10   So wild an air over it grew
That scarce in youth's increasing age
    Dared I the feeling to renew.
'Twas like a foretaste from the tomb,
    A warning voice to call me home.

15 In that mood I have watched the sun
    Go down upon my sire's domain,
Its long day's course of glory done,
    Its bower of roses spread again,
And, oh, how solemn seemed the wane;
20   Solemn—that word can never tell
The deadly sense of mental pain
    That wrung me as the evening-bell
Tolled out each castle sentinel.

And I beheld them measure slow
25   Their walk upon the flags below,
And heard them whistle clear and shrill
    My own wild woodland melodies,
The soft sweet plaintive airs that thrill
    Through all the land of lakes and [—]
30 And knew that they with [—]
      could gaze

I THOUGHT in my childhood how pleasant
      would be
The day when Life opened its portals for me,
When I should leave home, and go wandering away
Out into sunshine and forth into day
5 Shut in from the world serried [?] woods of the west
Silent and lonely and hidden from view.

I would sit in a chamber for hours alone.

I remember the time when years to come
    Seemed brighter than those gone by,
10 When I longed for my native woods and house
    Over the wide world to fly.

My native woods seemed a pleasant spot
   Sacred to calm and rest,
But all who lived there were soon forgot;
15   They never saw a guest.

Wild fruits and flowers and flocks of birds,
   And green grass through the year,
And deer in the park in graceful herds,
   But nothing else came there.

20 Life and marriage I have known,
   Things I dreamed of long ago.

LADY-BIRD! lady-bird! fly away home,
   Night is approaching and sunset is come,
The herons are flown to their trees by the Hall,
Felt but unseen the damp dew-drops fall.
5 This is the close of a still summer day.
Lady-bird! lady-bird, haste, fly away.

  The grand old Hall is wrapped in shade,
  The woodland park around it spread
  In gathering gloom in every glade.
10 This is the moment, this the hour
  To feel Romance in all her power.
  Is there not something in a name,
  In noble blood and ancient fame,
  Something in that ancestral pride
15 Which brings the memory of the dead
  Sailing adown time's hoary tide
  With sacred halos round it shed,
  Halos, oh far too bright to shine
  Round aught whose home is still below?
20 The starlight thoughts, the dreams divine
  From man's creative soul that flow

And stream upon the idols bright
He forms through all his earthly way
As if grown weary of the light
25   That smiles upon his own dull clay,
That clay he feels will not for ever
Cumber the spirit that would soar
To that deep and swelling river
Which bears the life-tree on its shore.
30   And he the hour would still foresee.
That sets his inward angel free.

        This Hall and park might wake such dreams.
They speak of pride of ancestry.
Yes every fading ray which gleams
35   On antique roof and hoary tree
Shews in gnarled bough and mossy slate
The grand remains of ancient state.

And thinks he of Patrician pride,
    He who sits lonely there
40   Where oaks and elms spread dark and wide
    Their huge arms in the air?

He wanders in the world of thought,
    He's left this world behind,
On that high brow are clearly wrought
45   A thousand dreams of mind.

And are they dreams of bliss or bale
    Of happiness or woe?
Methinks that face is all too pale
    For pleasure's rosy glow.

50   Methinks the mellowing haze of years
    Is o'er that tall form spread,
And time has poured her smiles and tears
    Full freely round that head.

He must have once been beautiful;
55   The relics still remain,
Though wasted sore with sorrow
    And darkened much with pain.

At morn he sought this lone retreat
    When the sun first crowned the hill,
60 And now the twilight calm and sweet
    Beholds him lingering still.

Yet not to reveries of woe
Clings Percy's wounded spirit so.
Scarce bound by its worn chains of
    clay
65 The soul has almost soared away
Lightened and soothed insensibly
By the lone home of wind and tree,
Where now his mental broodings
    dwell.
Vainly would man divine or tell
70 His upward look—his earnest eyes
Seem gazing ev'n beyond the skies.
Who calls him back to earth again
Will bring a wild revulse of pain,
And so thought he who glided now
75 With step as light as falling snow
Forth from the bowery arch of trees
That whispered in the gloaming breeze.
That step he might have used before
When stealing on to lady's bower
80 Even at the same still twilight hour,
For the moon now beaming mild above
Shewed him a son of war and love.
His eye was full of that sinful fire
Which oft unhallowed passions light,
85 It spoke of quickly kindled ire,
Of love too warm and wild and bright,

Bright but yet sullied, love which could never
Bring good in a rising, leave peace in decline;
Woe to the gifted, crime to the Giver,
90   Wherever reposed all the light of its shine.
Beauty had lavished her treasures upon him,
Youth's early sunshine was poured on his brow,
Alas that the magic of sin should have won him,
But he is her slave and her chained victim now.

95   Now from his curled and shining hair
Circling the brow of marble fair
His dark keen eyes on Percy gaze
With stern and yet repenting rays.
Sometimes they shimmer through the haze
100   Of sadly gushing tears,
And then a sudden flash of flame
Speaking wild feelings none could tame
        The dim suffusion clears.

Young savage! How he bends above
105   The object of his wrath and love,
How tenderly his fingers press
The hand that shrinks from their caress,
And from his lips in Percy's ear
Flow tones his blood congeals to hear.
110   Those tones were softer than the moan
Of echo when the sound is flown
And sweeter than a flute's reply
To skylark's song or wild wind's sigh.
Yet Percy heard them as they fell
115   Like the dull toll of a passing bell.
Sternly they summoned him back again
To a dark world of woe and pain.
The blood from his visage fell away
And left it as pallid as coffined clay.
120   Like clouds the charmed visions broke.
From his day-long dream at once he woke,

He woke to feel and see at his side
The very man who dared to roll
Marah's unsounded briny tide
125 Over the Eden of his soul,
Who dared to pluck his last fair flower
To quench his last star's cheering beam,
The last sweet drop of bliss to sour
That mingled with his Being's stream.

130 Up rose he and stretched forth his hand
In mingled menace and command.
With voice subdued and steady look
Thus to the man of sin he spoke,
'What brought you here? I called you not,
135 You've tracked me to a lonely spot.
Are you a Hawk to follow the prey
When mangled it flutters feebly away?
A sleuth-hound to track the deer by his
                  blood
When wounded he wins to the darkest
                  wood,
140 There if he can to die alone,
Unsought by the archer whose shaft has
                  flown
So right and true to its living mark
That it quenches even now the vital spark?

Zamorna, is this nobly done
145 To triumph o'er your Consort's sire?
Gladly to see his gory sun
Quench in the sea of tears its fire?

But haply you have news to tell,
Tidings that yet may cheer me well.
150 You've crushed at last my rose's bloom
And scattered its leaves on her mother's
                  tomb.

For its faded buds all ready lie
To deck my coffin when I die.
Bring them here—'twill not be long,
155   'Tis the last line of the woeful song;

And these final and dying words are sung
To the discord of lute-strings all unstrung.
O Adrian! do not harshly sweep
The chords that are quivering to voiceless sleep.'

160   'No! but I'd string them once more to a sound
That should startle the nations that rest around.
I'd call forth the glorious chorus again
Which flooded the earth with a bloody main.

Have I crushed you, Percy? I'd raise once more
165   The beacon-light on the rocky shore.
Percy, my love is so true and deep,
That though kingdoms should wail and worlds
        should weep
I'd fling the brand in the hissing sea,
The brand that must burn unquenchably.

170   Your rose is mine; when the sweet leaves fade,
They must be the chaplet to wreathe my head,
The blossoms to deck my home with the dead.

I repent not—that which my hand has done
Is as fixed as the orb of the burning sun;
175   But I swear by Heaven and the mighty sea
That, wherever I wander, my heart is with thee.

Bitterly, deeply, I've drunk of thy woe;
When thy stream was troubled, did mine calmly
        flow?
And yet I repent not: I'd crush thee again
180   If our vessels sailed adverse on life's stormy main.

But listen! The earth is our campaign of war,
Her children are rank, and her kingdoms spread far.
Who shall say "Hah!" to the mingling star?
Is there not havoc and carnage for thee
185   Unless thou couchest thy lance at me?

The heart in my bosom beats high at the thought
Of the deeds which by blended strength may be
                    wrought.
Then might thy Mary bloom blissfully still:
This hand should ne'er work her sorrow or ill.

190   No fear of grief in her bright eyes should quiver:
I'd love her and guard her for ever and ever.
What! shall Zamorna go down to the dead
With blood on his hand that he wept to have shed?

What! shall they carve on his tomb with the sword:
"The slayer of Percy, the scourge of the Lord?".'

Bright flashed the fire in the young duke's eye
    As he spoke in the tones of the trumpet swelling;
Then he stood still and watched earnestly
    How these tones were on Percy's spirit telling.

200   Nothing was heard but his quick short breath,
    And his fiery heart aroused panting;
The dark wood lay as hushed as death:
    Nor hum, nor murmur its valley haunting.

Then the low voice of Percy woke,
205   And thus in strange reponse he spoke.

.   .   .   .

OTHAT thy own loved son, thy noblest born,
　Should rise that tranquil vision to dispel,
And fresh and sparkling in his glorious morn
Should thunder forth to crush, destroy and quell,
5　That he should cause the trumpet strain to swell
And wring so many bosoms with its wail
And light the battle fire unquenchable,
Whose bloody glow the star of war might pale
And Sirius' burning beams with shrouding halos veil.

10　Gods of our land, withhold the radiant scourge,
Chain the young lion in his darkling den,
Hush the proud storm and soothe the wild white surge
And call us back to peace and rest again.
Let the sweet sunlight shine in each green glen
15　And light each shadowy mount with beams of peace
And still the voice that stirs the breast of men.
Cause the dread Glory of our land to cease,
And from the strong bright chain our fettered hearts
　　　release.

Now hush for evermore the minstrel's shell,
20　Lay by the flashing sword, lay by its sheath,
Let many lands moan to a burial knell
And skies grow dark above and seas beneath,
And lay the noble poet's withering wreath
With the young conqueror's o'er a regal tomb,
25　And let all flowers from rose to moorland heath
Scattered around the house of mourning bloom,
While thousands, millions weep the hero's early
　　　doom.

That were a glorious death so bright, so young.
No spot in all the lustrous orb grown dull,
30　The battle fought and gained, the rich strain sung,
The cup of honour to o'erflowing full,

The ship in harbour not a shattered hull,
But strong and swift and bounding as when first
With scarce a breeze to break the ocean's lull
35 She from her moorings with wild plunge burst,
And as she walked the waves dared storms to do
       their worst.

Think not upon the grave, the silent grave,
Think not upon the cold concealing earth.
When there are lands and lives and souls to save
40 What is a single transient mortal's worth,
Though he be noble, even of kingly, birth,
A very God for majesty and might,
In time of war and peace of woe and mirth,
The battle's guiding star, the banquet's light,
45 The worshipped of the fair, the idol of their sight?

Yet, crush remorse and quell the starting tear,
Grasp the sharp brand! look, yonder towers his crest.
Now, Patriot, rise o'er mercy, softness, fear.
Plunge to the red hilt in his noble breast,
50 Send the young Despot to his last high rest.
His heart's blood spouts, he heaves no moan, no sigh.
Now earth is by his blasted beauty prest.
Behold the radiant victor silent die,
Look on his fading brow, look on his closing eye.

55 He's with the Dead. That hand can lock no chain,
That head can wear no diadem, that tongue
Can give no mandate to his awe-struck brain.
No, all the chords of life are slacked, unstrung,
The flower is plucked, the tree to earth is flung.
60 Afric may triumph, let her drop no tear;
A hundred deaths would from his life have sprung.
He that lies powerless, voiceless, bleeding there
Held no man's life or good when classed with glory
       dear.

Bless him and leave him, seal his Royal tomb.
65 One kiss on the cold stone, one bursting sigh,
And then let darkness fold him in its gloom,
Then let corruption brood triumphantly
O'er what was once so proud, so bright, so high,
So like the imperial splendour of the sun
70 That men were dazzled as they passed him by.
But now his beauty's past, his glory gone,
He slumbers in his shroud still desolate [al]one.

WELL, the day's toils are over, with success.
    I've laboured since the morning, hand in hand
With those I love: and now our foes' distress
Seems gathering to its height; my stalwart band,
5   Desperate in purpose, cool and rock-like press
Near to their aim; before another day
We hope to smite our snared and stricken prey.

All seems in train for triumph; calm and stern
We see our clouded sun look out again;
10 Not like its summer dawn the white beams burn,
But withering chilly, still subdued by rain—
The rain of storms that pass and still return
In a dim shower sometimes, and momently
Cloud as with tears the light on land and sea.

15 Brief fits of weeping! They can ne'er subdue
The hidden yet glorious sense of victory nigh;
I feel it; all whose hearts to me are true
Feel and yet veil the impulse; still, no eye
That deep and secret consciousness may view,
20 Save that which would flash fierce with sympathy:
It is the Avenger's latest hope, and he
Waits for its full fruition—silently!

I've born too much to boast; even now I know,
While I advance to triumph, all my host
25 So sternly reckless to the conflict go
Because each charm and joy of life they've lost,
Because on their invaded thresholds grow
Grass from their children's graves, because the cost
Of their land's red redemption has been blood
30 From gallant hearts poured out in lavish flood.

Yet, oh! there is a sure and steadfast glory
In knowing that the state ascends again;
And that, when we with age are bent and hoary,
And when our children's children spring to men,
35 As we tell o'er this dark invasion's story,
How fires and war ran wild through every glen
And crowned each blue hill-top with crimson
     crest,
How then at last we found victorious rest,

And did not bow to demons, though their goad
40 With teeth of iron urged as to despair,
And though men called us rebels as they trode
Upon our yoke-bowed necks, and though the air—
The pure air of our mountains—felt the load
Of putrid plague, and corpses everywhere
45 Lay livid in our lonely homes, and tombs
Ceased to unclose in the rank churchyard's
     glooms,

For none had time to bury; if the rite
Were half-commenced, the summons of dismay,
The cry to arms, the strange appalling sight
50 Of squadrons charging, called each friend away;
And often thus, even at the dead of night,
Corpses were left alone 'midst clods of clay;
And the armed mourners hurried to repel
The whirlwind onslaught of the tribes of hell.

55 But the bare, ravaged land is swept and free:
Out of her shattered towns and blighted fields
The wind has driven the locusts; gallantly
We chased the scum before us; vengenance wields
A sword none can withstand, and as a tree
60 To the bleak autumn storm its foliage yields
So, scare resisting, the oppressor flew
As our tornado coming nearer drew.

Rising at once, the peasantry hemmed round
Arab and Scot retreating; hearths were quenched
65 And homes deserted if some hut was found
To yield a moment's shelter to the drenched
And starved and ravenous fiends; on the cold ground
No glowing fire gleamed; and trodden bread
And scattered flour to greet their eyes were spread.

70 Their corpses fell like famished wolves before us
Along the winter roads, spotting the waste
Of drifted snow; vindictive joy flashed o'er us
As the grim, belted skeletons we passed.
And were we wrong? And should remorse have
torn us
75 As we beheld them in black ditches cast,
Laid under leafless hedges, pale and gaunt,
Murdered with hardships, dead with grinding want?

Should we have wept? Shades of our fathers! say.
Spirits of our dead comrades! rise and tell.
80 Angels of those whose dying relics lay
On beds of pestilence! speak where ye dwell;
Should we have wept? Some in your early day,
The plague cut down: like shrunken flowers ye fell,
And withered hopeless in a land of slaves,
85 And knew that tyrants would tread o'er your
graves.

By the last sun ye saw, by the wild weeping
That closed your early pilgrimage in gloom,
By the unhallowed graves where, darkly sleeping,
You lie forgetful of the sorrowing home
90   That waits your long departure, vain the sweeping
Of the sweet native breezes o'er your tomb,
Icy and mute; you never can return,
But bow from Heaven, and hark what we have
      sworn.

Oh, by your memories, martyrs, there shall be
95   Bloody reprisal for your fearful fate:
My arm is strung with giant energy,
By the convulsing thought that all's too late.
New strength springs from that stinging agony,
And firmer resolutions, hotter hate,
100   Weep for the pangs of fiends. By God! by Heaven!
I'd kill the man who wept for that unshriven!

I am alone; it is the dead of night;
I am not gone to rest, because my mind
Is too much raised for sleep: the silent light
105   Of the dim taper streams its unseen wind,
And quite as voiceless, on the hearth, burns bright
The ruddy ember; now no ear could find
A sound, however faint, to break the lull
Of which the shadowy realm of dreams is full.

110   So, then, I've time to think of each event
That hath befallen of late to all below;
I've leisure to recall the sudden rent
That tore my heart a few short weeks ago.
'Twas at an Inn in Calais, and the faint
115   Cold sense of death, brought by that deadly blow,
Whitened my cheek and glazed my eyes awhile:
Darkness o'erswept the noon's soft sunny smile.

In a fair foreign land, with strangers round,
Reading a journal of my native West
120 Rung from the black-edged funeral-page the sound
Expected and yet dreaded: there the crest,
The arms, the name, were blazoned, and the ground
Marked where the corpse should lie, and all exprest
Even to the grim procession, hearse and pall,
125 The grave, the monument to cover all!

I went out sick and dizzy to the street;
The air revived me; something inward said:
'Tis but thine own work finished; time is fleet,
And early has the gloomy task been sped;
130 Yet still 'tis thy behest; now firmly meet
Its prompt fulfilment, turn thee from the dead
And go on prospering; thy way is free,
And they are punished, crushed, that thwarted
   thee.

Amongst the multitudes of thoughts that came
135 Rolling upon me, I remembered well
My feelings some months, since, before this aim
Of death was ripe, when it began to swell
And form within my breast, and like a dream
The keen and reeking recollections fell,
140 How I then watched my prey, and slowly wrought
My mind to union with the awful thought.

Nothing was bodied forth distinctly then:
I was too frantic; but at this lone hour
The bitter recollection comes again
145 Of many a night I spent within her bower;
Of all the musings that came o'er me when
Gently asleep beside me lay my flower
Blushing in blissful dreams, and pressing nigher
To the dark breast then filled with [—] fire.

150 Watching her thus, through many a sleepless night,
I never utterly resolved to slay;
I could not, when all young and soft and bright,
Trusting, adoring me, in dreams she lay,
Her fair cheek pillowed on the locks of light
155 That gleamed upon her delicate array
Veiling with gold her neck and shoulders white,
And varying with their rich and silken flow
Her forehead's smooth expanse of stainless snow.

Sometimes in sleep she'd put her hand on mine,
160 And fold it in her slight and fairy clasp,
As if my fatal thoughts she could divine;
And, as in terror she would faintly gasp,
And nearer, closer, all around me twine,
Holding me with an anxious, jealous grasp;
165 And when I woke and cheered her she would say
She dreamt I cast her scornfully away.

Often at night, after a long day spent
In hearing of her father's mad designs,
In toilsomely reclaiming projects bent
170 By his perverseness out of the set lines
I'd furrowed in the future, all I meant
With deepest thought to execute, the mines
I'd laid most carefully effaced and sprung,
And all that loved me by his insults stung;

175 Harrassed by his malignity so cold
And unprovoked and bitter, I've come home,
And full of stricken thoughts I never told,
Bearing upon my brow my spirit's gloom,
Entered the atmosphere of aerial gold,
180 Of light and fragrance in my lady's room,
And pressing her, unable to reply
To the warm wish of her saluting eye.

'Twas strange, but Mary never seemed to dread,
Or shun me in my ireful mood; she'd steal
185 Silently to my side and droop her head
And rest it on my knee, and gently kneel
Down at my feet, and then her raised glance said:
'Adrian, I do not fear, though I can feel
Your gaze is stern and dark; but I can brook
190 Even ferocity in that fixed look.'

Sometimes her lips as well as eyes would say:
'If you are here I'm happy, though in wrath;
But, when you keep through the long night away,
Repose, existence, luxury, I loathe.
195 Your presence forms the bright, the cheering ray
That makes life glorious. Adrian, what can
          soothe
Your ruffled mind? Tell me, and I will try
To light the gloom of that denouncing eye.'

'Trouble yourself no more with me,' I said
200 The last time she spoke thus; 'when I took you
Into my bosom, Mary, though your head
Was haloed with the lustre beauty threw,
And mind and youth and glowing feeling shed,
Yet then I swore that if your father drew
205 His hand from mine, I'd give him back his gift,
Of happiness and hope and fame bereft.'

Percy, the demon! playing with the feeling
Of an enthusiast's heart, he shall be paid
For his deceit, for his cold treacherous dealing,
210 In miseries keen as those himself has made,
Wounds festered deep beyond the power of healing;
My part in the great game is also played:
I've had his daughter, loved her, made her mine,
And now the bright deposit I'll resign.

215 'Fair love! before his sight consumed away;
    Reproach him with your dying gaze, my Mary;
    It is his fault; I love you each fresh day
    Intenslier than the last: I never weary
    Of gazing on that young pale face whose ray
220 Of deep, warm, anxious ardour, dashed with dreary
    Poetic melancholy, charms me more
    Than all the bloom which other eyes adore.'

    'You love me, yet you'll kill me!' she said, starting,
    While an electric thrill and passion woke
225 In all her veins, and wild reproaches darting
    From her dark eyes, in native heat she broke
    Fully upon me, all the calm departing
    And classic grace, as if the sudden stroke
    Had changed her nature, her most perfect form
230 Shaken, dilated, trembling in the storm.

    Anger and grief and most impassioned love
    Gathered upon her cheek in burning blushes,
    One with the other struggling, warning strove,
    And each by turn prevailed in whelming gushes;
235 She flashed a frantic glance to Heaven above;
    She called me cruel as the fiend that crushes
    Its victim after snaring it in toils
    Baited with rosy flowers and golden spoils.

    'Why have you chained me to you, Adrian, by
240 Such days of bliss, such hours of sweet caressing,
    Such looks of glory, words of melody,
    Glimpses of all on earth that's worth possessing
    And now, when I must live with you or die
    Out of your sight distracted, every blessing
245 Your hand withdraws, and, all my anguish
                  scorning,
    You go and bid me hope for no returning!'

Adrian, don't leave me—' then the gushing tears
Smothered her utterance, so I tried my power
To soothe her terrors and allay her fears,
250 And feed her passion with a sunny shower
Of my accustomed spells; as the sky clears
After a summer storm, in one brief hour
Happy and blest she'd given again her charms
Trembling but yet confiding to my arms.

255 Did I think then she'd die, and that forever
The grave would hide her from me? Did I deem
That after parting I should never, never
Behold her save in some delusive dream,
That she would cross death's cold and icy river
260 Alone, without one hope, one cheering beam
Of bliss to come? All dark, all spectral, dreary:
Was this thy fate, my loved, my sainted Mary?

Will no voice answer 'No'? Will no tongue say
That still she lives and longs and waits for me?
265 That burning still, though haply in decay,
The spark of life is lingering quenchlessly?
And that again the bright awakening ray
Of passion in her pale face I may see,
And watch the fervid, lightning thoughts whose
       shine
270 Kindled each feature with a beam divine?

Again o'er Hawkscliffe's wide green wilderness
The harvest moon her boundless smile will fling;
Again the savage woods will take that dress
Of dewy leaves from the refulgent spring,
275 Darken in summer and to autumn pass,—
In their wan robes of foliage withering
September's eyes will close with dreary light
Of moon and holy stars, foretelling night.

And shall I never wander in those shades
280 Where the trees sweep the earth o'ercharged with
    plumes?
Mary! among those solemn, moonlight glades,
Are all our roamings over? Will their glooms
Parting and bending as the breezes swayed
Shadow our love no more? Like natural tombs,
285 Where sound breathed out of darkest hush, each
    grove
Of giant oaks buried and watched that love.

Others I've met by night in field and wood,
Many a burnside has been my rendezvous.
And enviously, impatiently, I've stood
290 Under the sunless sky of sombre blue,
While the encroaching gloaming o'er the flood
Crept dark and still, and gathering drops of dew
Hung on the flowers, and twilight breezes swung
Chilly and low the whispering trees among.

295 And some bright eyes are closed that once to me
Were stars of hope, and hearts that loved me well
For years have stilled their beating 'neath some tree
Waving above the mounds, where mortals dwell
After they've put on immortality;
300 But long since I have learned the pangs to quell
Their memories brought, and now again, again,
Torture is wakened by reviving pain.

It cannot be; and has she cold and dying
Been stretched alone on her forsaken bed,
305 A stormy midnight's voice her requiem crying,
And hasting on the last dark hour of dread,
With speed none could avert, and Mary lying
Conscious that death was near, her spirit led
While her soul waved its wings prepared to soar
310 Back to the days she never might see more,

The ghostly trance increasing; and above
Her thorny pillow bent her father's brow
In agony; a clouded glance of love
The lady on her sire was seen to throw—
315   Of love and strange reproach. How thought will
        rove,
How scenes we think of suddenly will glow
Present before us! Oh, I see him bending
Over his child; I watch her soul ascending

Out of her dying eyes. Now is my time:
320   All rushes on me; could I speak the feeling!
Now, Percy, whom in spite of blood and crime
I loved intensely, dark thy doom is sealing.
Am I not well avenged? Struck in her prime,
Dies thy fair daughter, her last look revealing,
325   Her last word telling—to what hand she owes
Her grave beneath this avalanche of woes.

To thine! She's gone; aye, shudder and stoop
        lower;
Speak, call her back; the winged spirit may hear;
Paramount ruler, try thy utmost power;
330   Revive thy faded hope, thy blossom sere.
Vainly; the task of the last awful hour
Is finished: now the cloud, the pang, the tear
Are thine forever. Brow and heart and eye
Shall keep till death thy daughter's legacy.

335   Different it might have been. The actual doom
Is such as I have said, and Mary's gone
Floating away in light. Grief called her home;
Her angel heard and answered; and the sun
Smiles over Alnwick Church and o'er the tomb,
340   And balmy gales come murmuring from each glade
And pastoral walk where long ago she strayed.

I must forget her. I must cease to pine
After the days, the dreams, the hopes I cherished.
In truth, I could have wished to see the shine
345 Of her clear eyes before their lustre perished,
Their sad soft beam, like the subdued decline
Of twilight parting—could I but have nourished
Her languid, wasted strength and faded bloom,
And taken her to my breast, again her home.

350 But that is not vouchsafed, and so at last
I must shut out her image from my heart,
And mingling that with other glories past
Look back on what I leave before I start
On a divided track. A winter's blast
355 Howls o'er a desert where our journeys part;
And noon is past; the shades of eve draw nigh,
Dimly reflected from a stormy sky.

Turning amid the driving sleet and rain
I look along the pathway she has taken,
360 Now far away, a slip of emerald plain,
With lingering sun, and freshened foliage shaken
By a sweet Eden-breeze; and once again
I see her like an apparition beckon
In the bright distance in a moment gone.
365 She'll never return—'tis past, and I'm alone.

Victory the plumed one crowns; I hear her calling;
Again my diadem, my lands she flings
Redeemed before me; glorious sunlight falling
On the vermillion banner, lights its wings
370 With the true hue of conquest

And alone shall I be when the trumpet is sounding
To tell to the world that my kingdom is free;
Alone, while a thousand brave bosoms are bounding,
The yoke and the fetter-bolts shivered to see.

375 Alone, in the hall where the last flash is shining
Of embers that wane in their midnight decay,
How shall I feel as the wild gale's repining
Fitfully whispers and wanders away?

What will it tell me of days that will never
380 Smile on the life-weary mourner again?
What will it murmur of hours that for ever
Are past, like the spring-shower's glitter of rain?

Blown by the wind to the verge of the torrent,
Cluster the last leaves that fell long ago;
385 Some that are scattered by chance on its current
Withered and light fleet away in its flow.

Sooner shall these on the tree or the flower
Wave in their bloom as they waved ere they fell,
Then I shall behold the return of that hour
390 Whose sorrowful parting the night-breezes tell.

Then in the silence her picture will glimmer
Solemn and shadowy, high in the hall,
Still as the embers wax dimmer and dimmer
Stirring, like life, to their flicker and fall.

395 How shall I feel as the soft eyes, revealing
Sweetness and sorrow, gaze down through the
                   gloom?
How shall I feel when her image comes stealing
Over me such as she was in her bloom,

Twining around me, crowding the tresses
400 Curled on her white forehead into my breast,
Wooing the love that with passionate kisses
Wildly and warmly her beauty caressed?

Then shall I know that all mutely reposing
She's lulled in the slumbering gloom of her shrine,
405 With death on her white face, in shadow, disclosing
The trace of his truest and awfullest sign.

Then shall I know that her lip would not quiver,
Though with the pressure of love it met mine;
Then shall I know that no glance can dissever
410 The sealed lids that cover her eyes' ghastly shine.

All will be frozen, all cold and unfeeling:
Passion forgotten and sympathy gone;
Neither a motion nor murmur revealing
Life, in that colourless image of stone.

415 I shall not see it, for Mary is buried
Far from the Calabar's war-trampled strand;
And oh! her career to its dark close was hurried
Many a long league from her own native land.

Could she have died with its woods waving round
       her;
420 Could she have slept with their moan in her ear,
Rapt in romance the last slumber had found her
Fleeting away on the tone singing near.

Oh that the sun of the West had been beaming
Glorious and soft on the bed where she lay:
425 Then she had died not lamenting but dreaming,
Borne on the haloes of sunset away!

Had she but known all the love that I bore her,
Though I had left her in sorrow awhile,
Then when the wing of the sceptre swept o'er her
430 Her death-frozen freatures had fixed in a smile.

But she perished in exile, she perished in mourning;
Wild was the evening that closed her decline:
She withered for ever; I hope no returning;
And tears are so fruitful I need not repine.

435 God gave the summons: farewell then, my Mary;
Thou hast found haven when no tears may swell:
Hopeless and weary and joyless and dreary,
I must forget thee—For ever, Farewell!

BUT, oh, exult not. Hush thy joy.
That sunshine still is blent with rain,
And over that blue glimpse of sky
The stormy dim clouds may close again.

5 Kneel and look up and pierce with prayer
The far clear hollow arched above
And ask thy unseen Father's care
To fill the void of earthly love.

Then safe in haven o'er the sea
10 And o'er its wild white waves of foam
Look forth and cry triumphantly,
'What storm, what grief can vex my home?'

A WOODLAND dream! A vision dim
With umbrage from depending tree.

SIT still—a breath, a word may shake
The calm that like a tranquil lake
Falls settling slowly o'er my woes.
Perfect, unhoped-for sweet repose,
O leave me not—forever be
Thus more that Heaven than God for me.

An hour ago how lone I lay
Watching the taper's pallid ray,
As struggling through the night it shed
10   A light upon that statue's brow
To the cold rigid, marble head
Giving a strange half life-like glow
That startled sleep—and oftimes brought
Terror of night and dread of thought.
15   I scarce that dread may now recall,
For thou art here, mine own, my all.

Let me now in the silence tell
What I have felt when far away
The ocean's wide and weltering swell
20   Parted us further day by day,
And scarce as thou went wandering on
Could I in thought those lands portray
Where wrapt perchance in slumber lone
My lord 'mid foes and dangers lay—
25   Confused the dream of stormy waves
And battle-fields and gory graves
And woods untrodden—ways unknown
Still, round my midnight couch was
                    thrown.

If the soft evening star arose
30   To seal some cloudless day's repose
And would bring peace with tranquil ray
Where pain had tortured many a day,
Would touch the heart that yearned for thee
With a kind balm like sympathy,
35   How following on that glimpse of rest
Redoubling anguish wracked this breast,
Anguish because no [—] eye
Could see the light of that sweet sky.
And as to my wide halls I turned,
40   How dim the torch and hearthlight burned.

Beneath their gilded domes there fell
The gloom of lonely hermit's cell,
And music if awakened died
As if wild gales repining sighed
45 Through vaulted crypt, through columned
    aisle
Threading some old religious pile.

Is it so now? O, nearer still
Claps me and kiss the tear away
That starts—as that remembrance chill
50 Crosses with clouds my radiant day.
Close not thy dark eyes, for divine
To me their full and haughty shine.
Do I repent that long-past hour
Of moonlight-love and mystery
55 When the wide forest's arching bower
Heard me vow lasting faith to thee?
Suffering and loneliness and wrong
Are nothing to a heart like mine.
They only firmer knit the strong
60 True ties that twine its strings with thine.
I might reproach and chide thee now
For days when coldness dimmed thy brow,
But only burning love will speak
In tears, for words are far too weak.

O NEVER, NEVER LEAVE AGAIN

O NEVER, never leave again
The land that holds thy father's bower.

OBSCURE and little seen my way
　　Through life has ever been,
But winding from my earliest day
　　Through many a wondrous scene.
5　None ever asked what feelings moved
　　My heart, or flushed my cheek,
And if I hoped, or feared or loved
　　No voice was heard to speak.

I watched, I thought, I studied long,
10　The crowds I moved unmarked among,
I nought to them and they to me
But shapes of strange variety.
The Great with all the elusive shine
Of power and wealth and lofty line
15　I long have marked and well I know.

STANZAS ON
THE DEATH OF A CHRISTIAN

CALM on the bosom of thy God,
　　Fair spirit, rest thee now;
Even while with ours thy footsteps trod,
　　His soul was on thy brow.

5　Dust, to the narrow house beneath.
　　Soul, to its place on high.
They that have seen thy look in death
　　Will never fear to die.

THE TOWN BESIEGED

WITH moaning sound a stream
Sweeps past the Town's dark walls;
Within her streets a bugle's voice
Her troops to slumber calls.

5 The sentinels are set,
The wearied soldiers sleep;
But some shall know tomorrow night
A slumber far more deep.

A chill and hoary dew
10 On tower and bastion shines.
What dew shall fall when war arrays
Her fiery battle lines?

Trump and triumphant drum
Her conflict soon shall spread;
15 Who then will turn aside and say
'We mourn the noble dead'?

Strong hands, heroic hearts
Shall homeward throng again;
Redeemed from battle's gory grasp
20 Where will they leave the slain?

Beneath a foreign sod
Beside an alien wave;
Watched by the martyr's holy God
Shall sleep the martyred brave.

REVIEW AT GAZEMBA

ALL the summer plains of Angria were asleep in
      perfect peace
And the soldier as he rested deemed that foreign wars
      would cease;
All the slain were calmly buried—the survivors home
      returned,
Crossed again the silent thresholds—where their
      faithful consorts mourned.

5 Stained and soiled from Leyden's carnage—dark and
      stern from Evesham's fall
Every chieftain of the army sought once more his
      ancient hall;
And the proud commander slumbered on a couch's
      velvet swell,
Yea, beneath his lady's bower slept the gallant
      Arundel.

And the knight who never yielded in the battle to a
      foe
10 Now like Manoah's sun is fettered with encircling
      arms of snow;
The stalwart Thornton lingers by soft lawn and shady
      tree,
All the ills of war forgotten in his Julia's sorcery.

And why may not soldiers rest when the fiery charge
      is sped?
They may gather thornless flowers, who on bristled
      spears have bled,
15 They may lie without upbraiding in the mildest
      sunbeam's light
Who have watched through winter tempest and
      through cold December night.

Wherefore then that sound of trumpets sent at
    noonday through the land?
Why that rustling waft of banners and that gathering
    band by band?
Are there hosts upon the frontiers, are there ships
    upon the sea,
20 Are there chains in senates forging, for the children
    of the free?

No, though every foe is conquered and though every
    field is won,
Yet Zamorna thinks his labours for the Kingdom but
    begun
And those trumpets are his summons—those deep
    bugles are his call.
From bower, from couch and chamber he has roused
    his nobles all.

25 The horse again is saddled, that from conflict scarce
    has breathed,
The sabre flashed in daylight, that the peace had hardly
    sheathed,
And vaulting to their chargers, a hundred heroes
    spring;
Yea, ten thousand to Gazemba are gone to meet the
    King.

The morning just awaking lights the sky from pole to
    pole
30 Where the waters of a torrent through the arid deserts
    roll,
A banner from yon fortress waves brightly in the
    sun,
And from citadel and rampart peals deep the matin
    gun.

Heart-stirring, soul-exalting, whence bursts that
    warlike strain?
Whose are the armed battalions that fill Gazemba's
    plain?
35 On snow-white charger mounted, with snow-white
    plumes displayed
The herald of Arundel is at his horsemen's head.

To louder bursts of music the desert thrills again
As onward spurs Lord Hartford to marshal all his
    men,
And Etrei's jungles quiver, when the blood-hounds
    send afar
40 To greet their own Fernando the Bandit's wild
    Hourra!

Forth staff and plume and banner, forth crest and
    sword and lance
Amid the battery's thunder, the royal guards
    advance,
A flash from every cannon—a shout from every
    man—
For the king is dashing forward, he is spurring to the
    van.

45 Tall as a soldier should be and dark and quick of eye,
He rises in his stirrups the pageant to descry,
He cannot speak his answer to the sounds that hail him
    now,
But he reins his fiery horse and he halts to bare his
    brow.

There with eyes that meet the sun of the desert
    undismayed,
50 He bends before his warriors that curled and helmless
    head,

And then he signs for silence and he bids the charge
    begin;
The cheer is drowned, the shout is lost in the mimic
    battle's din.

They wheel, they close, they part, to the signal, to the
    word,
Every bosom, every heart by that Kingly voice is
    stirred;
55   The veterans of Benguela that voice before had
    known,
It had cheered the midnight march with its deep
    arousing tone.

By Cirhala's rapid waters that very Leader spoke
Ere the day that closed in slaughter over glorious
    Westwood broke,
And thus along the ranks had passed that haughty
    form [so tall]
60   With bare white brow, and gallant smile on the night
    of Evesham's fall!

And a faithful noble few could remember years ago
How young Douro led them through on a night of
    wail and woe,
When by far Guadima's shore and by Angria's sieged
    town
With blast and volleying roar the mountain storm
    rushed down.

65   Is there one in all that host 'neath Gazemba's rampart
    dread,
But would deem life nobly lost if for Adrian's sake he
    bled?
Is there one would shrink from death in the rudest
    rush of fight
If he gave his latent breath for his sake and in his sight?

You have followed me in dangers, says the monarch
    to his men,
70 When we scarce had hope to cheer us—will you follow
    me again?
While you keep my kingdom free—I will reign your
    sovereign true,
While your hearts are staunch for me shall my hand be
    strong for you.

To seal his haughty vow, and his solemn league to
    bind,
Once more he gave his brow, bare and glancing, to the
    wind.
75 The trumpets breathed a thrill, and then paused, then
    wild and high
Pipe and horn and clarion shrill, burst in triumph on
    the sky;
With hearts too rapt for words, stood the troops as
    still as death,
Then arose a clash of swords, but there never stirred a
    breath.

SIGH no more—it is a dream
  So vivid that it looks like life.

FAST, fast as snow-flakes, fled the legions,
  And the heart throbs, the blood runs fast
As gathering in from many regions
Returns the scattered, faded Past.

O THAT WORD NEVER,
DECEMBER 23RD

NOT many years, but long enough to see
No foe can deal such deadly misery
As the dear friend untimely called away
And still the more beloved, the greater still
5   Must be the aching void, the withering chill
Of each dark night and dim beclouded day.

THE Nurse believed the sick man slept,
For motionless he lay.
She rose and from the bedside crept
With cautious step away.

HOW far is night advanced? Oh, when will day
Reveal the vanished outline of my room?
I fear not yet—for not a glimmer grey
Steals through the familiar blank and solid gloom
5   Which shuts me in—would I could sleep away
The hours—till, skies all flushed with morning's
bloom
Shall open clear and red and cheer with light

LIKE wolf—and black bull or goblin hound,
Or come in guise of spirit
With wings and long wet waving hair
And at the fire its locks will dry,
5   Which will be certain sign
That one beneath the roof must die
Before the year's decline.

Forget not now what I have said,
Sit there till we return.
10 The hearth is hot—watch well the bread
Lest haply it may burn.

A T first I did attention give,
Observance—deep esteem;
His frown I failed not to forgive,
His smile—a boon to deem.

5 Attention rose to interest soon,
Respect to homage changed;
The smile became a relived [?] boon,
The frown like grief estranged.

The interest ceased not with his voice,
10 The homage tracked [?] him near.
Obedience was my heart's free choice—
Whate'er his mood severe [?].

His praise infrequent—favours rare,
Unruly deceivers [?] grew.
15 And too much power a haunting fear
Around his anger threw.

His coming was my hope each day,
His parting was my pain.
The chance that did his steps delay
20 Was ice in every vein.

I gave entire affection now,
I gave devotion sure,
And strong took root and fast did grow
One mighty feeling more.

25 The truest love that ever heart
Felt at its kindled core
Through my veins with quickened
        start
A tide of life did pour.

[A] halo played about the brows
30 Of life as seen by me,
And trailing [?] bliss within me rose,
And anxious ecstacy.

I dreamed it would be nameless bliss
As I loved loved to be,
35 And to this object did I press
As blind as eagerly.

But wild and pathless was the space
That lay our lives between,
And dangerous as the foaming race
40 Of ocean's surges green,

And haunted as a robber path
Through wilderness or wood,
For might and right, woe and wrath
Between our spirits stood.

45 I dangers dared, I hindrance scorned
I omens did defy;
Whatever menaced, harassed, warned
I passed impetuous by.

On sped my rainbow fast as light,
50 I flew as in a dream,
For glorious rose upon my sight
That child of shower and gleam,

And bright on clouds of suffering dim
Shone that soft solemn joy.
55   I care not then how dense and grim
Disasters gather nigh.

I care not in this moment sweet,
Though all I have rushed o'er
Should come on pinion strong and fleet
60   Proclaiming vengeance sore.

Hate struck me in his presence down,
Love barred approach to me,
My rival's joy with jealous frown
Declared hostility.

65   Wrath leagued with calumny transfused
Strong poison in his veins
And I stood at his feet accused
Of false [—] strains

Cold as a statue's grew his eye,
70   Hard as a rock his brow,
Cold hard to me—but tenderly
He kissed my rival now.

She seemed my rainbow to have seized,
Around her form it closed,
75   And soft its iris splendour blazed
Where love and she reposed.

NOTES

SECTION 1

p. 3 *Pilate's Wife's Dream* 'I've quenched my lamp, I struck it in that start'
Manuscript untraceable, and date of composition unknown, although perhaps late. A, p. 139. The first poem to appear in the Aylott and Jones collection has not received enough critical attention. The reconstruction of the feelings of Pontius Pilate's wife, imaginatively based upon the Gospel story, shows a conventional Christian hostility to Pilate, but an unconventional and perhaps unfair disloyalty to him from his wife.

TEXT p. 7 P correctly has God in l. 123, and man, his, he, and his in ll. 134–7. Pilate's wife can scarcely be expected to acknowledge the Deity of Christ.

p. 8 *Mementos* 'Arranging long-locked drawers and shelves'
Manuscript untraceable, but see p. 193 for two earlier very different versions, dated 1837. A, p. 118. The earlier draft appears at the end of a prose narrative describing the return of Zamorna. There are certain reminiscences of Branwell's poem, *Sir Henry Tunstall*.

TEXT p. 8 P has no stanza division at l. 8 and no indentation until ll. 117 and 120 on p. 11. On p. 12 there are no stanza divisions and no indentation at ll. 132 and 135. There is no indentation on pp. 13 and 14.

p. 15 l. 238 ripe, rife, P, presumably a misprint

p. 16 *The Wife's Will* 'Sit still—a word—a breath may break'
The poem on p. 325 has a similar opening, but is a very different poem. A, p. 169. The wife's contented constancy is a conventional contrast to the two previous poems.

TEXT   p. 16   l. 19   [Ay], Aye, P

p. 18   *The Wood*   'But two miles more, and then we rest!'
Manuscript untraceable. Presumably a continuation of the previous poem, with the loyal wife accompanying her husband on some dangerous cross-Channel venture in the wars between England and France.

TEXT   Only the last line in each stanza is indented in P.

p. 22   *Frances*   'She will not sleep, for fear of dreams'
Manuscript untraceable, but there is a manuscript in BCH, 1 p. (torn), $4\frac{1}{4}'' \times 4\frac{3}{4}''$ of stanzas 54–7. In normal handwriting, unsigned and undated, but around 1843. A, p. 94. The name Frances reminds us of the heroine of *The Professor*, but the sentiments are more akin to those of Lucy Snowe in *Villette* or even of Charlotte Brontë as she thought of M. Heger.

TEXT   There is no indentation in P, which also has many
                        unnecessary commas.
p. 28   l. 153   drunk, drank, P, but corrected in errata slip
p. 30   l. 214   retain, behold, BCH†
        l. 217   time may have changed him, he hope betraying,
                 BCH†
        l. 222   I am not loved, Loved I am not, BCH
        l. 224   mislead, delude, BCH

p. 31   *Gilbert*   'Above the city hung the moon'
Manuscript untraceable, but there is a manuscript of most of parts II and III in BCH, pp. 2–17 of *German Notebook*. In normal handwriting, unsigned and undated, but around 1843. Many corrections, most of them illegible. A, p. 95. Charlotte's most ambitious narrative poem sounds vaguely like the story of Mr Rochester, but hardly rings as true,

TEXT   p. 34 l. 104 [keep(?)], weep, P

p. 36 l. 179 so calm, this quiet, BCH

l. 182 advancing, to Gilbert, BCH

l. 183 Her sullen, [—], BCH

l. 184 She stands, [—], BCH

ll. 185-8 are in BCH

> His earthly frame indeed is here,
>   but not his spirit now.
> Read but the signs of dreadful fear
>   Imprinted on his brow.

l. 190 mark, note, BCH, see, BCH†

p. 37 ll. 197-204 appear to be omitted in the much corrected version of BCH

l. 216 is followed by four unpublished stanzas:

> But Gilbert is not guarded yet,
>   Not from himself secured.
> The same thoughts o'er his spirit flit
>   He never[?] alone endured.
> His cushioned chair shakes with the start
>   That shook the leafless tree,
> And fear and conscience throbs his heart
>   With the secret agony.

There is an alternative for these four last lines:

> He lays his hand upon his heart
>   It bounds with agony.
> The fireside chair shakes with each start
>   As shook the garden tree.

> The mother risen from her seat
>   Towards her children gazed.
> Her eyes with Gilbert do not meet,
>   With Gilbert's wildly raised.
> In his own home, by his own hearth
>   He sits in solitude,
> And circled round with light and mirth
>   [— — — — —] mood.

Delivered up to untold strife
  His frame seems sunk and crushed.
Twixt him and his unpitying[?] life
  Another world has rushed.
Twixt him and his a wondrous blast
  Deep toned and hollow blows,
And through this awful region[?] fast
  A sound of water flows.

That air all grim—all calm, all light
  So turbid, tired and dim.
And shapeless shades—all sunk in night
  [*One illegible line*]
A greenish gloom beclouds his eyes,
  A long roar fills his ear.
Nor gloom, nor roar can recognize
  This urgent sense of fear.

p. 38 l. 225 the nameless, this nameless, BCH
      l. 229 rushing, vast, ghastly, green, BCH†
      l. 231 dark, devouring, black, devouring, BCH,
              visionary, dreary, BCH†
      l. 239 of, to, P, but corrected in errata slip
      l. 243 The circling waters' crystal, The
              waters clear and limpid, BCH
      l. 248 Some trial lines, reminiscent of the paintings in
              Jane Eyre, follow ln BCH:

Dark streamed the hair—her gleaming arms
  At times moved with the billow.
In death's severe and marble charms
  She pressed her ocean pillow

or

The long curled wave arrested there
  Stood stirless with its fellow

or

Dark streams the hair—white floats the dress,
  The arms rise with the billow

or
> It lifeless rolls as rolls the wave

or
> Her face is young and lily-pale,
>> She seems a rain-drenched blossom.
> No sun will e'er again avail
>> To warm her snow-cold bosom

l. 250 ghastly, awful, BCH

l. 251 That, The, BCH

l. 256 Two unpublished verses follow in BCH, the second incomplete:

> And turned to him the pallid face,
>> The tresses long and streaming,
> Held fixed and motionless a place
>> Before his eyesight gleaming.
> His mind had failed before the weight
>> Of its own dark creation,
> Had not at length relenting fate
>> Ordained the dream's cessation.

> The storm that to the tortured sea
>> A transient truce had given
> Returned with doubled energy
>> From mightiest [?] impulse driven
> And yielding to the mighty sway
>> Of storm upon the billow
> The corse now swept a

p. 39 ll. 257–64 in BCH read:

> And straight before the corse was stretched,
>> So near his hand extending
> He could the lifeless limbs have reached
>> Or touched the wave impending.
> He saw the arms uplifted wave
>> With movement of the billow.
> The face lay sad and pale and grave
>> Upon its ocean pillow.

l. 266   The mass of waters raising, the whole great deep
           upraising, BCH

l. 275   in, by, BCH*

l. 276   slowly, rapid, BCH*

l. 278   defeated, divided, BCH

l. 280   Fear, faint and far subsided, BCH

l. 282   tempest, wreck, tumultuous seas, BCH
           sounding breeze, BCH*

l. 284   clung around his neck, eager climbed his knees,
           BCH

p. 40   l. 300   subtle, hardy, BCH

ll. 303–4   His face has taken a marble mask
              Unmoved, serene and bland, BCH

l. 311   Nor now, Not more, BCH

p. 41   l. 326   name, fame, BCH

l. 328   its, my, BCH*

l. 330   Some clouds are, The night is, BCH†

l. 335   smoothly, swiftly, BCH

l. 339   the portal, that mansion, BCH

p. 42   l. 354   His, The, BCH

l. 359   And, Soon, BCH†

l. 361   latchet, holds, latch upholds, BCH

l. 365   Lo, And, BCH†

l. 368   incessant, unceasing, BCH

l. 370   candle, taper, BCH

l. 374   blind, glazed, BCH†

l. 384   fail, quail, P, but corrected in errata slip

p. 43   l. 392   A cancelled stanza follows in BCH:

And Nature failed; the tide of life
    Stopped cancelled in its flow.
He fell as if a merciless knife
    Had sudden laid him low.
When through the hall the morning shone,
    Her early beams now shed
Upon the stone where stretched alone
    Lay Gilbert stiff and dead.

l. 402   vigorous, reckless, BCH

> After these final lines we have some more attempts
> at the appearance of the corpse on p. 39:
>
> And, oh, as near the pale corse lay,
>   Upheld by air or billow,
> It seemed he could have touched the spray
>   That churned around its pillow.
> The hollow anguish of that face
>   Had moved a fiend to sorrow,
> Yet such fixed calm of death could raze the trace
>   Of suffering's deep-worn furrow.

and

> Dishevelled streamed the brine-drenched hair

and

> And sad it was to see a form,
>   So young and early broken,
> Of mortal woe [?] and inward storm
>   Reveal so sure a token.
> [*Two illegible lines follow*]

and

> Around how pale and wan a brow
>   The brine drenched hair was streaming.
> How sunk and quenched with weary woe
>   The eyes were dimly gleaming.
> The lifeless head hung heavy back
>   And every limb showed token.

p. 44   *Life*   'Life, believe, is not a dream'
Manuscript untraceable, but identical manuscript in BCPML, pp.
17–18 of *Poems*. In normal handwriting, unsigned but dated 1839 and
said to be copied at Brussels, presumably around 1843, this being a
copy of a poem that forms part of the prose manuscript, *Henry Hastings*, in HCL, dated 26 March 1839 and signed Charles Townshend.
A, p. 110. The optimism of this poem, which Charlotte did not alter

between 1843 and 1845, is a jarring contrast to some of Emily's poetry, and the metaphor of elastic, unlike the comparison of the heart to indiarubber in *Jane Eyre* (and *Agnes Grey*), is frankly risible.

TEXT   p. 44   ll. 15–17   P has sorrow, hope, and hope.

p. 45   *The Letter*   'What is she writing? Watch her now'
Manuscript untraceable, but earlier version in BCH, 2 pp., 7¼″ × 4½″. In minuscule handwriting with many corrections, most of them illegible, unsigned, but dated, June 1837. A, p. 109. The early date is a useful reminder that we must not think of Charlotte writing to M. Heger here, and the grand house in which the letter is being written shows that this is an Angrian scene.

TEXT   p. 45   l. 17   unclosed, open, BCH*
              l. 22   Four illegible lines in BCH
              l. 25   Tall . . . spicy, And . . . fragrant, BCH
              l. 26   The polished threshold sweep, BCH
              l. 27   leaves and, clustered, BCH
              l. 28   deepening glow, radiance deep, BCH
         ll. 29–33   BCH reads:

                     Why does she not put down her hand
                         And gather one red rose,
                     And cast one glance o'er that rich land
                         Before the daylight close?

         p. 46   l. 35   fast her pen and, rapidly and, BCH
                 l. 37   [the], th', P
                         Her whole soul and appointed task, BCH
                 l. 40   serious, ardent, BCH
                 l. 42   [the], th', P
                 l. 43   the, that, BCH
                 l. 44   For something seemed to pine, BCH
                 l. 47   expanse, gloom, BCH
                 l. 49   Yet, But, BCH

l. 50   And o'er the couches soft, BCH
l. 51   as if leaning on the air, forward from the cornice fair, BCH
l. 52   A picture frowns aloft, BCH
l. 54   what form defines, each pencilled trace, BCH
l. 55   BCH has, with some corrections and some illegibility:

> That moss looks dark and shadowy
>   Those gilded mouldings grace,
> But still some feelings vague descend
>   Of youth all [?] wild and warm
> That strengthen as you lower bend
>   Your gaze upon that form.
> There seems a glossy flush of curls.
>   The eyes you well might deem
> A wild hawk's: like even pearls
>   The teeth of coral seem.
> And then so broad and white a brow
>   And features grandly cast
> In such a mould as tells us now
>   Of[—] and[—] past.

p. 47   l. 67   impending glorious, BCH*
       l. 77   BCH replaces by:

> The name, the place, 'tis all revealed,
>   You feel how lone she dwells,
> Though round her park and grounds [?] and field
>   So rich in radiance swells.
>
> You feel those clustering flowers may fade,
>   Un[—] unplucked, unmourned.
> You feel unmarked the twilight shade
>   May close where sunset burned.
> You know that ever in her ear
>   The sound of waves will be,
> For all her soul and heart holds dear
>   Is far beyond the sea,

> And neither hope nor silver dove,
> Nor Fear [—] carrion slave,
> Nor wildest wish inspired by love
> Can cross the rolling wave.

p. 47 *Regret* 'Long ago I wished to leave'
Manuscript untraceable, but earlier version in BCPML, pp. 9–10 of
Poems. In ordinary handwriting, unsigned but dated Haworth, July
1837, probably transcribed around 1843. Still earlier version in BCH,
1 p., $7\frac{1}{2}'' \times 4\frac{1}{2}''$, in minuscule handwriting, unsigned and undated. A,
pp. 143–4 says *Regret* was originally part of a prose manuscript and
that this is dated 21 July 1837. She also dates the BCH fragment
30 May 1837, but this seems to be a confusion with another poem.
Again we seem to have the same note of dutiful lament by a sailor's
wife to be found in *The Wife's Will* and *The Wood*.

TEXT p. 47 l. 5 rooms, wood, BCPML*, BCH
        l. 6 Were (was, BCH) full of gloom to me, BCPML, BCH
        l. 7 Saw I now that shadow broad, BCPML*, Saw I now
              its shadow broad, BCH
        l. 8 O'ercharged with exstacy, BCPML*, How happy
              should I be, BCH, BCPML*
     p. 48 l. 10 once, deemed, that seemed, BCPML, BCH
        l. 11 is, has, BCH
        l. 13 BCH reads:

> Mournful it is for hours to wait
>   And listen for a tread,
> Then to lie down desolate
>   Upon a lonely bed.

The BCH fragment then stops, although A thinks it continues with
the poem 'But, oh, exult not'.

        l. 23 One loved voice, Still one voice, BCPML

l. 25   Clear though sung the heavenly breeze, BCPML*
l. 26   O'er, of, BCPML*
l. 27   Even from Eden's bower and trees, BCPML*

p. 49   *Presentiment*   'Sister, you've sat there all the day'
Manuscript untraceable, but manuscript in BCPML in copperplate
and ordinary handwriting, pp. 4–7 of *Poems*, unsigned but dated May
1837, probably the original date of composition, and copied around
1843. Also in BCH a manuscript, 3 pp., 7¼″ × 4½″. In minuscule handwriting, signed C. Brontë and dated 11 July 1837. A, pp. 140–1. It is
odd to find a poem entitled *Presentiment* so sinisterly prophetic for
Charlotte.

TEXT   p. 49   l. 5   That open book, That book for hours, BCH†
          l. 9   field, park, BCPML, BCH
    After l. 9   BCPML and BCH continue:

A thick mist shuts the scene.
See how like night it closes dark
    Around those alleys green.
Aslant and small and sharp the showers
    Are driven by cold wild gales.
Through all our walks, in (through, BCH) all our
        bowers
    A saddening whisper wails.

How desolate, how lonely spread
    The slopes, the (long and, BCH) sweeping glades.
No ring dove's voice, no roe-buck's tread
    Awakes their shrouded shades.
How thin the rustle of the trees
    Sounds now from every tree;
The latest day of Autumn grieves
    In wan despondency.

Have you forgot how different shone
　　The summer past away?
Have you forgot how bright the sun
　　Rose smiling every day.
How flamed in fire its burning beams
　　In sunset pomp at night,
And stirred to life such glorious dreams
　　In us who watched their light.

In BCH these four lines read:

How still and beautiful its beams
　　Went calmly down at night,
And woke in us such glorious dreams,
　　Who watched their dying light.

Yes, Emma, I remember well
　　Those skies, those suns divine.
Yet mourn I not—for every dell
　　Shall see again their shine,
And every flower again shall blow,
　　And every tree unfold
Its foliage to the softest glow
　　Of summer skies of gold.

Hope, Jane, as you were born to hope,
　　Long be your life, and free,
　　(Live out your destiny, BCH)
But, sister, neither bower nor slope
(dearest sister, heaven's blue cope, BCH)
　　Shall smile again (no more, BCH) for me.
Forgive these tears, forgive the thought
　　Which brings that strange forebode;
I know my task is almost wrought,
　　My journey well-nigh trod.

Emma, the very pride of June
　　Burns high in heaven again.
A thousand birds their sweetest (choral, BCH†) tune
　　Pour forth in choral (sweetest, BCH†) strain.

Emma, the tranquil world asleep
　　On evening's bosom lies.
The river's breast (Thy father's lake, BCH, BCPML†)
　　　　　　　　　blue calm and deep.
　　Reflects uncluded skies.

Full (And, BCH) low in twilight's purple zone
　　The moon, set large (full, BCH) and mild,
Shines softly (glorious, BCH) as she ever shone
　　Since first in heaven she smiled.
　　(Smiles as she never smiled, BCH)
And Jane sits at an old tree's foot (oak's root, BCH),
　　Her feet on flowers repose,
The wild birds round her playful shoot
　　The sheep (deer, BCH, BCPML†) unstartled
　　　　　　　　　browze.

p. 50　l. 38　[bound], wound, P
After l. 50　P has no line of dots

p. 51　After omitting all preceding verses on pp. 49 and 50, BCH
and BCPML give the two final stanzas, although in BCH the last
stanza is added in ordinary handwriting.

l. 61　bier, corpse, BCPML, BCH
l. 64　in spring's first gleam, like thought or shade, BCPML,
　　　BCH
l. 65　how, left, BCH*
l. 66　Fades even as blossoms fade, BCPML, BCH**, To fade
　　　as blossoms fade, BCH

p. 51　*The Teacher's Monologue* 'The room is quiet, thoughts alone'
Manuscript untraceable, but earlier version in BCH, 3 pp. 7½″ × 4½″.
In minuscule handwriting, unsigned, but dated on the first page
15 May 1837, and on the second, oddly, 12 May 1837. The latter date
appears in the middle of a poem and may be irrelevant. The last sixteen
lines are in ordinary handwriting on a third page and may have been

added later. A, pp. 155–6. The poem, though a poor one, gives a useful insight into Charlotte's feelings as a teacher at Roe Head.

TEXT   No indentation in P or BCH.
p. 51   l. 3   long task, hard toil, BCH
          l. 7   waveless water, stirless, airless hill and waveless, BCH†
p. 52   l. 13   yon azure brow, what parts me so, BCH*, that pure brow, BCH
          l. 14   Parts me from all, From all this wide, BCH†
          l. 15   And . . . and, From . . . to, BCH†
          l. 17   [ay], aye, P, BCH
          l. 21   narrow, hardened, BCH
          l. 23   far, wide, BCH
          l. 35   sown, grown, BCH
          l. 37   Sorrow, grief may, BCH
          l. 39   But now I hear it darkly said, BCH
After l. 40   P begins a new stanza
p. 53   After l. 48 BCH inserts:

And look round on a house of gloom
And listen for a voice in vain
And feel that never even at home
My heart shall bound to joy again.
What shall I do?

and adds ll. 49–50 in the margin in ordinary handwriting.
          l. 55   wanted, asked for, BCH
          l. 56   Bright, For, BCH
          l. 57   sweet, soft, BCH
          l. 58   Though haply, And almost, BCH
After l. 62   BCH inserts:

A note such as a bird might sing,
   Its last and sweetest lay,
Before its little weary wing
   Was folded for the day.

l. 65   wild, deep, BCH
p. 54   l. 77   spring is, spirit, BCH
l. 78   Beneath the strain of, Submits to tyrant, BCH*
After l. 78   BCH inserts:

And wild repining fills the time
    That should be given to sleep,
While conscience speaks of sin and crime
    Because so fast I weep.
I have no want, I know no pain.
    Without the sun shines bright.
But, oh, I feel again, again,
    Within a starless night.

After l. 78   BCH continues in ordinary handwriting.
After l. 86   BCH inserts:

God, give me patience, give me faith,
Vouchsafe me strength to bear.
[*One illegible line*]

l. 88   A welcome, At least, BCH

p. 54   *Passion*   'Some have won a wild delight'
Manuscript untraceable, but earlier version in BCPML, pp. 13–16 of
Poems. In ordary handwriting, unsigned, but dated, finished at Upper-
wood, 12 December 1841. A, p. 138. An interesting adaptation of the
Peninsular War to Britain s Indian campaigns, with Douro being a
reminder of Angria.

TEXT   p. 54   l. 11   Could I deem, If I thought, BCPML
p. 55   l. 17   a trumpet sounds, remote and wild, BCPML*
ll. 19–20   Where Gaul and Briton meet in war
(Where tents are pitched and arms are piled*)
By Southern Douro's flow, BCPML
l. 21   Blood, War, BCPML*, Sutlej's, Douro's, BCPML
l. 22   scarlet, crimson, BCPML*

l. 23   Indus' borders, Spain's sierras, BCPML

ll. 25–33   BCPML omits and replaces by:

Bid me do some wilder thing,
    Angel, bid me be
False to country, false to King,
    True alone to thee.

l. 34   love, arms, BCPML

l. 36   my fire reprove, withdraw thy charms, BCPML

l. 37   By, In, BCPML

p. 56   l. 42   my triumph, that victory, BCPML

l. 50   Then, And, BCPML

p. 56   *Preference*   'Not in scorn do I reprove thee'
Manuscript untraceable, and no previous version can be found. A, p. 140. It may be coincidental, but it is fairly easy to read this poem in the light of Charlotte's experiences at Brussels, and imagine that the poem was written with M. Heger in mind, since the thoughtful hero bending over his papers does seem rather like him, and the narrator's feelings towards the rejected first hero probably corresponded to what Charlotte felt for M. Heger.

TEXT   No indentation in P.

p. 58   *Evening Solace*   'The human heart has hidden treasures'
Manuscript untraceable, but previous version in BCPML, pp. 8–9 of *Poems*, entitled *Remembrance*. In ordinary handwriting, unsigned and undated, but said to be written at Haworth. A, p. 91. Charlotte wrote another similar poem at Haworth in 1838 (p. 61), but I see no other evidence for the poem being originally composed in 1838. It was presumably copied around 1843.

TEXT   No indentation in P.

p. 59 ll. 13–16 BCPML has three alternatives for this stanza. The third reads as printed, with the substitutions 'round' for 'in' and 'heart' for 'souls'. The first reads:

> And then we tell our treasures over,
> Recall the past hours fled away,
> And then doth Memory's hand discover
> Its own realm of twilight grey

while the second reads:

> Then in our heart there seems to languish
> Thoughts of lost friends and early days,
> And griefs that once won tears of anguish
> Now scarce with dimness cloud our gaze.

l. 18 Float, Come, BCPML
l. 30 hour . . . room, room . . . hour, BCPML*

ll. 31–2 To thoughts that rise like stars in heaven
          With solemn shine and mystic power, BCPML*

l. 32 a, the, BCPML

p. 59 *Stanzas* 'If thou be in a lonely place'
Manuscript untraceable, but previous version in BCPML, pp. 18–20 of *Poems*. In ordinary handwriting, unsigned, but dated, 'written 14 May, 1837 at Roe Head. Copied at Haworth, 30 August, 1845.' Also in BCH this previous version, 1 p., $7\frac{1}{2}'' \times 4\frac{1}{2}''$. In minuscule handwriting, unsigned, but dated 14 May 1837. A, pp. 152–3. One of Charlotte's better poems, which improves in later versions.

TEXT p. 59   l. 6 look, looks, BCH
      p. 60 l. 16 silent, wandering, BCH, BCPML*
             l. 17 upon the wind, amid the hush, BCH, BCPML*
             l. 18 A murmur, whisper, sigh, BCPML, Wait for it
                    earnestly, BCH, BCPML*

ll. 19–20   Amid the stillness feel a rush
              Of happy thoughts of me, BCH, BCPML*
l. 21   blest, sweet, BCH, BCPML*
l. 22   P correctly indents
l. 22   seem, be, BCH, BCPML*
ll. 23–4   Which saw our severed spirits meet
              In magic memory, BCH, BCPML*
l. 30   eyes, eye, BCPML, BCH
l. 31   their changeful, its changeful, BCPML, its haughty,
          BCH
l. 35   deem, think, BCH, BCPML
l. 39   Till death the victor claims his hour, BCH, BCPML*
p. 61   ll. 5–8   BCH reads:

And peacefully my corse (grave†) will sleep (rest†)
    Beneath its guardian tree
If sometimes through thy veins shall leap (noble
    breast†)
    One pulse still true to me
    (One pulse shall strike for me†)

BCPML has two alternatives as well as the final version with 'will' for
'would' in l. 45 and 'bosom' for 'heart should' in 1.47:

And peacefully my corse would sleep
    Beneath a guardian tree,
If sometime in my bosom leap
    One pulse still true to me.

and

And sweet my sleep would be and sound
    Beneath the cypress tree,
If sometime in thy heart should bound
    One pulse still true to me.

p. 61   *Parting*   'There's no use in weeping'
Manuscript untraceable, but previous version in BCPML, pp. 16–17
of *Poems*. In ordinary handwriting, unsigned but dated 'Written at

Haworth, 1838; copied at Bruxelles, 1843'. Also in BCH this previous version, 1 p., 7½″ × 4½″. In minuscule handwriting, unsigned but dated 29 January 1838. A, p. 137 and AC, p. 169, giving the context of an impending departure for another term at Roe Head. Charlotte's forced cheerfulness strikes a very insincere note.

TEXT   No indentation in P.
     p. 61   l. 12   for, at, BCH
           l. 16   even, much, BCPML, BCH
   After l. 16   BCH inserts:

> We'll nurse romantic notions
> Of our own superior sense
> And despise the world's commotions
> As devoid of [—] or [—]

           l. 20   Whom, That, BCH

     p. 62   ll. 31–2   I could swear the Future's keeping
                     A reward for all this ill, BCH

p. 62   *Abostasy*   'This last denial of my faith'
Manuscript untraceable, but previous version in BCPML on inside cover and pp. 11–13 of *Poems*. In ordinary handwriting, unsigned but dated 29 May 1837, presumably the date of composition. Also in BCH this previous version, 2 pp., 7½″ × 4½″. In minuscule handwriting, unsigned but dated 29 May 1837. A, pp. 79–80. This poem, though of poor quality, is interesting for its hostility to Catholicism, shown in Charlotte's novels, and a general preference for love over religion, more reminiscent of Emily than Charlotte.

TEXT   p. 62   l. 1   Confession of my Christian faith, BCH
               l. 3   And, though, Though now, BCH
               l. 12   lifeless, placid, BCPML, radiant, BCH
       p. 63   l. 15   And I for this encircling ring, BCH
               l. 16   I, Have, BCH

l. 19 and God and, that Heaven that, BCH

l. 24 For he is far away, BCPML*, BCH

ll. 25–8 BCPML places these verses in the margin in pencil, prefacing them by:

> And did I need that thou shouldst tell
>   How long the green deep sea
> Has rolled between our last farewell
>   How long, how wearily.

BCH omits ll. 25–32 and has these four additional lines, followed by l. 32. BCPML has ll. 29–30 in pencil in the margin.

p. 64 ll. 45–8 BCH reads:

> But how my soul's mysterious sight
>   Beholds his image glow
> So fixed, so clear, so burning bright
>   Thou, father, dost not know.

l. 49 Talk, Speak, BCH

l. 52 dews upon, thin dews on, BCH

After l. 52 BCH reads:

> To him my childhood's faith is given
>   Beyond the wild deep's swell.
> I own no God, I hope no heaven,
>   I die an infidel.
> Oh, say no more of bliss above,
>   Of rest from sin's alarms.
> My bliss was in my bridegroom's love,
>   My rest was in his arms.
>
> Yet will I kiss the sacred sign
>   Thy faltering hand lifts now,
> I claim it mine as thou doest thine.
>   Oh, trace it on my brow.
> As the priest traced the cross she died
>   Without one prayer for grace.
> The monk with solemn accents cried
>   "Fare, spirit, to this place.

Tis done, and thou hast ceased to live.
    A too sad farewell to thee.
An awful God will not forgive
    Such dark apostasy.
I saw the bud unclose as fair
    As ever flower might bloom.
The fruit lies crushed and trampled there.
    How sorrowful her doom."

BCPML has in pen, replaced in pencil by the Shakespeare Head version with 'William's' for 'Walter's':

Oh, say no more of bliss above,
    Of rest from sin's alarms.
My bliss was in my bridegroom's love
    My rest was in his arms.

and then

Depress again the sacred sign
    Thy faltering hand lifts high.
Lay down the cross thou deems't divine
    And watch a human die.
    (Its virtue I deny*)

The BCPML manuscript then appears to stop, but the remaining two stanzas appear in pencil on the front cover of *Poems* in two versions. The first reads:

Now go—for at the door there knocks
    Another stranger guest.
I come—three wild and fearful shocks
    Have passed through brain and breast.
[*4 illegible lines*]

The second is more like the Shakespeare Head:

l. 67 I come—my weak (faint*) pulse scarcely beats,
      BCPML
ll. 73 ff. are replaced by:

> I'll rest not till daylight comes
>   However black the night.
> There is, we know, a moment when
>   God speaks and all is light.
> 'I'll rest, I'll sleep', she murmuring spoke,
>   Then still and voiceless lay.
> The slumber from which none ever woke
>   Had rapt her soul away.

p. 65   *Winter Stores*   'We take from life on little share'
Manuscript untraceable, but previous version in BCPML, pp. 1–2 of
Poems. In copperplate handwriting, unsigned and undated, but probably copied around 1843. Also in BCH a previous version, 1 p., 7¼″ ×
4½″. In minuscule handwriting, unsigned and undated, but probably
around 1837. A, pp. 170–1. Once again Charlotte's forced optimism
makes a poor poem.

TEXT   In both BCH and BCPML the stanzas have eight
                   lines, not four.
  p. 65   l. 5   unstrings his bow, withholds his hand, BCH†
          l. 6   apart, aside, BCH*
          l. 9   eve, day, BCH†
          l. 11   Our, And, BCH
          l. 17   viewlessly, silently, BCH
          l. 19   and, or, BCH, BCPML
          l. 20   silent, solemn, BCH
          l. 23   progress, swift flight, BCH
  p. 66   After l. 28   BCH and BCPML insert, omitting all subsequent
                   lines:

> And dying dreams of light are sealed
>   In marble urns, to be
> No more to ear or eye revealed
>   Save, Memory, by thee.

Thou with soft eyes and shadowy hair
Shall watch the sacred shrine,
And in some hour of dead despair
Unveil perchance its shine.

And then when faithless hope is gone,
And glowing Love is cold,
Shall thine and Heaven's pure (the pure and holy,
BCH) stars alone
The last sweet thought unfold.

p. 67 *The Missionary* 'Plough, vessel, plough the British main'
Manuscript untraceable and no previous versions. Possibly composed especially for publication. A, p. 122. An interesting preview of St John Rivers.

TEXT p. 70 l. 105 [demon—rage], demon-rage, P

p. 71 (*The Orphan Child*) 'My feet they are sore, and my limbs are weary'
Manuscript in BL as part of *Jane Eyre*. A, p. 125. TEXT as printed.

p. 72 (*Rochester's Song to Jane Eyre*) 'The truest love that ever heart'
Manuscript in BL as part of *Jane Eyre*. Early draft of last four lines in BCH, 1 p., 7¼″×4½″. In ordinary handwriting, unsigned and undated, but around 1843. For the history of this poem see note on 'At first I did attention give', p. 336. A, pp. 161–2.

TEXT p. 73 l. 27 The first edition of *Jane Eyre* read 'Far', but 'For' is the reading of the manuscript and all subsequent editions.

ll. 45–6   BCH has:

> My love has pledged (sworn*) with smile and kiss
> The holy bond (eternal link*) to tie.

p. 74   *The Orphans*   ' 'Twas New Year's night; the joyous throng'
Manuscript as sent to *The Manchester Athenæum Album* untraceable,
but previous version in BCPML, pp. 1–5 of French exercise-book. In
copperplate, signed Louis Belmontet, Fevrier, 1843. A, p. 134.

TEXT   l. 8   lonely, naked, BCPML†
                 l. 9   timid, faltering, BCPML
                 l. 12 Too gay to mark, All heedless of, BCPML
                 l. 14 The children's pale cheeks, Their pallid faces,
                        BCPML,† The children's white cheeks, BCPML
        After l. 24   there is an erased verse in BCPML:

> The stranger said, "My children's bread
>   I cannot give the poor.
> Go elsewhere; I must feed my own."
>   He sternly closed his door.
> His daughter wept, he saw her grief,
>   Yet deigned not to bestow relief.

                 l. 29 And, Oh, BCPML
        p. 75   l. 37 feebly, faintly, BCPML
                 l. 51 is, was, BCPML
                 l. 52 stilled, checked, BCPML†
                 l. 53 Mute, All, BCPML†
                 l. 56 a, the, BCPML†
        p. 76   l. 63 Now the proud rich their doom may weep, BCPML†

SECTION 2

p. 79   *Found in an Inn belonging to You* 'Thou art a sweet and lovely flower'

Manuscript in WS, 1 p., 2¼″ × 1½″. In minuscule handwriting, signed U.T. and dated 28 September 1829. A, p. 93. There is no other copy, and the note in the Shakespeare Head edition seems a rather desperate explanation for the discrepancies between the printed version and the manuscript, for which see Textual Introduction. In spite of the conventional nature of the vocabulary the poem is not bad for a girl aged thirteen.

TEXT p. 79   The title in the manuscript has 'You' not 'E.'.
            l. 10   [over-hanging], hanging, WS
            l. 11   [vivid lightings], lightning, WS
            l. 12   [roars], roaring, WS
            l. 14   [Through the night a], A gentle, WS
            l. 15   The mariners all hail it, WS
            l. 16   [Hails], As
        ll. 17–20   are in WS:

> When the sun shall rise in splendour
>   Bringing the coursing foam [?]
> With the colour of that gorgeous bow
>   Which anchors heaven's dome

            l. 22   [ocean's glassy], glassy ocean, WS
            l. 23   [flag shall flutter], red flag stirred by, WS
            l. 24   [sweet and soothing], sweetest, WS
      p. 80   l. 25   [Britannia's], Britain's, WS
            l. 26   [O'er], And, WS
            l. 27   [Over], O'er, WS
            l. 28   [Over], And, WS
            l. 30   [echo], music, WS
            l. 31   [Borne], Are borne, WS
            l. 32   [Float In], In, WS

p. 80   *Lines Addressed to 'The Tower of All Nations'*   'O, thou great, thou mighty tower!'
Manuscript in WS, 1 p., 2¼″ × 1½″, the opposite side of the previous poem. In minuscule handwriting, signed U.T. and dated 7 October 1829. The note of self-depreciation in the last stanza is healthy.

TEXT   p. 80   l. 1   [Oh], O, WS.
                l. 2   [Rising up], Rising, WS
                l. 6   [Like a], A, WS
                l. 7   [thy structure grey], thy structure, WS
                l. 9   [o'er thee hung], O'er thee, WS
                l. 10 [With its maze of], Hung with its, WS
                l. 11 [about thee spread], about thee, WS

p. 81   (*Sunset*)   'Beneath a shady tree I sat'
Manuscript in BCH, 1 p., 4¼″ × 4″. On the same page as *Sunrise* and some drawings. In minuscule handwriting, signed C.B. and dated 8 October 1829. A, p. 154.

TEXT   p. 81   l. 8   [a], the, BCH

p. 82   *Sunrise*   'Behold that silvery streak of light'
Manuscript in BCH, 1 p., 4¾″ × 4″. On the same page as *Sunset* and some drawings. In minuscule handwriting, signed Charlotte Brontë and dated 9 October 1829. A, p. 154.

TEXT   p. 82   l. 25   [blazing], flaming, BCH

p. 83   *The Churchyard*   ' 'Twas one fair evening,—when the closing day'
Manuscript in BCPML, pp. 1–2 of *Miscellaneous Poems*. In ordinary juvenile handwriting, signed Charlotte Brontë and dated 24 December

1829. The manuscript mentioned on p. 85 is untraceable. A, pp. 85–6. The blank verse and Gothic trappings, though immature, are nevertheless impressive. Less impressively, Charlotte gives the title as *The Churchyard. A Poemn.*

TEXT   p. 84   l. 39   [sombre], glazed, BCPML

p. 86   *Written upon the occasion of the dinner given to the literati of the Glass-Town* 'The splendid Hall is blazing'
Manuscript in BCH, 2 pp., 3½″ × 2¼″. In minuscule handwriting, signed C. Brontë and dated 8 January 1830. A, p. 173 and AC, p. 57. In the manuscript the poem is divided into stanzas with four short lines in each stanza replacing the two long lines of the Shakespeare Head version.

TEXT   p. 86   l. 7   [continuous], continual, BCH
         l. 22   common, vulgar, BCH*
                 [has], hath, BCH
       p. 87   l. 34   [These], All these, BCH

p. 87   *Written on the Summit of a High Mountain in the north of England* 'How lonely is this spot! Deep silence reigns'
Manuscript in BCPML, pp. 7–8 of *Miscellaneous Poems*. In ordinary juvenile handwriting, signed Charlotte Brontë and dated 14 January 1830. A, p. 173. The manuscript is not divided into stanzas, although in an earlier crossed-out version in the same notebook there is such a division. This ambitious if unsuccessful poem is worth studying for those interested in Charlotte's literary sources: one can detect traces of Scott, the Romantics, and the eighteenth century here.

TEXT   p. 88   l. 42   [grave], grove, BCPML

p. 89 *A Wretch in Prison, by Murry* 'Oh, for the song of the gladsome lark'
Manuscript in BCH, 1 p., 3½″ × 2¼″. In minuscule handwriting with many corrections, signed C. Brontë and dated 1 February 1830. A, p. 172. For Murr(a)y see AC, pp. 55, 265.

TEXT p. 89 l. 6 woodland's, mountain's, BCH†
l. 12 [And], With, BCH
l. 14 [Heard], Loud [?], BCH
l. 17 rush, flush, BCH†
l. 18 mighty, thundering, BCH†
l. 20 roaring, thundering, BCH†
p. 90 l. 22 heavens', thundering, BCH†

p. 90 *Winter. A Short Poem* 'Autumn has vanished with his train'
Manuscript in BCPML, pp. 8–9 of *Miscellaneous Poems* In ordinary juvenile handwriting, signed Charlotte Brontë and dated 3 February 1830. Charlotte is better at describing the gloom of winter than the joys of spring. The influence of Thomson's *Seasons* is marked.

TEXT   BCPML begins with a false start:

Autumn has vanished with his sickly train
Of withering forests and of falling leaves.
No more wide waving over the fruitful plain
Stands the ripe corn or bound in golden sheaves
Mixed with the vine a harvest garland weaves.

p. 91 l. 36 [snow-drop], snowdrop's, BCPML

p. 92 *Pleasure. (A Short Poem* or else not say I) 'True pleasure breathes not city air'
Manuscript in BCPML, pp. 5–6 of *Miscellaneous Poems*. In ordinary juvenile handwriting, signed Charlotte Brontë and dated 8 February 1830. A, p. 139. The influence of Thomson is again present.

TEXT   p. 92   l. 16   [winds], sounds, BCPML
       l. 23   [And], The, BCPML
               [valleys], valley's, BCPML puts the apostrophe in
               'vales'.
       p. 93   l. 43   The missing word appears to be 'aura'.

p. 94   (*Home-sickness*)   'Of College I am tired; I wish to be at home'
Manuscript in BCH, 1 p., 3½″ × 2¼″. In ordinary juvenile handwriting,
signed C.B., C.W. and dated 1 February 1830. A, p. 129 and AC, p. 54
for the context. Charles Wellesley, a schoolboy at Eton, is imagined as
pining for his African home.

TEXT   p. 94   l. 9   [in], all, BCH
       l. 10   [called poor, startled, withered wretch, and], cold
               and poor, starved withered wretch, a, BCH

p. 95   *The Vision. A Short Poem*   'The gentle showery Spring had
passed away'
Manuscript in BCPML, pp. 10–11 of *Miscellaneous Poems*. In ordinary
juvenile handwriting, signed C. Brontë and dated 13 April 1830. A,
p. 164 and AC, p. 65 for Branwell's criticisms of this poem. The
influence of Wordsworth is more prevalent here.

TEXT   There is in the manuscript an alternative first verse,
                difficult to decipher. It appears to read:

                Sweet spring had passed away
                The balmy breath of June had breathed on all the
                    rising corn
                Which waved in summer pride on fertile plain
                Or robed in green array
                The sloping side of many a cultured hill.

       p. 95   l. 10   [On Nature's], On all nature's, BCPML
               l. 19   [gale], star, BCPML

l. 23   No brackets in BCPML
l. 25   [rung], sung, BCPML
p. 96 l. 32   [my], the, BCPML
l. 45   [that], which, BCPML

p. 97 *Fragment* 'Now rolls the sounding ocean'
Manuscript in BCPML, p. 9 of *Miscellaneous Poems*. In ordinary juvenile writing, unsigned but dated 29 May 1830. A, p. 94.

TEXT   p. 97   l. 10   [aëriel], aerial, BCPML

p. 98 (*Reflections*) 'Now sweetly shines the golden sun'
Manuscript in BCPML, p. 12 of *Miscellaneous Poems*. In ordinary juvenile handwriting, signed C. Brontë and dated 31 May 1830. A, p. 129. This modest poem probably reflects the feelings of many people who have enjoyed a rare moment of summer on the moors above Haworth.

TEXT   l. 8   glows, shines, BCPML†
l. 25   azure deep, vault of blue, BCPML†

p. 99 *The Evening Walk* 'When August glowed with fervid summer pride'
Manuscript in BPM, 14 pp., 2″ × 1¼″. In minuscule handwriting, signed Marquis of Douro, C. Brontë and dated 28 June 1830.

TEXT   p. 101   l. 48   [to the], like, BCH
p. 107   l. 235   [Where], When, BCH

p. 109 *Morning* 'Lo! the light of the morning is flowing'
Manuscript in BCH, being 2 pp., 2″ × 1¼″ of *Young Men's Magazine* for 1830. According to A, p. 123 there is a later manuscript for a poem

printed in T. Wise, ed., *The Red Cross Knight and Other Poems* (London, 1917), but this is probably an inaccurate or dishonest transcription, for which see Textual Introduction. Wise's version is in fact identical to the manuscript, apart from 'glowing' in l. 1, clearly a mistake, 'enfold' for 'unfold' in l. 4, probably a mistake, the omission of 'It' on l. 32 of p. 110, and the replacement of ll. 49–53 by:

> But I love the evening's hour
> Whispering twilight to the breeze,
> And the dew's descending shower
> Falling lightly on the trees.

TEXT   p. 109   l. 20   [men], things, BCH
             l. 25   [hour], hours, BCH
             l. 27   [shower], showers, BCH

p. 111   *Young Man Naughty's Adventure*   'Murk was the night: nor star, nor moon'
Manuscript untraceable. A, p. 174 and AC, pp. 61–2 for Young Man Naughty. This is a curiously juvenile poem, and the date of 14 October 1830 given by Hatfield in BST 32 (1922), p. 109 may be too late.

p. 113   *The Violet*   'One eve, as all the radiant west'
Manuscript in RTP, with last 40 lines in BPM, pp. 3–7 of *The Violet*. In minuscule handwriting, signed Marquis of Douro, Charlotte Brontë, and dated, November 1830. A, p. 164. The classical learning, for which see AC, p. 22, though pretentious is impressive.

TEXT   p. 115   l. 58   [of this sunlit world], of the sons of earth, RTP
             p. 116   l. 70   [by], of, RTP
                      l. 91   she, from, RTP†
             p. 117   l. 98   [flows], flowed, RTP
                      l. 100   [glows], glowed, RTP
             p. 119   l. 160   RTP ends here and BPM begins
                      l. 165   [Sweet], A(s) sweet, BPM

p. 121   *Lines on Seeing the Portrait of——painted by De Lisle*   'Radiant creature! is thy birth'
Manuscript in BPM, p. 8 of *The Violet*. In minuscule handwriting, signed Marquis of Douro, Charlotte Brontë and dated 10 November 1830. A, p. 112 and AC, p. 72 for De Lisle's portrait of Marian Hume.

TEXT   p. 121   l. 9   [moon-lit], moonlight, BPM
              l. 18   [so], is, BPM
              l. 19   [of thy angel], Angel, of thy, BPM
              l. 21   [the], some, BPM
              l. 30   [Like golden], as gold as, BPM

p. 122   *Vesper*   'I'll hang my lyre amid these ancient trees'
Manuscript in BL, p. 9 of *The Violet*. In minuscule handwriting, signed Marquis of Douro, Charlotte Brontë and dated 11 November 1830. A, p. 163 says there is another manuscript, now untraceable, but as in the case of *Morning* (p. 109) this may be an incorrect or dishonest transcription. The differences between the manuscript in BL and the version recorded in C. Shorter, *Complete Poems* (London, 1923) follow the same pattern as in *Morning*.

TEXT   p. 122   l. 1   amid, upon, BL†
              l. 11   gentle, heavenly, BL†
              l. 13   [ear], car, BL
              l. 14   [heaven the dark], heaven dark, BL
      p. 123   l. 32   [silence], stillness, BL

p. 124   *Lines Addressed to Lady Z(enobia) E(llrington). Sent with my portrait which she had asked me to give her*   'Lady! this worthless gift I send'
Manuscript in RTP, p. 12 of *The Violet*. In minuscule handwriting, signed Marquis of Douro, Charlotte Brontë and dated 12 November

1830. A, p. 111 and AC, p. 61 for Lady Zenobia Ellrington, a blue-blooded bluestocking, rival to the humbler Marian Hume for Douro's affections. Zenobia subsequently marries Alexander Percy.

TEXT   p. 124   l. 21   [pearls], pearl, RTP
           l. 23   [queenly], single, RTP
      After l. 28   RTP inserts:

> And, oh, if ghastly death should break
>   The tie that binds us now,
> That token unto me shall speak
>   Of the imperial brow.

p. 125   *Matin*   'Long hath earth lain beneath the dark profound' Manuscript in BL and RTP, pp. 10–11 of *The Violet*. In minuscule handwriting, signed Marquis of Douro, Charlotte Brontë and dated 12 November 1830. A, p. 117 and AC, p. 72 for the context of this poem, the youthful Douro's love for Marian Hume, the daughter of his father's doctor.

TEXT   p. 125   l. 16   [awakening], awaking, BL
      p. 126   l. 25   [no], now, BL
            l. 32   The BL manuscript ends here and the RTP manuscript begins.

The increased number of errors in the Shakespeare Head edition is an interesting indication of the unreliability of this edition and the editions before it, when no manuscript was available for the editors to consult.

        l. 35   [And], Naught, RTP
        l. 36   [perchance], perhaps, RTP
        l. 38   [lambkins], lambkin, RTP
        l. 39   [whose], that, RTP
        l. 41   [Afric], Africa, RTP
        l. 42   [outpours his fervid], pours his most fervid, RTP

l. 44 [in wild and], even in, RTP
l. 46 [slumbers], slumber, RTP
l. 48 [Beam down upon my restless, spirit], Beaming upon me in unquiet, RTP
p. 127 l. 49 [but], how, RTP
l. 51 [stealing], flinging (?) RTP
l. 55 [from], o'er, RTP
l. 56 [Drew . . . that], What . . . then, RTP
l. 59 [win], bring back, RTP
l. 60 [That my], My sad, RTP
l. 61 [Oh], May, RTP

p. 128 *Reflections on the fate of neglected genius* 'Mighty winds that sing on high'
Manuscript in RTP, pp. 13–15 of *The Violet*. In minuscule handwriting, signed Marquis of Douro and dated 13 November 1830. A, p. 142. Whatever its Angrian context, the poem supplies useful evidence for the young Brontës' literary ambitions. It is possible that Wise's copyist may have been put off by the irregular metre and poor quality of some of the omitted lines.

TEXT p. 128 l. 12 [only], inly, RTP
After l. 14 RTP inserts: should burst to rage
l. 15 [vanquished], vanished, RTP
l. 23 [divinity], Divinity, RTP
p. 129 l. 29 But I to an unseen shadow speak, RTP
l. 36 [eye], eyes, RTP
l. 37 [purify], purifies, RTP
l. 47 [and], or, RTP
After l. 54 RTP inserts:

Or the blue moonlight heaven
　Bathed in a mystery of light
By myriads of glorious planets given
　Moving in orbits vast around the central light.

Then, when the high cerulean vault
  Quivers and trembles with their lustre strange,
Genius, thou dost thy votary's thoughts exalt
  To other mightier worlds that never never
    change.

And winged forms flit rapid o'er his brain
  Floating in radiance still and silently,
And on his ear swells some celestial strain
  Sounding from regions far beyond the sky.

None hear the unearthly song but him,
  And e'en to his entranced ear
Fitful, dreamlike and dim
  Those midnight sounds appear.

l. 55   [genius], Genius, RTP
p. 130   l. 60   [send], lend, RTP
After l. 62   RTP inserts:

The love of fame, the love of deathless glory
  Inspire alike the feeble and the strong.
The vigorous stripling and the ancient hoary
  Would each his name[?] to future years prolong.

l. 65   [soul], sole, RTP
l. 67   And thus in jostling strife he spends his breath,
       RTP†

p. 130   *Serenade*   'Awake! Awake! fair sleeper. Awake and view the night'
Manuscript in RTP, pp. 15–16 of *The Violet*. In minuscule handwriting, signed Marquis of Douro, Charlotte Brontë and dated 14 November 1830. Again Charlotte cannot quite handle the metre.

TEXT   p. 130   l. 4   [chiming], solemn chime, RTP
                l. 6   [for ever rushing], that ever rushes, RTP

p. 131   l. 12   [was], were, RTP
         l. 14   [thundering . . . are], thunder of . . . is, RTP

p. 132   (*Song*) 'The pearl within the shell concealed'
Manuscript untraceable. Part of the prose manuscript *Visits in Verreopolis* and dated 11 December 1830. A, p. 138 and AC, p. 292 for the image of the pearl.

p. 133   (*The Fairies' Farewell*) 'The trumpet hath sounded, its voice is gone forth'
Manuscript in HLH. In minuscule handwriting, signed C. Brontë and dated 11 December 1831. A, p. 162 and AC, p. 269, pointing out that this should not be taken, as it is by Miss Ratchford, as a grand finale to the Young Men's Play, consequent upon Charlotte going to school, although it may indicate a shift in the focus of the Angrian sagas with less part being played by the Genii. It may have been about this time that Anne and Emily embarked upon Gondal.

TEXT p. 133   l. 7   [sprang], sprung, HLH
                l. 8   [rang], rung, HLH
                l. 28   [tempest-], compact, HLH
      p. 134   l. 36   [troops], troop, HLH
                l. 44   [grave], hoarse, HLH
                l. 57   [rose], arose, HLH
      p. 135   l. 74   [bower], tower, HLH

p. 136   Oh! there is a land which the sun loves to lighten'
Manuscript in BCH, 2 pp., $3\frac{1}{2}'' \times 2\frac{1}{4}''$. In minuscule handwriting, unsigned but dated 25 December 1831. The bottom of the page is torn, and may conceal a signature; the last two words recorded in the Shakespeare Head version cannot be seen in the manuscript. A, p. 135

and AC, p. 76 for this description of the African Angrian scene, written in winter at Haworth before Charlotte's last term at Roe Head.

TEXT   p. 137   l. 38   [fair], dark (?), BCH
                     l. 44   [voice], roar, BCH

p. 138 *Lines on Bewick* 'The cloud of recent death is past away'
Manuscript untraceable. A, p. 86 gives the date as 27 November 1832 and the signature as C. Brontë. Thomas Bewick the painter died in 1828.

p. 141 (*Lament*) 'O Hyle! thy waves are like Babylon's streams'
Manuscript in BCH, 1 p., $7\frac{1}{4}'' \times 4\frac{1}{2}''$. In minuscule handwriting, unsigned and undated, although the prose manuscript, *The African Queen's Lament*, to which this is appended, is dated 12 February 1833, and the poem would seem to refer to this story. See A, p. 130. AC, p. 101 gives the context and on p. 273 discusses the literary influence of Byron and the Bible.

TEXT   p. 141   l. 5   shadowed, waned on, BCH†
                     l. 6   sweep, sigh, BCH†
                     l. 9   shines colder, is shining cold, BCH†
                     l. 10   Than, As, BCH†

p. 142 (*Death of Lord Rowan*) 'Fair forms of glistening marble stand around'
Manuscript in BCH, 1 p., $4\frac{1}{2}'' \times 3\frac{1}{2}''$. In minuscule handwriting, signed Charlotte Brontë, dated 26 May 1833. A, p. 92. On the back of the manuscript there is a note in prose, 'When Arthur had finished and his audience had yielded their tribute of applause, Marian exclaimed

in her lively way, "I think, my Lord, I know who you mean by Lord Rowan".' But the place of Lord Rowan in the Angrian saga is not known.

TEXT p. 142   l. 4   [thunder's], thunder, BCH
                l. 27   that, which, BCH†
                l. 28   [haven], heaven, BCH
                l. 29   it, him, BCH†

p. 143   (*Lord Edward and his Bride*)   'The night fell down all calm and still'
Manuscript in HRT, 1 p., 4½″ × 3½″, part of the prose manuscript *The Green Dwarf*, begun 10 July 1833 and finished 2 September 1833. Signed at beginning C. Wellesley and at end Charlotte Brontë. A, p. 127 and AC, pp. 97–101, for the story of *The Green Dwarf*, the abduction by Alexander Percy of the beautiful Lady Emily Charlesworth.

TEXT p. 143   l. 7   Toward me pensively, HRT†
       p. 144   l. 21   [teardrops], teardrop, HRT
                 l. 29   deep and, wildly, HRT†
                 l. 35   [deep], dim(?), HRT
                 l. 36   [soul's appalling], soul—appalling, HRT

p. 145   (*The Haunted Tower*)   'Oh! who has broke the stilly hush'
Manuscript in BCPML, 1 p., 4½″ × 3½″, part of the prose manuscript *Brushwood Hall*, itself part of *Arthuriana*. *Brushwood Hall* was completed on 1 October 1833. A, p. 135 and AC, pp. 104–5, which gives the story. Percy, ill, hides in the deserted hall, but is discovered.

TEXT p. 145   After l. 8   Two lines of prose intervene
                After l. 20   BCPML reads:

Hark to the wind so wild and dying
Through the black solemn fir grove sighing!
List to the unearthly voice that calls
The tongue that summons thee away!

p. 146 *The Red Cross Knight* 'To the desert sands of Palestine'
Manuscript in BCPML, 1 p., 4½″ × 3½″, part of *Arthuriana*. In minuscule handwriting, signed C. Brontë and dated 2 October 1833. A, p. 142. Charlotte's linking of the Crusades with the Angrian imperial mission in Africa is an interesting reflection of nineteenth-century historical attitudes.

TEXT p. 146 l. 11   [Then], They, BCPML
            l. 24   [each], the, BCPML
       After l. 24   the manuscript has no dots
            l. 26   [Sleeps], Was gathered, BCPML
      p. 147 l. 38   [bravest, best], bravest and best, BCPML
            l. 40   [Against], The war against, BCPML
            l. 44   [Call], Kingdoms call, BCPML
            l. 46   [blood, through], blood, through fire, through, BCPML
            l. 50   [Wring], And rescue, BCPML
            l. 51   [Win for], Take to, BCPML
            l. 52   [For], And pour on, BCPML

p. 148 *Memory* 'When the dead in their cold graves are lying'
Manuscripts in BCY, 5 pp., 7″ × 4¼″, BC, 4 pp., 6″ × 4″, and BPM, 2 pp., 6½″ × 5½″. The first in copperplate, signed C. Brontë and dated 2 October 1835, the second in copperplate, unsigned, but dated 2 August 1835, and the third in ordinary handwriting, signed C.B. and dated 13 February 1835. A, pp. 119–20. A raises the possibility of a fourth manuscript dated 2 October 1833, but this would seem to be a mistake by Hatfield.

TEXT p. 148   l. 6   that, which, BC
              l. 10   her, his, BPM
              l. 11   her, his, BPM
              l. 14   flee, fleet, BPM, BC
              l. 19   calm, still, BC

BCH omits ll. 17–20, 25–8. The alternative stanza on p. 149 is in the BC manuscript.

p. 149   *Lines Written beside a Fountain in the grounds of York Villa*
'Dear is the hour when, freed from toils and care'
Manuscript in BCPML, part of *Arthuriana*. In minuscule handwriting, signed C.B. and dated 7 October 1833. A, p. 113. See AC, p. 108 for this poem, written by Edward Sydney and stolen by the Marquis of Douro.

TEXT p. 150   l. 16   No dots follow this line
              l. 18   [shade], shades, BCPML

p. 151   *Richard Cœur de Lion and Blondel*   'The blush, the light, the gorgeous glow of eve'
Manuscript in BL, 27 pp., 6″ × 4″. In copperplate handwriting, signed Charlotte Brontë and dated 27 December 1833, Haworth, near Bradford. We find it difficult to admire Charlotte's conventional handling of this legend, although the verse is not bad.

TEXT p. 151   l. 8   [hoary waste, and], hoary, waste and, BL

p. 158   *Death of Darius Codomannus*   'The muffled clash of arms is past, as if it ne'er had been'
Manuscript in BCH, 23 pp., 6″ × 4¼″. In copperplate handwriting, signed Charlotte Brontë and dated 2 May 1834. Also a fragment in

BCPML, 2 pp., 5″ × 3¾″. In minuscule handwriting, signed Charlotte Brontë and dated 1 May 1834. A, pp. 88–9, AC, p. 240 shows Charlotte's interest in the Persian Empire, possibly used as a source for Angria.

TEXT　The manuscript, unlike most of Charlotte's, is well punctuated, but stanza divisions are difficult to detect. Even line divisions are obscured by the largeness of the handwriting and the smallness of the page.

p. 159	l. 38	wood, grove, BCH†
	l. 44	[*is*], is, BCH
p. 160	l. 76	[fatal], fated, BCH
p. 164	l. 184	The BCPML fragment begins here
p. 165	l. 217	rebel, Traitor, BCPML

p. 166　*Stanzas on the fate of Henry Percy*　'The tropic twilight falls, the deep is still'
Manuscript in HLC, 4 pp., 7½″ × 4½″, part of *Corner Dishes*. In minuscule handwriting, signed Charlotte Brontë and dated 15 June 1834. A, p. 153 and AC, pp. 107, 111 for the melodramatic story of Henry Percy, Marian Hume's first husband, murdered by Captain Steighton, a minion of Alexander Percy.

TEXT	p. 166	l. 9	swells, swell, HLC, but incorrectly
	p. 167	l. 12	rests on, has sought, HLC†
		l. 36	[shadow], shadow vast, HLC
		l. 38	[Long has], Loud as, HLC
	p. 168	l. 47	[fair], far, HLC
		l. 57	[brow], brows, HLC
	p. 169	l. 76	[gentlest], loveliest [?], HLC
		l. 97	[trembling o'er them], o'er them trembling, HLC
		l. 98	[lucid], coloured, HLC

p. 170   l. 103   [Wake] [?] they remembered from, Wakes thy remembered form, HLC

         l. 113   [his hand in hers], *his* hand to *hers*, HLC

p. 171   l. 134   [taper's], tapers', HLC

         l. 140   [from], far, HLC

         l. 149   [among], amongst, HLC

p. 172   l. 176   [as], to, HLC

         l. 185   [Lover she mourns not], Lover! She mourns not! HLC

p. 174   l. 244   [these], those, HLC

p. 176   *A National Ode for the Angrians*   'The sun is on the Calabar, the dawn is quenched in day'
Manuscript in BCH, 1 p., 7¼″ × 5¾″. In minuscule handwriting, signed Arthur Augustus Wellesley, C. Brontë and dated 17 July 1834. A, p. 127 and AC, pp. 125–6 for the founding of the new kingdom of Angria.

TEXT   p. 176   l. 1   [sun . . . dawn], Sun . . . Dawn, BCH

             l. 8   [on], and, BCH

             l. 15   [and], the, BCH

             l. 18   [its], his, BCH

      p. 177   l. 34   [The], And the, BCH

      p. 178   l. 44   [Aornu's], Aornus', BCH

             l. 56   [blood-red], bloody, BCH

      p. 179   l. 66   [The 'Slaves' Lament,' the 'Emperor's Hymn'], The slave's lament, the conqueror's hymn, BCH

p. 180   *Saul*   ' 'Neath the palms in Elah's valley'
Manuscript in BC, 8 pp., 6″ × 4″. In copperplate handwriting, signed C. Brontë and dated 7 October 1834. Much irregular punctuation. A, p. 147.

TEXT   p. 180   l. 25   [Saul is not a man], God is not in mind, BC
        p. 181   l. 57   [sullen], sunless, BC
                  l. 58   [Dark and], Darkly, BC
        p. 182   l. 76   [exiled], exile, BC
                  l. 79   [soothing], smoothly, BC

p. 182   *Lament*   'Lament for the Martyr who dies for his faith'
Manuscript in BL, 2 pp., 5″ × 3¾″, bound with the manuscript of *The
Spell*. In minuscule handwriting, signed C. Brontë, unfinished and
dated 28 November 1834. A, p. 108. See AC, p. 242 for Charlotte's
interest in St. Stephen, but the conclusion of the poem makes the
Christian interpretation less likely.

TEXT   p. 182   After l. 1   Lament for the warrior on battle's red sod BL
        p. 183   l. 29   secret, holy, BL†
        p. 184   The manuscript continues after l. 49:

                    But, Percy, for that rose of thine,
                    Maria Stuart, bright, divine,
                    Divine and bright the mortal form,
                    The eternal soul a venomed worm,
                    For her I'd never heave a sigh.
                    Unmoaned I'd let the fair fiend die,
                    Seductive in her treachery,
                    Most dazzling in her crimes.
                    The flower of France should fade away
                    And Scotland's heather Hell decay
                    Ere [?] her death mass left its chimes.
                    And I could smile vindictively
                    To know the earth I walked was free
                    From her who kissed her lord to death,
                    And poisoned him with kindness's breath,
                    One moment fondly oer him bending,
                    The next her gentle spirit lending

To plots that well might wake a shiver
In bosoms crime has deathed [?] forever.
Accursed woman o'er thy tomb
My scorn flings down its sternest gloom
(Thy sister snake stung well and deep†)

p. 184 (*Retrospection*) 'We wove a web in childhood'
Manuscript in HLC, 5 pp., 6¼″ × 3¾″. In minuscule handwriting, signed C. Brontë and dated 19 December, Haworth, 1835. A, p. 166. See AC, p. 140 for the context of this poem, important for Charlotte's awareness of the dangers of her Angrian visions.

TEXT p. 185 l. 42 As, When, HLC†
p. 188 After l. 114 HLC has, crossed out:

But other scenes I'd seen than this
Far wandering from that lordly bliss
[*A third, illegible line*]

l. 116 [ring], rang, HLC
l. 132 [And listened ... trembling], All listening ... lady's, HLC
l. 136 [lips'], lips, HLC
p. 190 l. 178 [Camilia's], Eamalia's, HLC

p. 191 *The Wounded Stag* 'Passing amid the deepest shade'
Manuscript in SUNY, pp. 11–12 of *The Wounded Stag*. In minuscule handwriting, unsigned and undated, but the final poem in this notebook is dated 19 January 1836. A, p. 172 and AC, p. 18 for a Christian interpretation of this poem.

TEXT p. 191 l. 7 Passed through, Fell on, SUNY†
l. 8 centred full, gently fell, SUNY*
l. 16 [bled], sobbed, SUNY
l. 20 breast, heart SUNY*

p. 192   'Turn not now for comfort here'
Manuscript in BCH, 1 p., 7¼″ × 4½″. In minuscule handwriting (last verse in normal handwriting, possibly not part of this poem), unsigned and undated. A, p. 162 and AC, p. 147, giving the context of Zamorna's army in retreat.

TEXT   p. 192   l. 2   [moors], guests, BCH
                 l. 4   [hills], halls, BCH

p. 193   *Mementos*   'Arranging in long-locked drawers, and shelves'
Manuscript untraceable. There is a manuscript in BCH, 4 pp., 7¼″ × 4½″. In normal handwriting, unsigned and undated, but around 1843. This however, apart from the first four lines, is a different poem from that printed here, although the general message is the same. See A, p. 118 for the date of 1837 for this poem and AC, p. 156 for the context. The BCH manuscript poem is printed below; we know nothing of Frances or Clara, although Frances might be the same as the heroine of the poem on p. 22.

> Arranging long-locked drawers and shelves
> Of cabinets, shut up for years,
> What a strange task have we set ourselves.
> How still the lonely room appears,
> (Look at those Chinese toys, those shells
> Gathered, no doubt, in Indian seas
> This Florence vase, the Venice glass†)
> How strange this mass of relics old
> In sullied pearl and tarnished gold,
> These volumes clasped with costly stone,
> With print all faded, gilding gone,
> Now stored [?] with cameos, vases, shells
> In this old chest's dusty cells.
> Why do the rich thus lay up treasures
> Which they forget or seldom see?
> They only think of present treasures
> And rarely turn to memory.

When Lady Frances leaves her home,
These English roads, this grey old tower,
And better loves, abroad to roam
Than live where she has land and power,
'Tis strange that she so little loves
Her own hereditary groves.
'Tis strange her bosom does not warm
To this old mansion's stately charm.
But if you saw what I have seen,
With what a sad and restless mien
She looks round on each panelled room
And seems to fear its pleasant gloom,
When at far intervals returning
She in her birthplace reappears,
Passes a single week of mourning,
Then leaves again her home for years.
Surely there is some old distress,
Some sorrow lingering here for her.
I scarce know what—yet partly guess
When to past time my thoughts recur.
These thoughts can thirty years retrace
Passed in the self-same scene and place.
So long my life has bounded been
By Aston's [?] park and woodlands green.
The house and forest seem the same
As the first day I hither came.
Old were they then, old are they now.
More moss upon the trees may grow,
More ivy round the gables cling
With each returning quickening spring,
But axe has never felled an oak
Nor change nor tillage scared a rook,
Nor Art one old carved chair displaced,
Nor stolen cup or vase enchased.
No one small ornament defaced, unhinged
No diamond latticed-frame it fringed.

Woodland and brier about them grew
An age since just as now they do.
But 'tis not so with living things.
To them warm sun and genial springs
Bring no renewal—they decay
Even in the arms they seek to cherish
When each one has fulfilled his day.
'Tis written he must pass and perish.
(Then comes the stone and marble urn
And dust must unto dust return†)
Full soon the grave remembrance swallows,
The heir succeeds—a new race follows.

This house is void and desert now,
'Twas peopled thirty years ago.
Master and mistress, youthful heir,
Daughters, both young, are passing fair,
Servants and guests and lordly cheer
Made all things gay and joyous here.
Clara and Frances were my care
To teach in childhood and in youth
To tend—each whim with mildness hear
When gay to guard—when sad to soothe.
Clara has beauty from her birth,
Always fine eyes and flowing hair.
Her mother knew that beauty's worth
And cultured (tended†) it with constant care
It prospered—she became each day
More perfect in her symmetry.
Her eyes acquired a brighter (softer†) ray,
Her face a sweeter harmony.
She was at length her parent's pride
And seldom left their fostering side.

p. 197 *Charge on the enemy* 'Charge on the enemy'
Manuscript in BCH, 1 p., 7¼″ × 4½″ with title on following page. In minuscule handwriting, unsigned and undated, but on the same page

as the Angrian poem, 'Well the day's toils are over, with success', signed Charlotte Brontë and dated 9 January 1837. A, p. 85.

TEXT   p. 197   l. 13   [an], in, BCH
           l. 14   [Risk], Riot, BCH

p. 197   (*The Ring*)   'This ring of gold, with one small curl'
Manuscript in BCH, 3 pp., 7¼″×4½″. In minuscule handwriting, unsigned and undated, but around 1837. A, p. 158. Although the Angrian context is hardly clear, and we do not know who the narrator is, this is a very fair example of Charlotte's Angrian fantasies with a strong emphasis on love, longing, and luxuriant scenery.

TEXT   p. 197   l. 1   [one], the, BCH
           l. 6   [green], grey, BCH
     p. 198   l. 24   gloom, shade, BCH†
           l. 29   [winter's], winter, BCH
           l. 35   panes, gigantic trees, windows at midnight, BCH†
           l. 42   remoter, distant, BCH†
           l. 43   dreams, thoughts, BCH†
     p. 199   l. 52   Traversed, Wandered, BCH†
           l. 60   that none would now remembered, I was no more remembered, BCH†
           l. 82   Of verdure to the, And to the wide, BCH†
     p. 200   l. 95   [though], though I, BCH
           l. 96   blent with the feeling, with love now mingled, BCH†
           l. 103   [Soon, O], Young, BCH
           l. 117   eve, night, BCH†
     p. 201   l. 129   [*felt*], felt, BCH

p. 201   (*The Harp*)   'No harp on earth can breathe a tone'
Manuscript in BCH, 1 p., 7¼″×4½″. In minuscule handwriting unsigned and undated. A, p. 127.

TEXT   p. 201   l. 9   played, played and sung, BCH†

p. 202   (*The Lonely Lady*) 'She was alone that evening—and alone'
Manuscript in BCH, 2 pp., 7¼″ × 4½″. In minuscule handwriting, unsigned and undated, but on the same page as the first draft of *Presentiment*, dated 11 July 1837. A, p. 149. AC, pp. 158–9 gives the context of
these poems of love and war.

TEXT   p. 202   l. 12   along, among, BCH†
                l. 24   Straight, Full, BCH†
        p. 203   l. 27   [hallowed], hollowed, BCH

p. 203   'It is not at an hour like this'
Manuscript in BCH, 1 p., 7¼″ × 4½″. In minuscule handwriting, unsigned and undated, but on the same pages as a poem dated 30 May
1837. Mr Nicolls, in a transcript of this poem in BCL, combines it
with the following poem, possibly correctly. A, p. 105.

TEXT   p. 203   l. 3   commingling, with trembling, BCH†
                l. 4   That grey and sunless heaven, salute the heavy
                       clouds, BCH†
        p. 204   l. 24   [twilight's], twilight, BCH

p. 204   (*My Dreams*) 'Again I find myself alone, and ever'
Manuscript in BCH, 1 p., 7¼″ × 4½″. In minuscule handwriting, unsigned and undated. Possibly part of previous poem, although A,
p. 177 and AC, p. 148 date it to 1836. Whatever the Angrian context,
the poem would seem to be a good indication of Charlotte's state of
mind at Roe Head, torn between the conflicting demands of her
religion and sexuality.

TEXT p. 204 l. 13 guide, lead, BCH†
          l. 16 sole, one, BCH†
          l. 18 Their sere leaves fall on, And float away to, BCH†
     p. 205 l. 32 dark, placid, clear darkness, BCH†

p. 205 'Dream of the West! the moor was wild'
Manuscript in BCH, 1 p., 7¼″ × 4½″. In minuscule handwriting, unsigned and undated, but around 1837. A, pp. 89–90. The Guadima is
an Angrian river. Charlotte's geography here is vague, owing more to
Haworth than to Africa.

TEXT p. 205 l. 2   [Guardina], Guadima, BCH
          l. 7   transcendent, seductive, BCH†
     p. 206 l. 13 [and], the, BCH
          l. 18 unfold, will spread, BCH†
          l. 20 [Nile], hill, BCH
                 dreary, trackless, BCH†
          l. 30 cold, soft, BCH†
          l. 35 Where, And, BCH†

p. 207 (*When thou sleepest*) 'When thou sleepest, lulled in night'
Manuscript in BCH, 2 pp., 7¼″ × 4½″. In minuscule handwriting, unsigned and undated, but around 1837. Many corrections, most of them
illegible. A, pp. 167–8. AC, p. 170 for this as another example of
Charlotte's unhappiness at Roe Head.

TEXT p. 207 l. 11 O'er, Through, BCH†
          l. 12 Muffled ... black, Muffled ... chill, BCH†
          l. 19 clouds, mists, BCH†
          l. 24 Come again, though distant flown, BCH†
     After l. 24 BCH adds:

                 Oh how happy, how unbroken
                 Seems that watchful hour to fly

l. 30   thy slumber blest, has been thy quest, BCH†

p. 208 l. 34   lonely watch-light's gleam, watch light's lonely ray, BCH†

l. 41   external things, the external world, BCH†

l. 56   Came, turned, BCH†

l. 58   [unfinished], half finished, BCH

p. 209 'The trees by the casement are moistened with dew'
Manuscript in BCH, 1 p., 7¼″ × 4½″. On the same page as 'Sweetly died both words and air', and thought by A, p. 161 to be part of the same poem. By the side of the manuscript of the latter poem Charlotte has written a list of numbers, but unfortunately these do not correspond to this poem or the preceding poems. Thus the two poems make up 38 lines, and separately 12 and 26, while the preceding poem has 66 lines. None of these figures occur in Charlotte's list. Unsigned and undated, but around 1837. AC, p. 170 for the context.

TEXT   p. 209   l. 3   from, on, BCH†

l. 8   her home, the past, BCH†

l. 9   the Hall in repose, the chamber was still, BCH†

l. 10   Lay, And, BCH†

l. 12   the lady still singing her vesper, the form of the lady still singing, BCH†

l. 24   may, can, BCH†

p. 210 After l. 38   there is no sign that the manuscript is unfinished

p. 210 'He could not sleep!—the couch of war'
Manuscript in BCH, 1 p., 7¼″ × 4½″. In minuscule handwriting, unsigned and undated, but around 1837. A, p. 98, AC, p. 170, saying this refers to Zamorna's sleeplessness after the battle of Evesham.

TEXT   p. 210   l. 20   [amid], amidst, BCH

p. 211   l. 21   Beneath, And by, BCH†

l. 23   [round], around, BCH
After l. 28   BCH adds:

> The morn will bring him back his power,
> His strength, his pride, his energy.

p. 211   (*Diving*) 'Look into thought and say what dost thou see'
Manuscript in BCH, 1 p., 7¼″ × 4½″, on the same page as the important diary fragment beginning, 'I'm just going to write because I cannot help it.' In minuscule handwriting, unsigned and undated. A, p. 114 dates this poem late 1836, but around 1837 is a more cautious date. AC, p. 292.

TEXT   p. 211   l. 2   how dark the waves flow, plunge through the foam, BCH†
            l. 3   [Sing], Sink, BCH
            l. 4   [ay], aye, BCH
            l. 5   none have I found, I find none to bring, BCH†
            l. 7   [sank], sunk, BCH

p. 211   'I scarce would let that restless eye'
Manuscript in BCH (A), 1 p., 7¼″ × 4½″. In minuscule handwriting, unsigned and undated, but around 1837. Another manuscript in BCH (B), 4″ × 4¾″ with the bottom torn off. In ordinary handwriting, unsigned and undated, and almost impossible to date. The Shakespeare Head version of the second manuscript is correct apart from the last two lines which are crossed out. A, p. 203.

TEXT   p. 211   l. 3   its, each, BCH (A)
            l. 8   Which, That, BCH (A)†
      p. 212   l. 10   feelings, thoughts would, BCH (A)†
            l. 11   bind, bid, BCH (A)

p. 212 'Is this my tomb, this humble stone'
Manuscript in BCH, 2 pp., 7¼″ × 4½″. In minuscule handwriting, unsigned but dated 4 June 1837. A, p. 104.

TEXT   p. 212   l. 4   quiet, sheltered, BCH†
       p. 213   l. 24   [face], free, BCH
       p. 214   l. 59   [soft and clear], soft, clear, BCH
       p. 215   l. 77   [lost], past, BCH

p. 215 (*The Pilgrimage*) 'Why should we ever mourn as those'
Manuscript in HRT, 1 p., 7¼″ × 4½″ at end of untitled prose manuscript
known as *Julia*. In minuscule handwriting, unsigned and undated,
although *Julia* is signed C. Brontë and dated 29 June 1837. A, p. 168.
Compare Branwell's poem with the same title.

TEXT   p. 215   After l. 8   HRT reads:

                            From Beulah's bowers the pilgrim gazed
                            On Danger conquered, dread defied

                l. 17   flood, stream, HRT†
       p. 216   l. 24   where they walk, pilgrims robed, HRT†
                l. 29   he, that, HRT†

p. 216 (*Watching and Wishing*) 'Oh, would I were the golden light'
Manuscript untraceable, though a copy by Mr Nicholls in BCL with
the text as printed. This copy dated 1837, although A, p. 136 says 1838.
The date of 21 July 1837 seems authentic, but may be a confusion with
the following poem.

p. 217 (*Marian*) 'But a recollection now'
Manuscript untraceable, though a copy by Mr Nicholls in BCL, and a
facsimile of the first 31 lines in A. Joline's *Meditations of an Autograph*

Collector (New York and London, 1902), p. 72. A, p. 83. The BCL copy is dated 21 July 1837.

TEXT BCL copy has eight-line stanzas. The facsimile in Joline is identical to the Shakespeare Head version, except for the addition of a trial line after l. 16, 'Does it not of moonlight tell'.

p. 217	l. 6	Nor, Nor yet, BCL
p. 218	l. 18	Looks, But looks, BCL
	l. 28	that, the, BCL
	l. 30	was, were, BCL
p. 219	l. 47	midnight's, moonlight's, BCL

p. 219 'A single word—a magic spring'
Manuscript in BCH, 2 pp., 7¼″ × 4½″. In minuscule handwriting, unsigned but dated 17 November 1837. A, p. 150 and AC, pp. 169–70 for this as Charlotte's analysis of what Angria meant to her.

TEXT	p. 219	l. 12	its, thy, BCH†
		l. 14	The lines in the footnote appear after l. 16 in BCH
	p. 220	l. 31	[Through the flowers], Through flowers, BCH
		ll. 35–8	These lines are crossed out in BCH
	p. 221	l. 55	mystic, mighty, BCH†
		l. 58	Yonder, That dim, BCH†

p. 221 (*Gods of the old Mythology*) 'Gods of the old mythology, arise in gloom and storm'
Manuscript in BCH, 2 pp., 4½″ × 3¾″. In a slightly unusual minuscule handwriting, unsigned and undated, but around 1837. A, p. 96. The learning and the style of this poem are reminiscent of Branwell, although the handwriting is not his.

TEXT p. 221   l. 4   [of vine], divine, BCH
      p. 222   l. 9   [Chaldæa], Chaldee, BCH
                l. 19   [brightly], bright, BCH
                l. 23   [blooms], gloom, BCH
                l. 25   [and], most, BCH
      p. 223   l. 53   [lands], hands (?), BCH

p. 224 'Yet sleep, my lord and know'
Manuscript in BCH, 1 p., 7¼" × 4½". In minuscule handwriting, unsigned and undated, but around 1838. A, p. 174.

TEXT p. 224   l. 6   host, foe, BCH†

p. 224 'Long, long ago—before the weight of pain'
Manuscript in BCH, 1 p., 7¼" × 4½", the same page as the previous
poem. In minuscule handwriting, unsigned and undated, but around
1838. A, p. 113. AC, p. 170 says this poem refers to Mary Percy's
disillusion with her husband. TEXT as printed.

p. 225 'What does she dream of, lingering all alone'
Manuscript in BCH, 1 p., 7¼" × 4½". In minuscule handwriting, unsigned and undated, but around 1838. A, p. 167. The context may be
the same as that of the previous poem.

TEXT p. 225   l. 2   [that], the, BCH
                l. 3   [dim, still], still, dim, BCH

p. 226 'The voice of Lowood speaks subdued'
Manuscript in BCH, 1 p., 7¼" × 4½". In minuscule handwriting,
unsigned and undated, but around 1838. A, p. 165. There is no cer-
tainty about the context of this poem, but the narrator may well be

Mina Laury, the governess mistress of Zamorna. The name Lowood is an odd reminder of *Jane Eyre*, and possibly a link between that novel and *Mina Laury*, the best constructed of the juvenilia.

TEXT   p. 226   l. 6   A plaintive tale, a mournful song, BCH†

p. 227   (*The Death of Lord Hartford*)   ' "Oh, let me be alone," he said'
Manuscript in BCH, 2 pp., 7¼" × 4½". In minuscule handwriting, unsigned and undated, but around 1838. A copy by Mr Nicholls in BCL does give the date as 1838. A, p. 130 and AC, pp. 166–7. Lord Hartford falls in love with Mina Laury, challenges Zamorna to a duel, is wounded, and hovers between life and death, with his love for Mina undiminished.

TEXT   p. 227   l. 8   How pain could quell his pride, BCH*
        l. 9   [still], still, BCH†, void, BCH
        l. 11   An iron sky with clouds o'erspread, BCH
        l. 12   [storms], sad storms, BCH
        l. 24   Told thoughts too strange for pain, BCH†

p. 230   (*Siesta*)   ' 'Tis the siesta's languid hour'
Manuscript in BCH, 1 p., 7¼" × 4½". In minuscule handwriting, signed C. Brontë and dated 7 July 1838. A, p. 159.

TEXT   p. 230   l. 12   Safe in her mountain, In her calm mountain, BCH†
        l. 14   fragrance, odours, BCH*
        l. 23   [that], those, BCH

p. 231   (*A Valentine*)   'A Roland for your Oliver'
Manuscript untraceable. The date of February 1840 is calculated correctly in the footnote. A, p. 146. The sending of this Valentine to

the Revd William Weightman is a well-known glimmer of light relief in the sombre Brontë story.

p. 233 *Napoleon* 'O Corsican! thou of the stern contour!'
Manuscript in BCPML, pp. 6–9 of French exercise-book. In copper-plate handwriting, signed in Charlotte's hand Auguste Barbier, and dated Mars, 1843. The fragmentary versions of the first 16 lines in BCH, both 1 p., 8″ × 5½″, both torn at the bottom, rendering a few additional lines indecipherable. In ordinary handwriting, unsigned and undated, but probably written shortly before fair copy. The first version is printed below, the second is much closer to the BCPML version, and is noted in the textual notes.

> Thy France, O straight-haired Corsican,
>   How bold and bright was she
> When the broad sun of Messidor
>   Woke her full energy.
>
> She was a young stallion steed
>   That rein or bridle spurned;
> Formed of a wild and fiery breed
>   Her veins with lava burned
>
> Her veins still hot with kingly blood
>   Gave not their strength to toil;
> Wild with the joy of liberty
>   Her free hoof struck the soil,
>
> The touch of violence or force
>   So far was yet unknown,
> Nor o'er his loins had foreign foe
>   The shameful harness thrown.
>
> She trampled generations in her course
>   For fifteen bloody years.

p. 233   l. 1   of the stern contour, of the straight dark hair, BCH*
          l. 5   [horse], mare, BCPML**
          l. 10   Insult by word or deed, insult or wrong or force, BCH,
                  BCPML*, No hand profane, BCH†
          l. 12   steed, horse, BCPML*, BCH
p. 234   l. 24   The ? fixed his hold, BCPML**
                  The missing stanza reads:

> Booted he mounted; since he knew full well
>   She loved the voice of war,
> Musket and beating drum and trumpet's swell
>   And cannon's roar.
> He gave the wide world for her hunting ground,
>   His sport was war and toil.
> Nor rest, nor might, nor sleep his charger found;
>   Ever the air and toil [?]

          l. 26   [Breast deep], Breast-deep, BCPML
          l. 32   hoof of iron, iron sabot, BCPML*
          l. 46   [to], on, BCPML
          l. 47   unhelmed, and crushed, BCPML*
          l. 48   Crushed on a, On a hard, BCPML*

p. 235   (*Master and Pupil*) 'I gave, at first, attention close'
Manuscript in BCPML in *The Professor*. Alternative manuscript in
BCH, pp. 18–24 of *German Notebook*. A, pp. 101–2. Compare 'At first
I did attention give', p. 336.

TEXT   p. 235   l. 2   Then ... warm, warm ... soon, BCH†
                  l. 3   From, Then, BCH†
                  l. 5   soon, now, BCH†
                  l. 7   a word, a glance alone, my lord's approving bow,
                          BCH†
                  l. 15   slight omission, slightest error, BCH†

After l. 20 there is an asterisk in the BCH manuscript, corresponding to the gap in *The Professor* between the first and second part of Frances Henri's narrative.

After l. 28   there are two crossed-out lines in BCH:

> when as a genial noon in May
> I once more breathed fresh air.

p. 236   l. 32   responsive, returning, BCH

After l. 36   as well as the rejected stanzas mentioned on p. 239, BCH has two crossed-out lines:

> When to the class I came again
>   With broken health renewed.

and a half-completed stanza:

> And left a   to cheer
>   school
> I once again returned to bear
>   rule.

l. 60   bees, trees, BCH
p. 237   l. 61   Yet, And, BCH†
l. 67   His brow relaxed his customed frown, BCH†
l. 68   An impetuous, stern, dark eye, BCH†
l. 81   Scant were the marks of praise bestowed, BCH†
l. 83   The glance that out his deep eye glowed, BCH†
After l. 84   there are two crossed-out lines in BCH:

> Even when he blamed for little cause
>   With bitter taunt and keen

l. 91   quail to, notice, BCH
l. 92   Upheld by, So strong was, BCH
p. 238   l. 96   throbbing, weary, BCH
l. 103   bleeding, gaping, BCH, BCPML†
l. 115   in, my, BCH
p. 239   l. 128   Protection, Thy refuge, BCH†

p. 239 'The Autumn day its course has run'
Manuscript in BCH, pp. 25–7 of *German Notebook*. In ordinary
handwriting, unsigned and undated, but around 1843. In three versions, all of which are difficult to read, A, pp. 81–2. The third version
is that printed in the Shakespeare Head, with one line in the manuscript
replacing two in the text.
The first reads:

A week ago September dead (gone* past*) October's moon set in,
For some days heavy mists were shed upon her crescent horn [?].
A night of rain the fog removed, then sunrise fresh and clear
With gentle smile the doubt repressed which mourned the failing year.
The autumn day its course has run—the autumn evening falls,
Already risen the autumn moon gleams quiet on these walls,
And casts [?] her light upon the fields, to silver bleaches pale.
The untrodden road a lustre yields as white as heavy hail,
But dark the line of woods whose heavy boughs embrowned
Still wait November's sleety storms to shed their honours round
Sable and pale the scene appears and [—] [—]
And Luna's gold. The landscape wears a mean and phaeton hue
    No blush or flush—no amber brightness
    A neutral shade—a tintless whiteness.
Chaste night and tranquil! not too chill.
No wintry frostiness breathes from the hill.
Bent from my lattice I feel no breeze
Sweep o'er those dark fields—steal through those trees.
Lone flows the water—my ear receives
Its sound like the murmur of light air and leaves.
Even from the road not a whisper comes,
Nor traveller nor wanderer its white track roams.
And my house is silent—in every room
There is but moonlight and vacant gloom.
How 'mid this marble, this darkness, this snow
Can my heart beat and my warm blood flow?
How where there is but shadow and gleam [?]
Can my mind vary its wonted dream?

I can only wonder as black as clouds.
I trace only [—] [—] as shrouds
In the starlight and moonlight darkly clear.
Hollow silence is in mine ear
Yet I think

The second reads:

My parents to the distant town this morning early went,
To meet them on the mountain road the servant I have sent.
The autumn day its course has run, the autumn evening falls,
Already risen the autumn moon gleams quiet on these walls,
And twilight to our lonely house a silent guest is come
In mask of gloom through every room she passes dusk and dumb.
I've followed her—through every door I've cautious glanced to see
That only shade and moonbeam filled each chamber's vacancy.

p. 240   'Early wrapt in slumber deep'
Manuscript in BCH, p. 28. In normal handwriting, unsigned and
undated, but around 1843. A, p. 90.

TEXT   p. 240   l. 8   drapery, curtain, BCH†
                l. 20 A, Like, BCH†

p. 241   (*On the Death of Emily Jane Brontë*)   'My darling, thou wilt
never know'
Manuscript in HLC, 1 p., 4″ × 4¾″. In minuscule handwriting, unsigned but dated 24 December at beginning, possibly as title. In this
and the following version the asterisked readings are the upper
versions. They look as if Charlotte was trying out alternatives.

TEXT   p. 241   l. 2   The, Such, HLC†
                l. 3   That ... borne, As ... felt, HLC*, As ... known,
                       HLC†
                l. 10 When, And, HLC*

l. 14   Looking forth, Exploring, HLC*, Beholding,
HLC*, streaming, tear dimmed, HLC†

l. 15   [On life's lone wilderness], On life's wilderness,
HLC, Life's lone wilderness, HLC*

l. 19   [Then], O, HLC** (lower version)

l. 22   help us, relieve, HLC†

p. 242   (*On the Death of Anne Brontë*)   'There's little joy in life for me'
Manuscript in HLC, 1 p., 3″ × 4″. In minuscule handwriting, unsigned but dated at beginning, possibly as title, 31 June 1849. A, p. 157.

TEXT   p. 242   l. 3   parting hour, lingering death, HLC

l. 5   the failing breath, each gasp of breath, HLC,† the
struggling for breath, HLC†

l. 6   Wishing, Hoping, HLC*, Still hoping, HLC*,
might, would, HLC*

l. 7   [shade], cloud, HLC** (lower version)

l. 9   cloud, shade, HLC*

l. 16   bear, meet, HLC†

p. 243   *Reason*   'Unloved I love, unwept I weep'
Manuscript in SUNY, pp. 13–14 of *The Wounded Stag*. In minuscule handwriting, unsigned and undated, but the final poem in this notebook is signed C. Brontë and dated 19 January 1836.

TEXT   p. 243   l. 4   [means], dreams, SUNY

l. 14   to ... belong, of ... am one SUNY†

l. 19   will, shall, SUNY†

l. 22   [heart], life, SUNY†, poor heart, SUNY

p. 244   After l. 28   SUNY has two lines that are difficult to read:

I hear your Thunder forcing near
Beyond whose waves I left all love

p. 244   l. 36   trampled, natural, SUNY†

p. 244 'He saw my heart's woe, discerned my soul's anguish'
Manuscript in BC, 1 p., 7¼" × 4½". In ordinary handwriting, unsigned and undated, but the fact that on the reverse of this poem there is a letter to W. S. Williams dated 13 November 1847 suggests that the poem is late. A, p. 99. The reference to the yearly whisper of anguish might seem to point to M. Heger, although Charlotte's letters to him were more frequent, and those that have survived were earlier than 1847.

TEXT   p. 244   l. 1   [discovered], discerned, BC
                l. 4   moans ... pangs, moaning ... travail, BC*
       p. 245   l. 15 Granite, marble, BC†
                l. 31 [overpast], over and, BC

p. 245 (*Eventide*) 'The house was still, the room was still'
Manuscript in BCH, 1 p., 7¼" × 4½". In ordinary handwriting, unsigned and undated, but around 1843. A, p. 100.

TEXT   After l. 8   BCH has: The prisoner to the free replied

p. 246 'On the bright scenes around them spread'
Manuscript in BPM inside the front cover of *Porny's Grammatical Exercises, English and French*, 1 p., 6¼" × 4". In minuscule handwriting, unsigned but dated 17 January 1831. A, p. 132. An early Angrian series of fragments.

TEXT   p. 246   l. 5   mighty, longest, BPM†
                l. 7   [amber-light], thick lights, BPM
                l. 12 [Elver's], river's, BPM
                l. 19 [as, in fancy], of infancy, BPM

p. 247 'Lo! stretched beneath the clustering palm'
Manuscript in BCH, 8 pp., 3½" × 2½". In minuscule handwriting, unsigned, but as A, p. 116 shows, this poem continues with 92 other

lines dated 11 July 1831, and is part of a prose manuscript entitled *A Fragment*. See AC, pp. 74–5 for this story. The full text of this poem will be published in Dr Alexander's forthcoming edition of the juvenilia.

TEXT p. 248   l. 5   fan, pass, BCH†
              l. 9   lair, den, BCH†
              l. 12 [for], of, BCH
              l. 29 while, though, BCH†
                     [bewildered ocean], the ocean 'wildered, BCH
              l. 30 Her liquid realm between, BCH†
              l. 35 passion's, darkest, BCH†
      p. 249 l. 37 [whose], those, BCH
              l. 39 But, And, BCH†

p. 250   (*The Rose*)   'On its bending stalk a bonny flower'
Manuscript in BC, 2 pp., 5″ × 3″. In minuscule handwriting, unsigned and undated. A, p. 130.

TEXT p. 250   l. 14 [grow both day and night], it by day and by night, BC

g. 251   (*Morning*)   'Morning was in its freshness still'
Manuscript in BPM, 3 pp., 6″ × 4″. In ordinary handwriting, unsigned and undated, but around 1843. A, p. 124.

TEXT p. 251   l. 8   Disturb, Enter, BCH†
      p. 253 Before l. 41   there are two cancelled lines in BCH:

              If ever smiling eye met mine
                Or kind face turned to me.

              l. 42 fair, sweet, BCH†
              l. 44 wear, share, BCH*
              l. 48 But to dissolve in air, BCH†

p. 253   (*Lost in the Hills*)   'I now had only to retrace'
Manuscript in BCH, 1 p., 7¼″ × 4½″. Unsigned and undated but around 1843. A, p. 102. TEXT as printed.

p. 254   (*Alfred the Great*)   'Look, wife, the clouds are full of snow'
Manuscript in BCH, 2 pp., 7¼″ × 4½″. In ordinary handwriting, unsigned and undated, but around 1843. A, p. 115.

TEXT   p. 254   l. 3   A cold north, By night the, BCH†
                     l. 16   fierce these forests, dangerous, BCH*
                     l. 21   [buffet], tripod, BCH**

SECTION 3

p. 259 'High minded Frenchmen love not the Ghost'
Manuscript in BCH, 1 p., 5″ × 2¾″. In normal juvenile handwriting, very difficult to read, signed Young Soult, C. Brontë and dated 17 July 1829. A, p. 99. Young Soult was Branwell's pseudonym, and this may be a joint effort. TEXT as printed, although I have not been able to decipher the crossings out.

p. 259 'I've been wandering in the greenwoods'
Manuscript in RB, 1 p., 2¾″ × 2¾″. In minuscule handwriting, signed C. Brontë and dated 14 December 1829. A, p. 106, showing the former attribution to Emily. The signature could be that of Emily, as the C could be an E, but the handwriting and date point to Charlotte. TEXT as printed.

p. 260 *Verses by Lord Charles Wellesley* 'Once more I view thy happy shores'
Manuscript in RTP, 1 p., 3½″ × 3½″. In normal juvenile handwriting, signed C. Brontë and dated 11 February 1830. A, p. 163 and AC, pp. 59–61 for the persona of Lord Charles Wellesley. TEXT as printed.

p. 261 *Miss Hume's Dream* 'One summer eve, as Marianne stood'
Manuscript in BCPML, 2 pp., 3¾″ × 2″. In minuscule handwriting, signed Islander Lord C. Wellesley and dated 29 June 1830. There is an additional note, 'I wrote this in half an hour, C. Brontë'. A, p. 121 and AC, pp. 71–2 for the love affair between Marian Hume and Arthur Wellesley.

TEXT p. 262 l. 28 lane, hedge, BCPML†
            l. 51 A hollow breeze blows, The hollow wind sways, BCPML†
       p. 263 l. 64 raised her head, oped her eye, BCPML†

p. 263 'He is gone, and all grandeur has fled from the mountain'
Manuscript in BCH, 2 pp., 3½″ × 2¼″. In minuscule handwriting, unsigned but dated 20 August 1832. A, p. 98, who says there are two
manuscripts, but the former may be a faulty copy by Wise.

TEXT   p. 263   l. 11   Then, O, May the, BCH†
             l. 12   Thy, his, BCH†
    p. 264   l. 21   he, thou, BCH†
             l. 24   his, thy, BCH†
             l. 28   be unfurled on high, wave in England's sky, BCH†

p. 264   *St. John in the Island of Patmos*   'The holy exile lies all desolate'
Manuscript untraceable, but transcript by Mr Nicholls in BCL, said
to be by C. Brontë and dated 30 August 1832. A, p. 154 and AC,
pp. 259, 271.

TEXT   The sixth stanza appears to be crossed out, perhaps because it
seems to refer to John the Baptist.

p. 266   'Justine, upon thy silent tomb the dews of evening weep'
Manuscript in BCH, 1 p., 7¼″ × 4½″. In minuscule handwriting, unsigned and undated, but probably around February 1833 because on
the back of this manuscript is *The African Queen's Lament*, which is
thus dated. A, p. 106 and AC, p. 214 for the context of this poem.
Justine is Mina Laury's mother and Zamorna's nurse.

p. 268   'The moon dawned slow in the dusky gloaming'
Manuscript in BPM, 2 pp., 4½″ × 3½″. In minuscule handwriting,
unsigned and undated, but the prose story *A Leaf from an Unopened
Volume*, to which this is attached, is dated 17 January 1834. Also in
in BCH two earlier versions, 4 pp., 5″ × 2¾″. In minuscule hand-

writing, unsigned and undated, but around 1834. A, p. 122 and AC, p. 236 with an illustration.

TEXT   The first version in BCH, very difficult to read, only includes the first part of the poem. It runs as follows:

> Slow dawns the moon on the brow of the gloaming,
> Dimly beside it shimmers a star,
> All broken it shines on the waves wildy foaming,
> Which rush on the course of the wild Calabar
>
> The light of the moon the wail of the river
> Wake the sweet voice . . .
> [6 illegible lines]
>
> From the caverned earth I rose
>   Mortal like to thee.
> On my tribute streamlet flows
>   To the monarch sea,
> Even as thy career will close
>   Dark in eternity.
>
> And then I asked the crescent moon
>   O'er what her bow was bent,
> And thus the sweet response came down
>   From Heaven Earthward sent.
>
> Beneath my midnight wandering
>   All widely lies the earth.
> I view the stream's meandering
>   To the ocean from its birth

The second version in BCH is much closer to BPM.

p. 268	l. 2	Dimly, Dim, BCH
	l. 3	they shone, it shines, BCH
p. 269	l. 13	from the wave like a sound in a dream, BCH
	l. 40	The desert hearth and home, BCH
p. 270	l. 52	softest, lightest, BCH
	l. 57	This verse precedes the previous one in BCH

l. 67   my beams in peace, in peace my beams, BCH
p. 271 l. 86   round, on, BCH
        l. 88   Above, Around, BCH

p. 271 'The day is closed, that spectral sun'
Manuscript in BCPML, 4 pp., 4½″ × 3¾″. In minuscule handwriting, unsigned and undated, but around 1834. A, p. 87. AC does not mention this poem, but it would seem to refer to the death of Henry Percy, discussed on p. 107.

TEXT   The last section of the poem is written in pencil and is very difficult to read.

p. 271 l. 2   Whose full light never glowed on earth, BCPML†
p. 273 l. 55 breeze, wind, BCPML†
        l. 81 bark, brat, BCPML†

p. 274 'Come now, I am alone, the day's wild riot'
Manuscript in SUNY, p. 1 of *The Wounded Stag*. In minuscule handwriting, unsigned and undated, but there is the signature C. Brontë and the date of 19 January 1836 at the end of the last poem in this volume. This poem would seem to have a Roe Head context. A, p. 13. TEXT as printed.

p. 275 'All is change—the night, the day'
Manuscript in SUNY, p. 4 of *The Wounded Stag*. In minuscule handwriting, unsigned and undated. Possibly before the other poems in this volume, as it appears in the middle of 'Long since, as I remember well' at the bottom of one sheet that has to be read upside-down. TEXT as printed.

p. 275 'Long since, as I remember well'
Manuscript in SUNY, pp. 1–8 of *The Wounded Stag*. In minuscule

handwriting, unsigned and undated, but there is the signature C. Brontë and the date of 19 January 1836 at the end of the last poem in this volume. A, p. 114. AC, pp. 279, 280, 291 for this poem as evidence for Charlotte's state of mind at Roe Head.

TEXT	p. 275	l. 9	gain, know, SUNY†
		l. 10	Which, That, SUNY†
	p. 276	l. 30	Oh, And, SUNY†
		l. 41	ray, breath, SUNY†
	p. 277	l. 53	flowed, ran, SUNY†
		l. 62	being alone, solitude, SUNY†
	p. 278	l. 92	like a giant, grimly, sternly, SUNY†
	p. 279	l. 131	While, And, SUNY†
	p. 280	l. 164	That untimely, The midnight, SUNY†
	p. 283	l. 246	glancing lightning, following glory, SUNY†
		l. 250	give, tell, SUNY†
	p. 284	l. 274	pray, weep, SUNY†
	p. 286	l. 347	gentle, silver, SUNY†

p. 289 'But once again, but once again'
Manuscript in SUNY, pp. 15–20 of *The Wounded Stag*. In minuscule handwriting, signed C. Brontë and dated 19 January 1836. A, p. 83 and AC, p. 142. Both this poem and its predecessor are interesting but chaotic. In both poems I have only recorded the more obvious of the many corrections.

TEXT	p. 292	l. 116	stern, dark, SUNY†
	p. 294	l. 161	strange, vague, SUNY†
	p. 298	l. 295	clear, sweet, SUNY†

p. 299 'And not alone seems she from pillared halls'
Manuscript in BCH, 1 p., 7¼″ × 4½″. In minuscule handwriting, unsigned and undated. A, p. 78 does not even hazard a guess at the date, but around 1836.

TEXT p. 299 l. 6 broad, wide, BCH†

p. 299 'A single word so seen at such a time'
Manuscript in BCH, 1 p., 7¼″ × 4½″. In minuscule handwriting, unsigned and undated, but around 1837. On the same page as 'Turn not now for comfort here'. A, p. 81. TEXT as printed.

p. 299 'And few have felt the avenging steel'
Manuscript in BCH, 1 p. (torn), 4¼″ × 4¾″. In minuscule handwriting, unsigned and undated, but around 1837. A, p. 78. TEXT as printed.

p. 300 'I never sought my mother's face'
Manuscript in BCH, 1 p. (torn), 4¼″ × 4¾″. Reverse of previous manuscript. In minuscule handwriting, unsigned and undated, but around 1837. A, p. 102. TEXT as printed.

p. 301 'I thought in my childhood how pleasant would be'
Manuscript in BCH, 1 p., 7¼″ × 4½″. In minuscule handwriting, unsigned and undated, but around 1837. A, p. 105. TEXT as printed.

p. 302 'Lady-bird! lady-bird! fly away home'
Manuscript in BC and BCH, 4 pp., 4½″ × 3½″. In minuscule handwriting, unsigned and undated, but around 1837. A, p. 107. TEXT as printed.

p. 309 'O that thy own loved son, thy noblest born'
Manuscript in BPM, 1 p., 9″ × 6½″. In minuscule handwriting, unsigned and undated, although on the back of a letter from Charlotte to her father, dated 17 May 1831. A, p. 134, however, dates this around 1837.

TEXT p. 309 l. 8   And hush for ever more the minstrels' shell, BCH†
            l. 12 proud, wild, BCH†
            l. 23 lay, leave, BCH†
    p. 310 l. 38 cold, damp, BCH†
            l. 47 sharp, red, BCH†, look, spring, BCH†
            l. 58 slacked, now, BCH†
    p. 311 l. 72 desolate and lone, BCH†

p. 311 'Well, the day's toils are over, with success'
Manuscript in BCH, 10 pp., 7¼″ × 4½″. In minuscule handwriting, signed Charlotte Brontë and dated 9 January 1837. A, p. 166. TEXT as printed. I have not been able to decipher any but the most trivial crossings out.

p. 325 'But, oh, exult not. Hush thy joy'
Manuscript in BCH, 1 p., 7¼″ × 4½″. In minuscule handwriting, unsigned, but dated 30 May 1837. Not in A.

TEXT p. 325 l. 4 dim, sad, BCH†, wild, BCH†

p. 325 'A woodland dream! A vision dim'
Manuscript in BCH, 1 p., 7¼″ × 4½″. In minuscule handwriting, unsigned and undated. On same page as previous poem, and therefore around 1837. Not in A. TEXT as printed.

p. 325 'Sit still—a breath, a word may shake'
Manuscript in BCH, 2 pp., 7¼″ × 4½″. In minuscule handwriting, unsigned and undated. A, p. 169 takes this as an early version of *The Wife's Will*, p. 16, but apart from the partial similarity of the first line there is no resemblance between the two poems. Probably around 1837. TEXT as printed.

p. 327   *O Never, never leave again*   'O never, never leave again'
Manuscript in BCH, 1 p., 7¼″×4½″. In minuscule handwriting, unsigned and undated, but around 1837. On same pages as previous poem. Not in A. TEXT as printed.

p. 328   'Obscure and little seen my way'
Manuscript in BCH, 1 p. In minuscule handwriting, unsigned and undated, but around 1837. The poem looks autobiographical, but may be Angrian. Not in A. TEXT as printed.

p. 328   *Stanzas on the Death of a Christian*   'Calm on the bosom of thy God'
Manuscript in BPM, 1 p., 10″×7¾″. In copperplate handwriting, signed C. Brontë, Haworth and dated 27 July 1837. A, p. 153. TEXT as printed.

p. 329   *The Town besieged*   'With moaning sound a stream'
Manuscript in BCPML, pp. 3–4 of *Poems*. In copperplate handwriting, dated June 1838, but probably copied around 1843. Alternative version in BCH, 2 pp., 7¼″×4½″. In minuscule handwriting, unsigned but dated 28 June 1838. A, p. 160 and AC, pp. 171–9 for the plot of *Stancliffe's Hotel* in which this poem originally appeared.

TEXT   The alternative version in BCH reads:

> Deep the Cirhala flows
>   And Evesham o'er it swells,
> The last night she shall smile upon
>   In silence round her dwells.
>
> All lean upon their spears,
>   All rest within, around,
> But some shall know tomorrow night
>   A slumber far more sound.

The summer dew unseen
On tent and turret shines.
What dew shall fall when battle's voice
Is heard along the lines?

Trump and triumphant drum
The conflict war shall spread.
Who then will turn as we and say
"We mourn our noble dead?"

Strong hands, heroic hearts
Shall homeward throng again,
Redeemed from battle's bloody grasp
Where will they leave the slain?

Beneath a foreign sod
Beside an alien wave
(They found an exile's grave†)
Watched by the martyr's holy God
Who guards the martyrs grave?
(Repose the martyred brave†)

p. 330 *Review at Gazemba* 'All the summer plains of Angria were asleep in perfect peace'
Manuscript in BCH, 2 pp., 7¼″ × 4½″. Unsigned, but dated 7 July 1838.
A, p. 144 and AC, p. 182.

TEXT p. 330   l. 6   once more, again, BCH†
        p. 331   l. 26   flashed, waved, BCH†

p. 334 'Sigh no more—it is a dream'
Manuscript in BCH, 1 p., 7¼″ × 4½″. In minuscule handwriting, unsigned and undated, but around 1838, as there is a one-line mention of the review at Gazemba (see previous poem) on the same page. Not in A. TEXT as printed.

p. 334 'Fast, fast as snow-flakes, fled the legions'
Manuscript in BCH, 1 p., 7¼"×4½". In ordinary handwriting, unsigned and undated. On the same page as the previous poem, and
therefore probably around 1838, but Charlotte may have written
these lines later. A reminder of the last verse of the poem on p. 188.
Not in A. TEXT as printed.

p. 335   *O That Word Never*   'Not many years, but long enough to
see'
Manuscript in BC, 1 p., 1"×4". In minuscule handwriting, unsigned,
but dated 23 December, possibly as title. See A, p. 128 for the attribution to Emily, but the handwriting is clearly Charlotte's. The date
1839 is a conjecture, made when the poem was thought to be by
Emily, and it is possible that this moving poem is in fact Charlotte's
response to Emily's death in December 1848.

TEXT   p. 335   l. 6   each, the, BC†
The words 'O that word never' are written along the margin.

p. 335   'The Nurse believed the sick man slept'
Manuscript in BCH, 1 p., 3½"×5" (torn). In ordinary handwriting,
unsigned and undated, but around 1843. A, p. 129.

TEXT   p. 335   l. 3   She left the bed and softly crept, BCH†

p. 335   'How far is night advanced? Oh, when will day'
Manuscript in BCH, 1 p., 3½"×5" (torn), the same as the preceding
poem. In ordinary handwriting, unsigned and undated, but around
1843. A, p. 100. TEXT as printed.

p. 335   'Like wolf—and black bull or goblin hound'
Manuscript in BCH, 1 p., 3½"×5" (torn). In ordinary handwriting,

unsigned and undated, but around 1843, probably a fragment of the poem on p. 254. A, p. 111. TEXT as printed.

p. 336   'At first I did attention give'
Manuscript in BC, 4 pp., 7¼″ × 4½″. In ordinary handwriting, unsigned and undated, but around 1845. I discuss this poem, its relationship to two poems in *Jane Eyre* and *The Professor*, and its autobiographical implications in CW, pp. 1–12. A, p. 81.

TEXT   p. 336   l. 10   him near, his tread, BC†
                  l. 18   pain, grief, BC†
                  l. 22   sure, deep, BC†

        p. 337   ll. 27–8   Then did the veil of doubt depart
                              And life a glory wore, BC†

                  l. 29   It played about the awful brow, BC†
                  l. 37   But, And, BC†
                  l. 40   surges, brilliant, BC†
                  l. 41   robber path, barren track, BC†
                  l. 43   For hate and love, delight and wrath, BC†
                  l. 46   omens, feelings BC†
        p. 338   l. 56   gather nigh, [?] brings nigh, BC†

                  ll. 57–9   The hate, the love, the joy the sweet
                              The wrath I had passed over
                              These came on pinion strong and fleet, BC*

                  l. 66   veins, soul, BC†
                  l. 73   seized, reached, BC†

APPENDIX
PRELIMINARY LIST OF OTHER POEMS BY CHARLOTTE BRONTË, NOT PUBLISHED IN THIS EDITION

'A better lot is thine, fair maid'. Around March 1839. Published in W. Gérin, *Five Novelettes* (London, 1971), p. 283.

'And when you left me what thoughts had I then'. 19 July 1836. Published in SHCBM, vol. II, p. 240.

'And with that thought came an impulse'. 26 March 1839. Published in W. Gérin, *Five Novelettes*, p. 245.

'Beneath Fidena's Minster'. 21 July 1838. Published in SHCBM, vol. II, p. 370.

Captain Flower's Last Novel. 'Each sound of woe has died away upon the summer air'. 20 November 1833. Published in SHCBM, vol. I, p. 307.

'Dark is the mansion of the dead'. 7 November 1833. Published in W. Holtz, *Two Tales by Charlotte Brontë* (Columbia, 1978).

'Death is here, I feel his power'. 28 August 1830. Published in BST, 52 (1942), p. 112.

'Eamala is a gurt bellaring bull'. 27 June 1833. Published in SHCBM, vol. I, p. 228.

Harvest in Spain. 'Now all is joy and gladness, the ripe fruits'. 9 December 1829. Published in SHCBM, vol. I, p. 15.

'Haste, bring us the wine cup'. 4 September 1830. Unpublished.

'Hearken, O Mortal, to the wail'. 18 December 1830. Published in SHCBM, vol. I, p. 59.

'Holy St. Cyprian! thy waters stray'. 17 January 1838. Published in W. Gérin, *Five Novelettes*, p. 167.

Hurrah for the Gemini. 'Hurrah for the Gemini! Blessed be the Star!' 14 October 1834. Published in SHCBM, vol. II, p. 44.

Interior of a Pothouse by Young Soult. 'The cheerful fire is blazing bright'. 21 August 1829. Unpublished.

'In this fairy land of light'. 17 August 1829. Published in T. Burnett, *The Search after Hapiness* (London, 1969), p. 34.

'I think of thee when the moonbeams play'. 12 August 1830. Published in SHCBM, vol. I, p. 31.

'I've a free hand and a merry heart'. 21 April 1836. Published in SHCBM, vol. II, p. 127.

'Jeffry, my turtle, fare thee well'. Around 1835. Published in SHCBM, vol. II, p. 86.

'Lanes were sweet at summer midnight'. 29 April 1836. Published in SHCBM, vol. II, p. 150.

'Last Branch of Murdered Royalty'. 12 February 1833. Published in SHCBM, vol. I, p. 216.

'Let us drive care away'. 1 May 1833. Published in C. Alexander, *Something about Arthur* (Austin, 1981), p. 47.

'Life, believe, is not a scene'. 26 March 1839. Published in W. Gérin, *Five Novelettes*, p. 269.

Lines by one who has tired of dullness upon the same occasion. 'Sweep the sounding harp string'. 21 November 1829. Published in BST, 29 (1919), p. 271.

Lines spoken by a lawyer on the occasion of the transfer of this magazine. 'All soberness is past and gone'. 20 November 1829. Published in BST, 29 (1919), p. 270.

Lines to the Aragua, a river of the Caucasian Mountains. By D. 'Mighty river, bold gushing'. 13 August 1830. Unpublished.

'Long my anxious ear hath listened'. 12 October 1830. Published in SHCBM, vol. I, p. 34.

'Lo, our mighty chieftains'. 20 August 1829. Unpublished.

'Merry England, land of glory'. December 1829. Published in SHCBM, vol. I, p. 16.

'My lady turned her from the light'. 20 February 1834. Published in SHCBM, vol. I, p. 334.

'Now fall the last drops of the shower'. 11 December 1830. Published in SHCBM, vol. I, p. 50.

'Oh, spirits of the sky were there'. 23 August 1830. Unpublished.

'Oh, when shall our brave land be free'. 24 July 1829. Unpublished.

On seeing a beautiful statue. 'See that golden goblet shine'. 2 September 1829. Unpublished.

On seeing an ancient Dirk. 'Dagger, what heart hath quivered neath thy blow'. 30 August 1830. Published in SHCBM, vol. I, p. 22.

On seeing the Garden of A Genius. 'How pleasant is the world'. 9 September 1829. Unpublished.

On the great Bay of the Glass Town. ''Tis pleasant on some evening fair'. 2 November 1829. Published in BST, 5 (1919), p. 266.

'On the shore of the dark wild sea'. 7 November 1833. Published in W. Holtz, *Two Tales by Charlotte Brontë*, p. 110.

'O wind that o'er the ocean'. 27 June 1833. Published in SHCBM, vol. I, pp. 266–7.

'Proudly the sun has sunk to rest'. 25 May 1830. Published in C. Shorter, *The Twelve Adventurers* (London, 1925), p. 68.

Serenade. 'Gently the moonbeams are kissing the deep'. 27 June 1833. Published in SHCBM, vol. I, p. 256.

'Silver moon, how sweet thou shinest'. 6 July 1830. Unpublished.

Song by Lord Wellesley. 'Some love sorrows dismal howls'. 27 August 1830. Unpublished.

'Sound a lament in the halls of his father'. 27 July 1833. Published in SHCBM, vol. I, p. 286.

The Bridal. 'Oh, there is a wood in a still and deep'. 14 July 1832. Published in SHCBM, vol. I, p. 202.

'The chapelle stood and watched the way'. 29 April 1836. Published in SHCBM, vol. I, p. 151.

'The Crypt, the Nave, the Chancel past'. 8 October 1834. Published in SHCBM, vol. II, p. 38.

The fallen soldier's hymn. 'Almighty, hush the dying cries'. 1 May 1833. Published in C. Alexander, *Something about Arthur*, p. 53.

'The gale that breathed from that blue sky'. 20 March 1834. Published in SHCBM, vol. I, p. 341.

The Glass Town. ''Tis sunset and the golden orb'. 25 August 1829. Unpublished.

The Rivals. ''Tis eve. How that rich sunlight streameth through'. 11 December 1830. Published in SHCBM, vol. I, p. 45.

'The rumour of invaders through all Zamorna ran'. 28 June 1838. Unpublished.

The Song of the Ancient Britons on leaving the Geni Land. 'Farewell, O thou pleasant land'. 2 September 1829. Unpublished.

The Swiss Emigrant's Return. 'Long have I sighed for my home in the mountain'. 27 June 1833. Published in SHCBM, vol. I, p. 255.

'The wave of Death's river'. 21 June 1834. Published in SHCBM, vol. I, p. 382.

'The wild waves of the Geni deep'. 20 November 1833. Published in SHCBM, vol. I, p. 308.

'There are lands where scents of flowers'. 20 November 1833. Published in SHCBM, vol. I, p. 310.

'There's not always'. Around July 1839. Unpublished.

'To the forest in the wilderness'. 8 May 1830. Unpublished.

A Translation into English Verse of the First Book of Voltaire's Henriade from the French. 11 August 1830. Published in C. Shorter, *Voltaire's 'Henriade', Book 1* (London, 1917).

A Traveller's Meditations by the Marquis of Douro. 'This wide world I have compassed round'. 3 September 1830. Unpublished.

'What is more glorious in nature or art'. August 1829. Unpublished.

'Where has Arthur been this night'. 8 May 1830. Unpublished.

'Why do you linger and why do you roam'. 21 July 1838. Published in SHCBM, vol. II, p. 372.

'Your mama's in the dairy, your father's in the field'. 21 July 1838. Published in SHCBM, vol. II, p. 372.

INDEX OF FIRST LINES AND TITLES